PROPERTY OF U.P.E.I.

D1259971

THE
AMERICAN
LEFT

THE AMERICAN LEFT

Failures and Fortunes

Mark E. Kann
foreword by
DEREK SHEARER

HX
89
· K285
1982

PRAEGER

PRAEGER SPECIAL STUDIES • PRAEGER SCIENTIFIC

160651

Library of Congress Cataloging in Publication Data

Kann, Mark E.
    The American left.

    Includes index.
    1. Socialism--United States.   2. Radicalism--
United States.   I. Title.
HX89.K285   1982   320.5'3'0973   82-13184
ISBN 0-03-061772-3

Published in 1982 by Praeger Publishers
CBS Educational and Professional Publishing
a Division of CBS Inc.
521 Fifth Avenue, New York, New York 10175 U.S.A.

© 1982 by Praeger Publishers

All rights reserved

23456789   052   987654321

Printed in the United States of America

To my teachers and friends,

Judith Hicks Stiehm

and

Robert Booth Fowler

CONTENTS

FOREWORD
Derek Shearer

The greatest revival of the American Left since the New Deal and the rise of the Congress of Industrial Organizations (CIO) could occur in the 1980s. It will be a time of political opportunity. There will be circumstances where acts of political will can transform situations, create new mass democratic movements, and win significant political victories. Will activists on the Left be up to the task?

The answer, of course, cannot be known in advance, but it is more likely that political openings will be grasped if the political terrain on which one acts is seen clearly. Mark Kann's book serves to clear away many obstacles to political navigation. He helps us to take correct bearings before we commit our resources and ourselves to arduous political journeys.

It is important, as Kann reminds us, not to be unduly pessimistic. The country has not shifted massively to the Right. Reagan was elected because he was not Jimmy Carter. Reagan's major television advertisements in the closing weeks of the campaign reminded voters over and over that he was the first union president to run for the presidency of the United States and stressed that he pledged to defend the sanctity of the social security system. He won by appearing moderate, reasonable, and above all, more competent than Carter.

It was adroit of Reagan and his conservative advisers to claim more for the victory than was there. By interpreting his election to the media as a conservative mandate and by acting in office as if it were such a mandate, Reagan hoped to shift the country to the Right, both ideologically and institutionally.

By the summer of 1982, it is clear that Reagan has not succeeded in his purpose. Public opinion has swung against him in his handling of the economy and of foreign affairs. Reaganomics is perceived as biased toward the rich. Blue-collar workers who might have voted for Reagan are disillusioned by plant shutdowns, rising unemployment, and high interest rates. The Reagan-Haig bellicosity on El Salvador and their unwillingness to consider nuclear détente is wildly out of line with majority public opinion.[1] Demonstrators

---

Derek Shearer is Director of Urban Studies at Occidental College. He is coauthor, with Martin Carnoy, of Economic Democracy: The Challenge of the 1980s. He is a member of the Santa Monica Planning Commission and has managed winning municipal campaigns for Santa Monicans for Renters Rights.

greet the president at public appearances around the country, and
Reagan has even been booed as he arrived at the ballet in Washington,
D. C. Unless Reagan retreats from his hard-line conservative posi-
tions, his popularity will continue to decline, and he will almost cer-
tainly be a one-term president. He could well be another Herbert
Hoover and destroy Republican electoral hopes for a generation.

While the new American renaissance promised by Reagan has
failed to materialize (and cannot under the laissez-faire policies he
espouses), the Democrats are not, at present, waiting in the wings
with a workable, alternative set of policies. Many Democratic leaders in Congress have tried to outdo Reagan in giving tax cuts to business or in advocating a tougher military policy.

The Democratic Party is not a coherent Left. It has been,
since the New Deal, the party of regulated capitalism. It is likely
that it will remain so, at least through the 1984 elections. The only
major policy direction coming from the Democrats is for a more
sophisticated form of regulation and national planning. The major
proponents of this outlook include the New York investment banker
Felix Rohatyn and Massachusetts Institute of Technology economist
Lester Thurow. It would not be surprising to find Rohatyn named as
secretary of the treasury and Thurow as head of the Council of Economic Advisors in the next Democratic administration. Both Rohatyn
and Thurow are admirably frank in admitting that the goal of their
policies is to save the system from its own instabilities. Certainly,
their proposals for a new Reconstruction Finance Corporation and
for new taxes on consumption are not aimed at democratic structural
reform. These are simply rationalizing mechanisms for an even
more centralized, regulated capitalism.

There is an American Left. It is an indigenous Left, rooted in
communities and various mainstream institutions, such as trade
unions, universities, newspapers, and government agencies. It is
not ideologically coherent. It is not organized by one national group,
but it is alive and well and engaged in politics.

What's left of the Left that one should view with optimism?

The New Left arose, took form, and had political impact in the
mass movements of the 1960s: civil rights, antiwar, women's rights,
consumer and environmental protection. What began as essentially a
student movement grew to have tremendous influence on the country.
Although many activists themselves did not realize it, these issue-
oriented movements were very effective at changing American public
opinion. A careful reading of the polling data shows that by the end
of the 1970s the country had shifted significantly in a more liberal direction in attitudes on race, women, the environment, big business,
and intervention in Third World countries. [2]

The underground and alternative press, particularly publications
such as _Ramparts_, pushed the mainstream media (publishing and tele-

vision) into investigative journalism and led to a more critical attitude toward government activities and the operation of large corporations. This more critical stance toward official government pronouncements is evidenced daily in the critical coverage given of the civil war in El Salvador by "CBS News," the New York Times, and the Washington Post.

The women's movement has grown tremendously beyond its early radical feminist base. Through organizations like the Coalition of Labor Union Women (CLUW) and the national 925 union for women office workers, the movement has begun to reach out to working-class women.

Starting with Ralph Nader's exposé on the Corvair, the consumer movement has reached into almost every community. Most state and city governments have offices of consumer affairs, and most local television stations feature consumer reporters. Stories about unsafe products or illegal business practices are no longer suppressed or hidden from public view.

In the universities, there is a new generation of critical Left scholars in almost every discipline.[3] Students have access to a variety of texts and monographs that present views critical of American society and the economy, and students can study with teachers who offer courses and programs of study that prepare them for a politically active life.

Many of the alternative institutions of the 1960s have survived— food cooperatives, printing collectives, bookstores, alternative schools, restaurants, research centers, progressive foundations, publications, and so on. These institutions provide some measure of alternative democratic culture for activists around the country. In our hometown of Santa Monica, California, my family shops at Co-Opportunity, a food cooperative, where we save 10 percent to 20 percent on our monthly bill, purchase healthy food, and see our friends while we shop. Our children attend the Santa Monica Alternative School (SMASH), which is a public school, but run in a democratic manner, with student and parent participation. I shop for books at the Midnight Special or Papa Bach, both run by political activists. The Liberty Hill Foundation, located in the nearby Ocean Park Church, gives donations to a variety of community action groups in the Los Angeles area. We take our children to hear benefit concerts by artists like Pete Seeger for In These Times or Jackson Brown to raise money for the statewide nuclear freeze campaign. Mother Jones, Working Papers, Democracy, and other publications regularly arrive at our house with news and political information.

In Santa Monica we are also fortunate to belong to a local political organization—Santa Monicans for Renters Rights (SMRR)—that has won five successive elections, put numerous activists into political office, won majority control of the city council, and brought the city the honor of being dubbed by the press as the People's Republic of Santa Monica. The electoral victories by the Left in Santa Monica are no fluke.[4] Similar victories have been occurring in other cities in California (Santa Cruz and Chico) and in other states (Vermont, Pennsylvania, and Texas). These electoral successes reflect a maturing of the New Left and offer some hope for building a presence for a national democratic Left. It took almost a decade or more for many activists, trained in Alinsky-style community organizing, to understand that community organizing and electoral politics need not be mutually exclusive.[5]

How then to proceed?

Mark Kann analyzes the historical failures of the American Left to take advantage of its opportunities. In particular, he criticizes Left ideologies that distance radicals from the American people. As Jim Hightower, a political activist and populist candidate for public office in Texas, says, "You can't have a mass movement without the masses." Hightower also advises, "Run at the bastards." Activists on the Left spend far too much time at conferences in the ethereal realm of abstractions and not enough time rooting themselves in America's radical traditions and contending in the political arena.

I have argued elsewhere at length for a set of policies that combines greater public control of capital with greater democratic participation in decision making—best described as economic democracy and best argued for politically in the United States under this rubric.[6] What is needed is for more people and organizations to take economic democracy and run with it politically. Kann provides a grounding for these policies by tracing trends in American Left thought, language, and politics that point to a convergence on "radical democratic" terrain. The fortunes of the Left, he argues, depend on its attachment to "democratic dialogue, participation, and control" as the main focus for political action.

Left activists should believe strongly enough in themselves and in a democratic vision to be willing to offer it to the majority of citizens in a context with which most Americans are comfortable, to be as concrete and specific as possible about needed structural reforms, and to explain these policies in clear American terms. Above all, as Mark Kann rightly says, we should not be timid in reassessing our own past and taking practical steps toward building a national democratic movement needed to avoid economic and political chaos in the coming years.

NOTES

1. Adam Clymer, "Public Opinion, Too, Is Running against the White House," New York Times, March 21, 1982, reporting on

xii

the Times-CBS poll, shows a sharp drop in Reagan's popularity; Robert Scheer, "Majority in U.S. Back Nuclear Arms Freeze," Los Angeles Times, March 21, 1982; and Steven V. Roberts, "Poll Shows a Majority Want U.S. to Stay Out of El Salvador," New York Times, March 21, 1982.

2. Everett Carll Ladd, Jr., Where Have All the Voters Gone? (New York: Norton, 1977), pp. 30-31, summarizes data on public attitudes toward government spending.

3. Bertell Ollman and Edward Vernoff, The Left Academy (New York: McGraw-Hill, 1982) reports on the resurgence of Left scholarship on campuses.

4. Derek Shearer, "How the Progressives Won in Santa Monica," Social Policy 12, no. 3 (Winter 1982): 7-14.

5. In 1981 the Midwest Academy, a leading training center of community organizers, began including electoral organizing in its curriculum. A state and local leadership electoral effort has been started by Midwest Academy founder Heather Booth.

6. Martin Carnoy and Derek Shearer, Economic Democracy: The Challenge of the 1980s (White Plains, N.Y.: M. E. Sharpe, 1980) discusses it in great detail.

ACKNOWLEDGMENTS

In large measure, this book was made possible by the two teachers to whom it is dedicated. First in the 1960s and then in the 1970s, Judith Hicks Stiehm and Robert Booth Fowler provided me the "space" to pursue lines of thought that sometimes bordered on the absurd. They participated with me by being my critics. They allowed me enough independence to fail so that I could try again. I do not associate either of them with the American Left discussed in this book, but I cannot imagine a worthy American Left that does not take seriously their commitment to democratic community.

The actual writing and rewriting of this book was a nine-year process, during which I received invaluable help from many people. The earliest drafts were read and criticized by Edward Friedman, James C. Scott, Patrick Riley, and Robert Booth Fowler. Some of my ideas were tested against (and fell short of) the wisdom of Murray Edelman. Thankfully, years of discussion and disagreement with Carol Thompson, Nora Hamilton, and Kitty Kovacs forced me to make major revisions in later drafts. Supportive advice from Thomas Hone and Ben Agger helped me to shape those revisions. More recently, I have benefited from interchanges with Sheldon Wolin, Jack Diggins, Jane Flax, Robert Alford, Maurice Zeitlin, Tom Hayden, Robert Kargon, Donna Haraway, Peter Bachrach, and Fred Harris; their imprint is evident in the final draft. In addition, several brief discussions with Carl Boggs, Elizabeth Rapoport, and Derek Shearer helped me to finalize this book. Let me acknowledge the contribution of these fine scholars and friends, thank them sincerely, and then take full responsibility for having distorted their wonderful ideas to fit my own agenda.

That agenda involves coming to terms with my bewilderment over the American Left. I have long identified with it but have never felt comfortable in it. It has always seemed "too something" to me: too American or too European, too theoretical or too pragmatic, too liberal or too Marxist, too reformist or too revolutionist. The list goes on. From out of this chaos I have tried to develop some creative disorder that I call radical democracy. I must thank my wife, Kathy, and my son, Simon, for having tolerated my years of chaos and for helping me live the creative disorder that is our lives together.

INTRODUCTION

THE AMERICAN LEFT
AND DEMOCRACY

If the men of the future are ever to break the chains of
the present, they will have to understand the forces
that forged them.

Barrington Moore, Jr.

A major political contest is now taking place over the future of
America. At stake is democracy. And it is as yet uncertain what
role, if any, the American Left will play. This book focuses on
whether the American Left can get into the contest, win some political leverage, and at the very least, legitimate democratic public control as a serious option for the future.

THE POLITICAL CONTEST

In the 1970s it became increasingly common to hear that American democracy was suffering from too much success. For example,
historian Daniel Boorstin said that "we have probably come closer to
attaining our professed objectives than any other society of comparable size and extent, and it is from this that our peculiarly American
problems arise."[1] Consider our national parks. "We, the people"
have set aside 15 million acres of wilderness for our common benefit
and enjoyment. However, our national parks have become so attractive that they are now plagued by overuse, traffic jams, pollution,
crime, and other problems more generally associated with urban
blight and congestion. Political scientist Samuel P. Huntington applied the same logic to the U.S. government.[2] Our government has
been so successful in accommodating popular demands that more and
more groups have brought their problems to it. As a result, U.S.

1

government suffers from a political overload that undermines its authority and its ability to govern.

The idea that too much democracy is a bad thing was mostly talk until it became the centerpiece of Ronald Reagan's 1980 presidential campaign. Since Reagan moved into the White House, his administration has doled out offshore oil leases, public land usage rights, and state authority faster than private entrepreneurs can use them. Democratic space in America is now shrinking—literally!

Conservatives have taken it upon themselves to justify the shrinking process. In 1978, for example, the Institute for Educational Affairs was founded to funnel corporate largesse into books and journals, conferences and media events, and even student publication ventures that legitimate democratic reducing and make the diet more palatable to Americans.[3] In 1980 organizations like the National Conservative Political Action Committee demonstrated their ability to build huge war chests with which to finance the electoral victories of antidemocratic politicians and to underwrite the defeat of welfare-state liberals.[4] Since then, the conservative juggernaut has rolled over many of the democratic rights and entitlements that most of us had learned to take for granted. Lest we forget, it was just a few years ago that these conservative ideas were mostly considered anachronisms, the nineteenth century rantings and ravings of a handful of eccentrics. Today, the assault on democracy is not only respectable, it bears the presidential seal of approval.

What has happened to the welfare-state liberals who exercised political hegemony for the last 50 years? Certainly, they had had many indications that their reign was imperiled. The political centralization, overbloated bureaucracies, and multinational corporations associated with welfare statism had generated considerable and growing political alienation among Americans for decades. Jimmy Carter had been forced to plead with Americans for their trust, only to fall victim to popular distrust a few years later. Nonetheless, the Reagan victory shocked these liberals. Reagan won his first budget and tax cut skirmishes in 1981, while liberals primarily watched in disbelief. They consoled themselves that Reagan's triumphs in Congress would give his policies a fair chance to fail; Reaganism would be its own undoing. But Reagan was not easily undone. He blamed continuing crises in foreign policy and the economy on 50 years of liberal government. To date, he evidences few signs of retreating from his defense-spending policies, his attack on entitlements, or his assault on citizens' rights.

Welfare-state liberals now seem to be moving in two directions. First, some liberals have implicitly hopped on the antidemocratic bandwagon. They argue that the Democratic party has been spoiled by its past successes. It has accommodated too many groups, and the party reforms of the early 1970s invited too much participation. The party now suffers a political overload, which weakens it at the polls. The key to reinvigorating the Democratic party, and thus liberal fortunes, is to give more power to party professionals, bureaucrats, and insiders, thereby limiting the participation of outside groups. This is what the Democratic Party Commission on Presidential Nominations (the Hunt Commission) recently recommended. [5] Having assimilated conservative logic, these liberals apparently believe that less democracy means more democracy.

Second, perhaps most welfare-state liberals have begun to take more initiative to resist the conservative attack on the welfare state. They are building their own war chests to finance mass media campaigns and mass mailings. They are mobilizing interest groups in opposition to Reagan. In September 1981, they organized a Solidarity Day that was highlighted by 125,000 people marching in Washington, D.C., in protest against most facets of Reaganism. So far, these liberal initiatives have had little effect. The Democratic party's response to Reagan's 1982 State of the Union Address was slick and critical but offered no concrete alternatives. The many mailings that I receive attack the scourge of neoconservative thinking, but their tone is defensive rather than constructive. The Solidarity Day march attracted many interest groups that are Reagan's victims, but it provided no basis for unifying these groups into a cohesive democratic movement. "The message," writes Sheldon Wolin, "is that there is no vision. . . . There is only the common urge for catharsis that is satisfied when each interest is allowed to voice its fears."[6] Liberals are paralyzed by a dilemma of their own making. They can oppose the conservative assault on the welfare state and hope to pick up some support among the current victims; however, they cannot wholeheartedly defend the welfare state as the democratic alternative, because it has largely been discredited.

The political topography of mainstream America now consists of conservatives who are attacking even tame manifestations of democracy and welfare-state liberals, who are either complicit in the attack or paralyzed in their defense. At the very center of the political map is a large void. No major political force is seriously defending democratic terrain; and almost no one with influence even imagines extending democratic space. It is not even certain that major social groups like organized labor, in themselves, have enough leverage to ensure that democracy will remain on the American political agenda. To the extent that it does remain on the agenda, it is being redefined as limiting public influence on the private sector rather than as empowering the public to determine the shared future.

This is a void that makes it conceivable for the American Left to articulate growing mass discontents, to organize them into a mass movement, and to focus that movement on issues of democratic public control. The American Left could become the prime defender of democratic space, arguing that the best cure for our democratic ailments is more democracy—more democratic dialogue, more democratic participation, and more democratic control over the decisions that affect our lives. Is it possible or likely that the American Left will assume this role in today's political contest?

THE FAILURES OF THE AMERICAN LEFT

If the past is a guide to the present, then we can expect that the American Left will fail to play a significant role in the struggle for American democracy. Though the American Left has been able to stake out what Peter Clecak describes as a "narrow ground of hope,"[7] it has never established itself as an influential, abiding actor in the American political drama. Part of the reason for this concerns the "exceptional" nature of the American experience. However, the thesis in Part I is that the American Left has forged its own chains.

The American Left has never had political leverage comparable to that of European social democratic, socialist, or Marxist parties and movements. Instead, the American Left has had brief moments of influence that quickly disappeared. American exceptionalism is only part of the explanation. Certainly, America's political system has done much to accommodate and cushion popular discontents; America's capitalist economy has produced the material abundance and opportunities necessary for the "embourgeoisement" of the working class; and America's frontiers have siphoned off dissatisfactions while absorbing people's ideals. This has meant that the American Left has had more than its share of difficulties in building mass support. However, both scholars and radicals exaggerate the significance and exceptionality of these phenomena. Often, the Left uses this explanation as an excuse for its failures and, thus, redirects blame away from itself.

The American Left has not appreciated its own arena of operations. It exists within the historical confines of a Lockean political culture that blunts the radical edge of "radical liberalism" and makes unintelligible the theory, language, and politics of "socialism." Nonetheless, the Left has continued to advocate radical liberal and socialist ideologies, which provide few useful guidelines for American activists and few attractions for the American people. Having failed to achieve much and to build mass support, the Left has compounded its problems by devaluing the American people either as an "ignorant" mass or as victims of "false consciousness." This politics of devaluation gives rise to three self-defeating facets of the

Left. First, it focuses radicals' attention on the power of elites to shape mass consciousness rather than on the vulnerability of elites, which opens the door to change. Second, it legitimates various brands of Left elitism, ranging from a progressive investment in expertise to Leninist vanguardism, which distances the Left from the American people. Third, it creates a gap between Left rhetoric in support of democratic ideals and Left politics that invests little trust in the American demos. Thus, Americans have good historical reasons for being suspicious of the Left's democratic credentials; without strong democratic credentials, the Left has little chance of assuming a significant role in the political contest today.

RADICAL DEMOCRACY

Historically, the Left has not heeded Emerson's command, "Trust thyself: every heart vibrates to that iron string."[8] Instead, the Left has advocated European ideologies, used European terminologies, and justified the European politics of reformism versus revolutionism—all of which have little relation to the American experience. This may be changing today. Part II extracts from twentieth century Left thought some trends that suggest that the American Left may be converging on the terrain of radical democracy. This terrain is familiar enough to Americans to attract mass support and is also a basis for transforming America by extending democratic space.

The old ideological foundations of the Left may be undergoing renovation. The Lockean liberalism that informs radical liberalism increasingly legitimates the politicization of private centers of power; the Marxism that shapes American socialism is being reinterpreted to upgrade the importance of the social struggle for political power. To an extent, Left ideologies are converging on a theory of democratic popular control. Furthermore, the esoteric and constricting language of the Left may be undergoing metamorphosis. Some Marxists have discovered ways to transform their messages into a more familiar and accessible vernacular, and some radicals have been able to infuse that vernacular with unmistakably radical meanings. To a degree, the Left is discovering its American voice, which speaks in democratic accents and facilitates democratic dialogue. Finally, contemporary Left politics may be gravitating toward "nonreformist reforms." The Left is engaged in a multifaceted search for democratic reforms that are located in current political struggles and that better position people to assume greater control over their lives. In this sense, the Left is firming up its democratic credentials by arguing that democratic means are the surest route to democratic ends.

Today, the American Left stands at the intersection, first, of its own history of fragmentation, assimilation and isolation, and political failings and, second, of its current attraction to democratic ideologies, languages, and politics. We know that the historical route leads to repeated failures. Does the radical democratic road hold out more hope for better fortunes?

THE FORTUNES OF THE AMERICAN LEFT

In my view, the fortunes of the American Left depend on its ability to persuade Americans that democratic changes are possible, desirable, and at least partly achievable within the contemporary historical context. Promises about future possibilities, visions, and achievements may keep alive hope but do not particularly attract mass support. Part III examines the potentials for the democratic Left to reveal the elites' vulnerabilities, to legitimate opposition to elites and support for the enrichment of democracy, and to practice politics that can conceivably retard if not reverse the conservatives' antidemocratic momentum today.

To the extent that the American experience has been exceptional, it no longer is. Political elites now face a legitimation crisis in which mass discontents build; corporate elites face an economic crisis that shatters Americans' material expectations; and the United States, as a national entity, may have reached the end of its geographical and intellectual frontiers, forcing Americans to face today's alienation rather than to defer to tomorrow's dreams. The fact that U.S. elites have yet to agree on solutions to these crises constitutes a crack in elite hegemony that offers possibilities for change; the fact that U.S. elites do agree that they need more concentrated power to administer any solutions suggests that they are especially vulnerable to the claims for greater public accountability and the greater decentralization of power, which issue from democratic movements.

With the modesty that stems from personal experiences on the Left, I offer a theory of radical democracy that is meant not as a "truth" that resolves differences among radicals but as an example of how democratic movements can be legitimated. The theory is framed in terms familiar enough to make radical democracy seem desirable to mass audiences in the United States; it is constructed out of concepts radical enough to justify the extension of democratic norms into significant areas of everyday social life. The theory is not only an example of a Left vision that might unite democratic elements in American society; it is also a general set of guidelines for focusing radical democratic politics. In particular, it suggests that democratic reform efforts within the mainstream and democratic resistance outside the mainstream can complement one another, both to enlarge the cracks in elite hegemony and to avoid the historical perils of assimilation and isolation.

Were the American Left fortunate enough to reveal the possibilities for change, convey the desirability of change, and practice a politics in support of change, it will have at best succeeded to get its concerns for egalitarianism and human liberation into today's political contest. This is a modest accomplishment but not an insignificant one. After all, the American Left has generally been the "invisible man" of American politics, its egalitarian visions mainly hidden from the public's everyday encounters with politics. At an historical moment when democratic terrain is shrinking, a visible Left situated to communicate its visions may be the only ground of hope to "repair the democratic fabric where it has been rent and to invent and encourage new arrangements that will point toward a better society."[9]

NOTES

1. Daniel Boorstin, Democracy and Its Discontents: Reflections on Everyday America (New York: Vintage, 1974), p. 103.

2. See Samuel P. Huntington, "The United States," in The Crisis of Democracy: Report on the Governability of Democracies to the Trilateral Commission, ed. Michel Crozier, Samuel P. Huntington, and Joji Watanuki (New York: New York University Press, 1975), pp. 59–118.

3. See Peter H. Stone, "The I. E. A. —Teaching the 'Right' Stuff," Nation, September 19, 1981, pp. 231–35; and Fran R. Schumer, "The New Right's Campus Press," Nation, April 3, 1982, pp. 395–98.

4. See Richard A. Viguerie, The New Right: We're Ready to Lead (Falls Church, Va.: Viguerie, 1981).

5. Compare Fred R. Harris, "Let's Not Give Up on Democracy: A Normative Approach to Contemporary Democratic Theory," in The Future of American Democracy: Views from the Left, ed. Mark E. Kann (Philadelphia: Temple University Press, 1982), chap. 9; and Sheldon Wolin, "Editorial," Democracy 2, no. 2 (April 1982): 2–4.

6. Sheldon Wolin, "Editorial," Democracy 2, no. 1 (January 1982): 2.

7. See Peter Clecak, Crooked Paths: Reflections on Socialism, Conservativism, and the Welfare State (New York: Harper & Row, 1977), p. 23.

8. Ralph Waldo Emerson, "Self-Reliance," in The Norton Anthology of American Literature, ed. Ronald Gottesman, Laurence B. Holland, David Kalstone, Francis Murphy, Hershel Parker, and William H. Pritchard, shorter ed. (New York: Norton, 1980), p. 301.

9. Sheldon Wolin, "Why Democracy?" Democracy 1, no. 1 (January 1981): 4.

PART I

FAILURES

INTRODUCTION TO PART I

> A major problem with left histories is the preference for
> the "heroic" presentation. The contending forces are the
> side of virtue and the side of villany. . . . The difficulty
> with such analysis is the failure to analyze the weaknesses
> of one's own forces, the failure to consider the incapacities
> of the defeated side.
>
> Richard F. Hamilton

The theme of Part I is that the American Left has failed and is
largely responsible for its own failures. It has failed to become an
abiding, influential force in American politics; it has failed to honor
its rhetorical commitment to democracy; and it has failed to sustain
whatever mass support that has been within its grasp. While the
American Left has had its historical moments, it consistently allows
those moments to pass by, giving in to patterns of internal fragmentation, assimilation and isolation, and an ineffective politics of reformism or an unwanted politics of revolutionism. American exceptionalism only explains the difficulty of the Left project in the United
States; the ideologies and practices of the Left itself best explain the
failures.

Chapter 1 identifies the American Left and its patterned failures.
It then gauges the extent to which American exceptionalism explains
those failures. My argument is that America's political structures,
capitalist economy, and broad frontiers are neither as accommodating
nor as exceptional as scholars and radicals would have us believe.
They are simply barriers to Left influence, which at most, are slightly
stronger than the barriers erected by European elites, who nonetheless, today face the challenge of powerful Left movements.

Perhaps the most exceptional facet of the American experience
is the nation's Lockean political culture, which acts as a "Gothic"
sorting device for distinguishing patriots and aliens. This is a culture well suited for assimilating the reformism of radical liberals
and isolating the revolutionism of socialists. There is, however, no
necessary reason why the Left should facilitate rather than contest
the process.

Chapter 2 identifies the main currents of Left thinking, currents
that flow through U.S. history and reappear with each new generation
of radicals. I argue that traditional Left ideologies have in fact been
structured to facilitate assimilation and isolation. Furthermore,
these ideologies belie democratic ideals by advocating elitist means
of change and by devaluing the democratic potentials of Americans.
This not only leaves radical activists without a vision that might inspire commitment to a Left movement; it also forces activists to

overcome the antidemocratic stigma that inhibits their organizing efforts among Americans.

Did the Left have any other choice? Absolutely! It could have sought out ways to root itself in the political culture without becoming its captive. But this would have required it to reassess its received ideologies and enmities and to transcend its historical intolerance for those who do not affirm its truths. It could have affirmed democracy as a means of change and a vision of change. But it preferred to trust its European forebears more than its American audiences. Ultimately, the Left's attachment to old orthodoxies has prevented it from cultivating the New World.

Part I is a "photographic" portrait of Left failures—the defeated side's incapacities. It attempts to freeze patterns of self-defeat in order to examine them. Part II, however, is more a cinematic study, which juxtaposes old patterns to new trends, suggesting that some segments of the American Left have and are attempting to situate themselves in familiar and radical democratic terrain.

1

A POLITICS WITHOUT
A COUNTRY

Can the American Left establish for itself an abiding role in shaping America's future? When we look to history for guidance, we find no more than moments of Left influence. More often, the American Left has suffered the statelessness of Philip Nolan, fiction's man without a country. Both experience an acute identity crisis regarding their place in America; both live with the homelessness of having been substantially disavowed by their countrymen. Unlike the European Left, the American Left cannot draw on a history of vision, support, and influence as a foundation for its political future. Why?

PERPETUAL ATROPHY

"Revolution," writes Sheldon Wolin, "is the most radical action that a people can undertake collectively. . . . The gravity of the act requires a people to ask themselves who they are as a collectivity, what justifies the destruction of their prior identity, and who they hope to become by reconstituting themselves."[1] The year 1776 signals a time when Americans were free to conceive new visions of the good society, to experiment with innovative institutions, and to reconstruct their relations along egalitarian lines. America was, after all, "a benign state of nature" and the special preserve "of virtue and liberty," where old traditions could be put away in the name of a reborn humanism.[2] Radical ideas pervaded the colonies, and nowhere did they have a greater impact than in Pennsylvania.

Pennsylvania radicals articulated and institutionalized their new vision in the 1776 state constitution, "intended to bring the entire government—legislature and executive—within the control of the people."[3] The radicals created a unicameral legislature, opened its doors to

13

the public, required that bills be printed in the free press before they could become laws, published assembly votes, extended the franchise, and opened previously appointive offices to public election and instruction. Their emphasis lay in democratic discourse, mass participation, and local-based control as the best guarantees of people's liberty and welfare. They did not hesitate to use government, the local militia, or direct action in the streets to reshape the economy according to egalitarian norms. Hoarders, speculators, and profiteers were punished; the plight of the debtor classes was alleviated. Theoretically, exploitation by the rich was to give way to a more just distribution of wealth.

What Gordon S. Wood calls the Pennsylvania Revolution—the democratic revolution within the American Revolution—was a short-lived experiment. [4] The old authorities soon reestablished their power. A few years later, the new federal government established its hegemony in Philadelphia. Its attitude toward the radicals was the same as John Adams's attitude toward Tom Paine: "a mongrel between pig and puppy, begotten by a wild boar on a bitch wolf." [5] U.S. elites would no longer tolerate efforts aimed at radical democracy and redistributionist politics; and the American Left would never again get as firm a grip on constitution making or state power.

In a sense, the 1776 Pennsylvania Revolution is the high point of American Left history. The remaining chapters are episodic and disconnected. They tell of occasional Left unity, based more on common enemies during a particular crisis than on shared democratic visions that outlast particular moments. They report periods of popular support but not decades of sustained recruitment and mass affection. They record moderate, temporary political influence rather than a permanent role in the competition for power over the future. The failure of the American Left to sink deep roots into U.S. history has had a debilitating effect on new Lefts. Each generation of radicals must begin to build ideas, support, and influence from ground zero; each generation can find little to emulate in its predecessors and often looks to Europe more recently, to Cuba, Asia, and Africa) for successful models to follow. However, the Left's new beginnings with alien models rarely result in unity, popularity, or leverage. The American Left, according to John Diggins, "has been something of a spontaneous moral stance, mercurial and sporadic." [6] Its legacy generally consists of atrophied roots that are nearly useless for cultivating a more egalitarian future.

This perpetual atrophy makes it difficult to identify the Left. The Democratic Clubs of the 1793-95 period had a vague Enlightenment identity, which involved support for the French Revolution, antielitism, equal rights for men and women, rational penal reforms, popular education, antislavery, and social egalitarianism. [7] Even this vague identity was a model of self-certainty compared with what followed in the nineteenth century. Tom Paine, Thomas Jefferson, Thomas Skidmore, Frances Wright, Henry David Thoreau, Ralph Waldo Emerson, Margaret Fuller, Frederick Douglass, Wendell Phillips, Susan B. Anthony, Edward Bellamy, Henry George, Charlotte Perkins Gilman, W. E. B. DuBois, Daniel De Leon, and Eugene V. Debs—to name a few significant figures—all had visions of the good society, which might have given definition to the Left. But their visions were inconsistent and often antagonistic. Emerson's self-reliant individual would have fared poorly in Bellamy's state socialist society. Conceivably, the core of an American Left identity might have emerged from the family of values radicals advocated. Their support for egalitarianism and emancipation was manifest in calls for liberty, equality, justice, democracy, fraternity, and community. However, these values never distinguished or defined the Left. American conservatives and liberals have often harnessed these values to their own visions and politics. And radicals rarely agreed on their meanings or priorities. Recall this exchange between Susan Anthony and Eugene Debs: " 'Give us suffrage,' Miss Anthony said laughingly, 'and we'll give you socialism.' To which Debs blithely replied: 'Give us socialism and we'll give you suffrage.' "[8]

Without a unifying vision, the Left could only establish itself as a series of oppositional movements during particular national crises. The American Civil War era witnessed a pattern of radical cohesion in opposition to the South, slaveholders, and slavery. A few decades later, radical political parties, newborn unions, and progressive groups experienced some unity in opposition to the robber barons during the recurring crises of capitalism. These episodes cast the mold for the twentieth-century Left. Opposition to banks and corporations, conservative politicians, and then the Nazi peril during the Great Depression was the basis of some Left coalitions in the 1930s. And "the Establishment," which supported racism, militarism, and bureaucratism in the 1960s, fostered some alliances between the strange bedfellows of the New Left. Historically, the American Left is perhaps best identified by its "philosophical temperament," consisting of a "sense of negation."[9]

Movements founded more on negation than vision rapidly exhaust themselves. This is especially true in the United States, where a pervasive faith in the future tempers the malaise rooted in the present. Good enemies (as a focus of negation) are hard to find. America has never had the aristocracy that in Europe spawned a class-conscious bourgeoisie as an adequate opponent for radicals.[10] American capitalists have not made good enemies. They have promoted benign self-images, like Andrew Carnegie's "Christian Stewardship," or George Pullman's "paternalism," or more recently, scientific manag-

ers and experts serving the citizens' welfare. [11] In addition, capitalists tend to be hidden away in corporate boardrooms or bureaucratic mazes, where their persons and activities are shielded from
public view. Nor have American politicians made good enemies.
Ever since King George III lost the colonies, the "Big Brother" role
has been vacant. Overtly corrupt politicians disappear during periodic elections, if not sooner. Presidents are not especially good objects of protest because they usually can lay claim to some public
support, and they usually have redeeming records in some policy
areas. Thus, Lyndon Johnson may have been despised for his militarism, but such spite was tempered by his respectable record in
civil rights and welfare policies. As U. S. political power has become
more centralized, enmeshed in bureaucracies, and interdependent on
the international marketplace, it has become increasingly difficult to
settle convincingly on any individual or group of individuals as responsible for the crises addressed by the Left.

The problem of good enemies is compounded by radical analyses
that pin the blame for crises not on people per se but on processes and
structures. It is difficult to organize a mass movement against an
impersonal system of checks and balances that undermines democratic
initiatives; it is difficult to sustain an oppositional movement against
capitalist structures while arguing that capitalists are as much victims
as workers. For a while, George Wallace and Lester Maddox may
have been wonderful antagonists, but they soon disappeared; what remains is the "institutional racism" elusive enough to make everyone,
and therefore no one in particular, blameworthy. Without good enemies, Left opposition quickly degenerates into the theoretical disputes
that take the place of political organization and action.

The crises that provoke the search for good enemies are themselves fickle creatures. [12] Crises are phenomena that we hear about
in the media but that affect our everyday lives in uncertain, indirect,
and uneven ways. Is there a crisis in higher education today? If so,
what is its impact on administrators, faculty, students, businesses,
or communities? Does it make much difference to the millions of
Americans who do not attend college? In virtually all crises, the
answers to such questions are not obvious or the same for everyone;
they are contingent on people's varying experiences and expectations.
Crises are also, by definition, temporary phenomena. A dramatic
act like reform legislation or military victory is one possible end;
the gradual transformation of a "crisis" into a set of "problems" for
expert solution is another possible end. Thus, the crisis of carnage
on the nation's highways becomes a problem for traffic engineers;
the crisis of stagflation becomes a problem for professional economists. Finally, crises are subject to manipulation by elites. Economic
elites may transform a recession into justification for government

subsidies to the automobile and steel industries; political elites may convert Third World discontents into an excuse for bigger defense expenditures and decreased welfare outlays. In a sense, elites can monopolize the means of crisis production, management, and resolution so that they, rather than radicals, become the prime beneficiaries of mass unrest.

The disappearance of good enemies and the end of crises correlate well with the historical atrophy of the American Left. For example, let us consider the concluding chapters of the Civil War. The South, slaveholders, and slavery were defeated and were thus no longer good enemies. The immediate crisis of violent confrontation was over. Most leftists knew that manumission was not the same as racial equality or full emancipation for blacks, but they believed that working through established channels was the best means for further progress. Indeed, some important reforms were enacted. Other leftists were more skeptical. Unless the exslaves had "forty acres and a mule," they would lack the resources necessary for gaining an education, establishing economic independence, winning political power, or even defending past gains. In fact, many of the early advances toward racial equality were soon bargained away by white elites. Still other radicals were not particularly concerned with the race issue. Their own visions, values, and interests motivated them to fight what Howard Zinn calls the Other Civil War against the bosses and the exploitation of labor. [13] Sometimes, radicals fought this war by accommodating racism or even promoting it. Without a common enemy to negate or an immediate crisis to bind it into a cohesive opposition movement, the American Left has repeatedly fragmented into larger and smaller groups that rarely cooperate and sometimes condemn one another. This story has been more common than unique in the last 100 years.

The fragmentation of the Left follows a general pattern of assimilation and isolation, which deprives it of coherence, mass support, and political influence. The radicals who work for progress through established political channels involve themselves in a Madisonian politics of checks and balances, electioneering and lobbying, pork-barreling and bargaining, interest group vetoes, and major temptations to co-optation. On an issue-by-issue basis, they become participants in a process of routinized conflict in which minor victories are possible on the basis of coalition-building and compromising radical values. Success in this arena ultimately depends on radicals' willingness to make piecemeal proposals that do not alienate their more conventional allies.

Radicals' participation in mainstream politics often adds up to what James Weinstein calls the subordination to liberalism. [14] Radical goals and ideology are deemphasized, only to deprive the Left of a distinct identity upon which to build mass support. Coalition politics forces leftists to devote most of their time and energy to nurturing contacts among powerful elites, which deprives radicals of time and energy for nurturing mass support. Like mainstream politics itself, the Left's participation in it is signally uninspiring and, thus, links the Left to the political distrust Americans harbor for their politicians and to the mass boredom Americans feel for their politics. By playing according to Madisonian rules, the American Left has never been able to develop a distinct identity or lasting public allegiance. The Communist party tried it in the 1930s, and helped win some important victories for labor, but was easily purged from the labor movement in the 1940s.

These costs may conceivably be justified by the beneficial leftist influence that results. Few American radicals deny that the Thirteenth Amendment, the Wagner Act and the founding of the CIO, the Environmental Protection Act, or the Occupational Safety and Health Act are important gains made possible, in part, by Left participation in conventional politics. What is questionable are the ultimate effects of this reformism. On the one hand, Madisonian politics favors established elites, who have the power and resources to win most political competitions, to veto initiatives that contest their interests, and most important, to remold reforms to suit their own interests. For example, the Wagner Act provided organized labor with the right to engage in collective bargaining, but according to Stanley Aronowitz, the terms were such "to bring the class struggle under the aegis of government supervision."[15] The short-term victory may have damaged the long-term struggle. On the other hand, radicals' own complicity in Madisonian politics tends to legitimate it and its results. When Ronald Reagan destroys the Environmental Protection Act or the Occupational Safety and Health Act in the 1980s, radicals have no effective response. These outcomes stem from the rules of the political game, which radicals have accepted; and radicals lack the mass support that will allow them to stop Reagan in accord with those rules.

Historically, Left participation in mainstream politics has meant assimilation to mainstream politics. The shocks of elitism may be cushioned, but elitist power structures stay intact. This is not to imply that the American Left's other historical alternative carries with it more positive results. It does not.

One major segment of the American Left has always kept its distance from mainstream politics. This allowed it the "luxury" of ideological purism, experimentation with more or less exotic theories and strategies of change, and the employment of a broad range of unconventional political tactics. This segment has invested itself not in reformism but in revolutionism. Only an overhaul of the political and economic system can be the basis for human equality and emancipation; only action outside and against the mainstream is conducive to progressive change. Ultimately, revolutionary ends justify virtually any means. In practice, revolutionary politics in the United States usually has consisted of attacks on those radicals who assimilate and a halfhearted involvement in reformist activities aimed not at reforms but at the recruitment of more revolutionaries. Except during rare moments of Left unity and influence, revolutionary radicals have been isolated on the fringes of the Left and especially on the most distant shores of American life. This isolation rarely breeds anything other than more isolation. [16]

U. S. history is short on mass revolutionary impulses that might provide the revolutionary Left any sense of rootedness. However, the United States does have a long-standing tradition of popular rebellions—Shays's Rebellion, the Whiskey Rebellion, the Dorr Rebellion as well as slave rebellions, ghetto rebellions, and more—which conceivably could have provided these radicals with a popular base of support. In fact, this has not been the case. Most American rebellions are inspired not by revolutionary visions but by people defending themselves against those who would deny "their rights, traditions, and institutions."[17] The defensive nature of American rebellions provides little room for revolutionaries.

First, rebels generally perceive themselves as law-abiding. They literally take the law into their own hands to defend it against incursions, even by the state. They seek to vindicate their constitutional rights, common law traditions, local ordinances, or perhaps their religious and ethical canons by opposing corrupt politicians or the destructive extension of marketplace moralities and practices. From the protests against the Alien and Sedition acts of the 1790s to Martin Luther King, Jr.'s nonviolence campaign against racism in the 1960s, most American rebels have perceived themselves as the upholders of the U.S. Constitution and Bill of Rights who must break laws in order to defeat those who abuse them. Rebels have not been particularly sympathetic to revolutionary radicals, who do not want to defend older, higher law but wish to create new, untried social orders.

Second, American rebels generally see unconventional, direct action politics as a temporary proposition. In many cases, they simultaneously participate in rebellions and pursue reforms; in most cases, they repudiate rebellions when confronted with the stick of state repression and the carrot of state reforms. Consider upstate New York's Anti-Renter Movement of the 1840s. Facing evictions issued by a monopolistic landowning family, tenant farmers organized guerrilla actions to stop the evictions and foreclosures; they also organized political pressure to secure their right to the land in the state legislature. Eventually, government forces crushed the guerrillas, but the legislature did enact remedial reforms. Howard Zinn draws this conclusion: "The farmers had fought, been crushed by the law, their struggle diverted into voting and the system stabilized by enlarging the class of small landowners, leaving the basic structures of rich and poor intact. It was a common sequence in American history."[18] Whether or not the reforms stabilized the system of injustice, they have been acceptable outcomes to most American rebels, especially when the alternative has been destruction by the police and army. The revolutionary radicals who reject reforms in these circumstances and who, for ideological or tactical reasons, continue to support the deepening of rebellion in the face of almost certain defeat find themselves isolated from other rebels, most of the Left, and virtually all of the American people.

Isolation feeds on itself. Why have the others "sold out" or why do they suffer from "false consciousness?" American thinkers offer few answers. Most American intellectuals accept with Tocqueville "the general equality of condition among the people," which breeds respect for diverse political viewpoints; or most intellectuals preach a pragmatism that views reality as "dynamic and unfolding, and man active and creative" to justify experimental reforms.[19] Lacking answers rooted in American culture, revolutionary radicals look abroad. In Marx's The German Ideology, Lenin's What Is to Be Done?, or other foreign works, they discover theories that explain false consciousness and even provide blueprints for overcoming it. Their new knowledge, however, serves only to perfect their isolation. Their "alien" theories are communicated in special languages and codes only the "knowing" few can decipher; their "alienating" theories appear reprehensible because they demean the intelligence of educated Americans and offer deterministic or quasi-deterministic views repugnant to Americans' sense of free will and unlimited opportunities.[20]

At the extreme, revolutionary radicals retreat into small vanguardist sects or even into academic cells, where they argue out "true consciousness" among themselves, confirm their own role as historical avant-garde, and overvalue revolutionaries abroad and devalue the American people as cowards and idiots. Sometimes they engage in symbolic violence, propaganda of the deed, to demonstrate the vulnerability of elites or to spark the coming revolution; more often, they engage in symbolic talk to assure themselves that the revolution is coming—somehow. Whatever they do, their extreme isolation prevents them from building a mass base of support or wielding political influence. Instead, it opens them to police infiltration and elimination.

The American Left has long been caught between the rock of assimilation and the hard place of isolation, with no apparent way out.

Most assimilate, and some bear isolation. Unhappy with both alternatives, many leftists withdraw to community or single-issue politics,
where overriding structures of domination can be ignored; or they
simply tire of the fray, withdraw from it, and practice sympathy from
a distance, radical apathy and cynicism, or in a few instances, a life
devoted to revealing "the God that failed."[21]

In this respect, the New Left of the 1960s and early 1970s was
not new. It began as a repudiation of the compromises and ideological
orthodoxies of the Old Left of the 1930s. Lacking a clear-cut enemy
who could be blamed for mass alienation in a technological society,
it latched onto the crises of racism and militarism to glue together
an oppositional movement. However, these crises were literally
wound down. Civil rights legislation and massive federal expenditures
in places like Watts defused some radicalism and fostered divisions
between radicals; a draft lottery and then the withdrawal of troops
from Vietnam had the same effect on the antiwar movement. When
police and National Guard violence escalated in black communities
and on college campuses, New Leftists were increasingly faced with
the choice of accepting modest reforms or pursuing revolution at the
price of obliteration.

Hopes for reform waxed, first in the Eugene McCarthy and Robert Kennedy campaigns and then in the George McGovern campaign.
Most members of the New Left cultivated these hopes and went on to
help spearhead many of the progressive reforms of the 1970s, only to
witness many of these reforms easily reversed in the 1980s. Some
members of the New Left withstood assimilationist pressures, com-
mandeered organizations like Students for a Democratic Society (SDS),
and soon found themselves isolated (if not hidden) underground like
the Weathermen, only to resurface in the 1980s when conservative
victories highlighted revolutionary failures. Reflecting on her own
experiences in the underground, Jane Alpert recently said, "The idea
that we were actually going to make a revolution that would eventually
overthrow the government was its own kind of unreality."[22] The fragmentation of the New Left also gave rise to an antipolitical counterculture, some nascent community activists, some born-again Chris-
tians, and an army of New Left veterans who decided to reenlist, not
in the Left, but in what Christopher Lach has popularized as "the culture of narcissism."[23] Like so many new Lefts before it, this one
ended in the same compromises, orthodoxies, and failures of its pre-
cursors.

To be sure, the American Left has won some significant skirmishes in the last 200 years. The New Left, for example, did help
to make life better for America's minorities, end the war in Vietnam,
initiate important reforms, and by its own shortcomings, midwife the
birth of a new generation of feminists as well as environmentalists

and peace advocates. Other historical Lefts can claim accomplishments of equal or greater stature. The point is that the American Left has failed to establish itself as a permanent and powerful force in the making of America. During the historical moments when it begins to sink roots in native soil, those roots immediately begin to atrophy. Fragmentation, assimilation and isolation, and long-term political impotence follow. The American Left lacks an identity upon which to found mass support, which might give it more than momentary influence. "Every morning," writes Philip Slater, "all 200 million of us get out of bed and put a lot of energy into recreating the social calamities that oppress, infuriate, and exhaust us."[24] In part, we do this because we cannot count on the American Left to articulate, organize, and effectively pursue egalitarian, democratic alternatives.

AMERICAN EXCEPTIONALISM?

The American Left's past weighs heavily on its present, diminishing its future prospects. Why has it suffered this perpetual atrophy when left-wing movements everywhere have sunk national roots? Why is the American Left more vulnerable to assimilation and isolation than European Lefts? Why can the American Left do little to oppose the conservative drift today while the French and Greek Lefts, for example, are growing in power and influence? The current answers to these questions, given by scholars and radicals alike, are largely refinements of Werner Sombart's 1906 argument: the exceptional nature of the American experience has generated structural barriers to social democratic and socialist movements in the United States.[25] Briefly, I will consider three facets of this argument to reveal its limitations.

One facet of the argument points out that U.S. politics and political structures are historically unique. Americans never fought a democratic revolution because their nation was founded on democratic norms and processes. From the beginning, traditional authority was sacrificed on the altar of democratic individualism; the people were sovereign, and public opinion was the voice that ruled.[26] Americans viewed the state as a benign instrument of their collective will rather than as a malignant threat to their freedoms. The U.S. Constitution contained a Bill of Rights, which guaranteed individuals the freedoms to participate in public discourse and to register their opinions. It also supported widespread political rights by which public opinion could be translated into official government policies. The wealthy and the impoverished, the contented and the alienated alike were able to voice their views with some expectation that the state would rectify injustices, ban unfair practices, and solve pressing social problems.

Of course, not everyone shared these democratic freedoms. Jefferson warned that some bloodshed in their defense might be necessary. But the expectation steadily grew among Americans that these freedoms would be the birthright of every American child. The relatively peaceful establishment and extension of democratic freedoms in U. S. history was an exceptional phenomenon. Americans could take for granted their rights and, therefore, did not have to fight democratic revolutions, which in Europe had a radicalizing influence on the masses.

The American political experiment succeeded because the nation's economic abundance and opportunities eased class conflict. "Democracy in America," writes John Diggins, "never posed a direct threat to capitalism."[27] Democratic freedoms could be extended to the people because widespread abundance and economic growth eliminated the necessity of using the state as an arena of class conflict. People made modest demands on the state because U.S. capitalism provided them access to cheap land, social mobility, rising standards of living, and real hopes of fulfilling their acquisitive desires. As long as people made modest demands on the state, the state could accommodate their demands without suffering the wrath of capitalist elites. Sombart's conclusion was that "the American . . . perceives a kind of divine revelation in the Constitution of his country, and consequently he reveres it with divine awe."[28] Henceforth, radicals who challenged either the Constitution or the state would be stigmatized by such sacrilege.

Certainly the American state has never been a "neutral" protector of people's rights or a neutral processor of people's demands; it may even be best characterized as "a committee for managing the common affairs of the whole bourgeoisie," as some Marxists argue.[29] Nonetheless, the American state has been exceptionally flexible in accommodating the frustrations and demands of America's discontented. When necessary, it has enacted reforms that cushion the shocks of economic change and deprivations. It has even legislated into reality the public education and progressive taxation that were part of Marx's political platform in the Communist Manifesto. Leon Samson pointed out in 1935, and Michael Harrington and Peter Clecak recently reaffirmed, that the U. S. political system has been quite adept at stealing radicals' thunder by appropriating, tempering, and institutionalizing radicals' demands and, thereby, maintaining mass support for the political system.[30] As a result, most Americans continue to believe that the American state is legitimate; the pervasiveness of this belief forces the Left either to assimilate to it if they want an audience or to reject it and suffer isolation. Part of what Daniel Boorstin calls the genius of American politics has been its ability to cater to radical impulses and so contain them.

Furthermore, U.S. politics is structured in a way that systematically deprives the Left of a base of operations. The signal achieve-
ment of the Founding Fathers was to develop a "science of politics"
that simultaneously provided a steady stream of legitimation to the
state and deprived people with democratic sentiments from influence
in the state.[31] Democratic norms, processes, and rights were the
basis for winning the consent of the governed. But government itself
was a Rube Goldberg contraption, which made it unwieldly as an instrument for democratically inspired actions. Checks and balances, separation of powers, federalism, appointive and elective offices, stag-
gered elections, multiple layers of suffrage, and constitutional prohi-
bitions were mechanisms that empowered elites to veto radical proposals and to accommodate moderate reforms. Never again would the
Pennsylvania Revolution be repeated.

If radicals could not gain a foothold in federal government, they
could not gain a foothold in political party competition either. Sombart suggested that the "monopolistic position of the two dominant
parties" served to defuse serious political discourse, eliminate antagonistic competition, and devour third-party efforts. In addition,
America's two-party system fragments mass discontents. The two
major parties cut across class, racial, sexual, and ethnic lines and
also harbor a "populist streak," whereby they welcome into their
ranks the moderately disaffected.[32] Within this context, radicals can
hardly hope to invigorate democratic dialogue, influence the major
parties, or build third parties that garner mass support. America's
exceptional combination of intricate checks and balances and two-
party politics allows the Left to voice its protests as catharsis but
provides it with no effective political instruments for formulating and
acting on its radical will.

Let me suggest that the strongest conclusion one can draw from
these arguments about the exceptional nature of the American political
system is that it has been a powerful barrier to Left political influence.
However, these arguments do not demonstrate that the political system has been an impenetrable barrier or even dramatically exceptional. Throughout U.S. history, people have opposed the state, while
the Left has failed to attract or organize that opposition; throughout
European history, the state has also accommodated discontents,
though European radicals have been able to build mass support.

Have most Americans viewed the state as a benign instrument
of their collective will? Today's fears of big government and bureaucracy are more than components of today's legitimation crisis; they
are deeply etched into an American past, lined with persistent, even
obsessive fears of political authority as a source of political tyranny.[33]
A good "people's history" of the United States tells of innumerable
groups, large and small, persistent and sporadic, that have opposed

the state because it did not accommodate them and have sought major changes in opposition to and outside the purview of the state.[34] A new generation of social historians is now recapturing the stories of the American poor, workers, farmers, blacks, immigrants and migrants, and women who have participated in rebellions, vigilantism, violence, civil disobedience, and other protests against the state and its allies. The very fact that the U.S. government has always had to use its coercive apparatus to enforce tax and draft laws and that, nonetheless, millions of Americans evade them lends support to the idea that many Americans, throughout our history, have viewed the state with something less than divine awe. If Americans have been ambivalent about the state and have demonstrated an abiding willingness to challenge it, then it is conceivable that the American Left could have built a mass base of support in opposition to state elitism.

Are America's politics and political structures so exceptional? Americans never fought a democratic revolution that spawned the radicalism of 1848 Europe, but Americans have repeatedly fought democratic skirmishes that gave birth to radical sentiments. For example, Thomas Skidmore's struggle for workers' political rights in Jacksonian America carried with it some mass enthusiasm for people's "equal right to property."[35] Women's rights, minorities' rights, and even consumers' rights movements have also had radicalizing effects. In most cases, however, the effects dissipated rather than gave birth to a radical movement. Moreover, the radicalism of 1848 Europe produced states that have been equally and even more accommodating to the discontented than the U.S. government. Within a global context, European governments have been quite progressive in areas of civil and political liberties; they have been extremely flexible in enacting reforms that cushion and contain radical discontents. European states also have checks and balances as well as pressures toward multiparty coalitions that are barriers to radical organizing. In sum, the American and European political experiences are not as different as Sombart and others would have us believe; the differences do not fully explain why the American Left has failed to make a real mark while the European Lefts have left indelible imprints in their nations' histories.

A second facet of the American exceptionalism argument focuses on the history and structures of the U.S. economy. Marx predicted that successful capitalism would generate a class-conscious proletariat, which would overthrow it. Not in the United States. Capitalism in the United States was successful beyond Marx's dreams but produced a working class that suffered "embourgeoisement." American workers supported rather than opposed capitalism. "I believe," wrote Sombart, "that emotionally the American worker has a share in capitalism; I believe that he loves it."[36] More than a few American radicals agree that the working class has been bought off by rising standards of living and mass consumption, and that it therefore opposes the Left's movements that serve workers' "objective" interests.

This argument assumes that the Horatio Alger myth has some basis in reality. America's wealth of natural resources, Protestant work force, and "Yankee ingenuity" have been the foundation for the dramatic growth of U.S. capitalism. Economic growth and expansion have meant tremendous profits for capitalists, who continue to extract surplus value from their workers; but growth and expansion also provide enough wealth to finance workers' rising standards of living; mass access to necessities and moderate luxuries; and new government programs to ease suffering among the displaced, underemployed, unemployed, and unemployable. Even those workers who have shared little in the expanding pie have been able to hope that their hard work, thrift, and education would unlock the door to plenty, if not for them then certainly for their children.

If newfound wealth and opportunity were not enough to wed American workers to capitalism, American capitalists have been ingenious at building structures that tied the knot. They engineered the first managerial revolution, which replaced traditional class distinctions with the blurred gradations of a stratification system. They pioneered mass production and mass marketing, which destroyed cultural distinctions between classes by homogenizing social life. They blueprinted profit-sharing schemes and pension plans, which attached workers' own fortunes to the stable growth of capitalism. They took the first step in recognizing bread-and-butter unions, tolerating collective bargaining, and integrating the "aristocracy of labor" into their peacetime and wartime planning processes. Because of the kind of capitalism that evolved in the United States, capitalists made a certain amount of sense when arguing that the good of business is also the good of the working class.

American capitalists were also brilliant at structuring the economy in ways that defused working-class discontents. They set native-born workers, immigrant groups, ethnic groups, racial groups, unionists and nonunionists, and men and women at each others' throats. They negotiated union contracts with differential benefits for different job categories to arouse jealousies between workers. They promoted the professionalism that replaces owner-worker conflict with collegial discussion among experts, consensus planning, and group compromise. Workers were still exploited and even alienated, but they had little chance of developing a class consciousness.[37]

Sombart argued that all Left "utopias came to nothing on roast beef and apple pie."[38] The American working class was too fat and too contented to accept condemnations of the capitalist economy that catered to workers' acquisitiveness. For capitalists and workers alike, conventional wisdom has been stated in the following manner: "If we just have more growth, we can have more good jobs for everyone. . . . More is obviously better than less, and economic growth . . . the social lubricant that can keep different groups working together."[39] Economic growth has kept capitalists and workers from the class conflict Marx predicted. Viewed from the Left, it seems that American workers believe in the "false promises" of their trade unionism and are thereby accomplices in America's "one-dimensional society."[40] Even if American workers were to transcend their false or one-dimensional consciousness, it is not clear that they can overcome the fragmentation structured into American working-class life.

Without a class-conscious proletariat in the United States, the Left has been unable to build mass support in the one class that has fueled radicalism throughout Europe. Without this mass support, pressures toward assimilation and isolation become irresistible. At the very least, the absence of working-class support creates an ever-present tear in the fabric of the Left. Political radicals see their role as educating the working class to its true interests or at least speaking for the working class, which has yet to recognize its true interests; cultural radicals often forsake the working class as a force for change and, instead, look to an avant-garde intelligentsia to lead the way.[41] This coupling of Left unpopularity to internal divisiveness has condemned the Left to sterility.

The embourgeoisement argument again demonstrates that U.S. history and its structures do present powerful barriers to Left growth or recruitment. But the argument suffers a partial blindness, which makes it a less-than-satisfactory account of Left failures.

Has the American working class been so completely bought off by U.S. capitalism? Workers' acquisitiveness and trade union consciousness must be juxtaposed to their religious, ethnic, communal, and family traditions as well as to their historical standards of self-respect and self-growth, which undercut their allegiances to capitalism. "Traditional relations that constitute a sense of personhood," writes Harry Boyte in the tradition of E. P. Thompson, "are always a complex ensemble, containing parochial, elite, and popular-democratic themes alike."[42] I would suggest that American workers are more ambivalent about capitalism than enamored of it. One reason they have so often resolved that ambivalence in favor of capitalism is that the American Left has not offered them alternatives "that resist assimilation, uprooting, and forcible 'modernization.'"[43] Like its revolutionary segment, the American Left as a whole has often neglected the concrete cultures of workers in favor of some abstract vision of modernized, rationalized, economic life.

Moreover, there is little reason to believe that social mobility or hope for it necessarily makes radical ideas less attractive.[44]

Most radicals themselves come from relatively affluent backgrounds, which afford them the education and even the luxury to question received structures. Today's feminist, environmental, and antinuke movements draw their support mainly from the middle classes, just as yesterday's New Left won support from middle-class college students. Often, it is America's better-off workers rather than its impoverished workers who make the most radical demands in union caucuses or on the shop floor. Rising standards of living simply do not explain why the American Left has not been able to attract a mass following either among prosperous workers or among the millions of workers who still do not share in the fruits of economic growth.

Finally, the embourgeoisement argument does not adequately demonstrate that the U.S. economic experience is that exceptional. From a worldwide perspective, European economies have been amazingly successful in providing people opportunities for social mobility. Europe's social democracies may even foster more opportunities for upward mobility than the U.S. economy. [45] Certainly, European capitalists have been brilliant both at adapting American techniques to integrate workers into capitalism and at engineering their own structural innovations. When faced with the radical Factory Council movement in Italy in 1920, Giovanni Agnelli of Fiat was prophetic in his strategy for defeating it. He threatened to export capital and jobs; he offered concessions that split the workers' movement; and he helped construct a coalition of capitalists, liberal politicians, and moderate workers' parties and unions to "reindustrialize" postwar Italy. [46] Only after World War II did America's multinational capitalists seriously adapt Agnelli's techniques to their own ends. Yet, Italy developed an influential Left, while the United States has not.

A third facet of American exceptionalism is symbolized by Frederick Jackson Turner's 1893 "frontier thesis." America's spacious landscape and then its expansionism have served as a safety valve for letting off the steam of mass discontents. America's frontiers have made available cheap farmland and economic opportunities, which provided hope in the West for people who despaired in the East. Oppressed Americans could "escape into freedom" by becoming pioneers rather than contest their oppression by enrolling in radical movements. [47]

The option of going West was never a simple one. Groups of people, like slaves, indentured servants, and debtors, were not free to move at will. Communal, religious, family, and economic ties bound many to the East. The hardships, dangers, and uncertain outcomes of migration made it a less-than-desirable alternative for many. Perhaps more important than the actual opportunities for escape was the perception that escape and new opportunities were always available. Sombart suggested a frontier psychology.

> The mere knowledge that he <u>could</u> become a free farmer
> at any time could not but make the American worker feel
> secure and content, a state of mind that is unknown to
> his European counterpart. One tolerates any oppressive
> situation more easily if one lives under the illusion of be-
> ing able to withdraw from it if really forced to.[48]

One could tolerate or even ignore today's malaise by investing one's
hopes in tomorrow's possibilities. This frontier psychology has been
adapted and used throughout the twentieth century.

During World War I, President Woodrow Wilson portrayed the
world as a frontier for American democracy and deeply split the radical movement. After World War II, California served as a frontier
of hope for those returning from the war in the Pacific to settle there.
In the early 1960s, President John Kennedy invited citizens to pioneer
the "New Frontier" of the Peace Corps, of science, and of outerspace
explorations. To a degree, Americans have been able to live with
terrible problems because they could look forward to a better future.
The more they invested of themselves in future frontiers, the less
they faced and contested today's dilemmas.

The safety-valve function of American frontiers, I would argue,
is generally overstated. The immense perils of westward migration
may have made eastern radicalism appear as a safer alternative.
Those who did migrate often brought their radicalism with them.
Western farmers in Massachusetts and Pennsylvania, respectively,
made Shays's Rebellion and the Whiskey Rebellion. The American
West was a prime basis for support for radicals like Eugene Debs,
Big Bill Haywood, and Upton Sinclair. At most, America's continen-
tal frontiers diffused, not defused, radical sentiments. Furthermore,
the frontier psychology must be juxtaposed to people's disappointments
and daily experiences. Those who invested their hopes in the Peace
Corps and joined it sometimes came home disillusioned and added
weight to the New Left. Those who never lived on the frontiers of
land or knowledge might have felt pride in their nation's accomplishments and prospects but still had to face the injustices of everyday
life. The gap between future hopes and today's fears can be as ener-
gizing as enervating.

In the long view, American frontiersmanship has been an ama-
teur effort compared with the European experience. Americans had
an accessible frontier, but Europe had the entire world. In the seventeenth century, John Locke spoke of "the vacant places of America"
as a destination for Europe's disenchanted.[49] In a sense, America
was Europe's frontier. In the following centuries, European nations
took advantage of the entire globe as a colonial and imperialist safety
valve. George Orwell's <u>Burmese Days</u> is one of many chronicles
about alienated Europeans who escaped into the colonial apparatus to

put on the trappings of upper-class or middle-class life.[50] Even with this immense frontier, however, Europe did not let off enough steam to forestall the development of abiding left-wing movements at home. We have little reason to believe that America's more modest frontiers could have so much greater an effect on the Left.

If the American history, structures, and environment discussed here are exceptional, they are exceptional only in degrees. Sombart's argument and its recent refinements are excellent mappings of the difficult terrain that the American Left must cross if it is to win mass support. It pinpoints the very real barriers to Left progress. But elites have always put barriers before left-wing movements, which have always found the terrain difficult. What may be more exceptional than the barriers themselves is that the American Left has dwelled so often on the historical determinants of its impotence that it has not appreciated the thread of mass ambivalence that runs throughout U.S. history. That Americans have been accommodated by the political system, bought off by abundance, or focused on future hopes in no way means that they have not continued to harbor feelings of political alienation, economic exploitation, and everyday injustice. In part, the American Left has failed to articulate this side of the American experience, because it has used history as an excuse for its failures rather than as a source of knowledge for change.

THE AMERICAN GOTHIC CULTURE

Why has Americans' ambivalence been so difficult to detect? One important reason is that American culture provides few opportunities for people to express it. Ours is a Lockean political culture built on Gothic oppositions, which urge people to declare themselves for or against their received political world. In itself, this political culture is not a cause of Left failures but an environment that the Left must appreciate if it is to avoid failures.

"Americans are Lockeans first, last, and always," writes William T. Bluhm.[51] The most elaborate statement of this view is Louis Hartz's The Liberal Tradition in America, where he argues that American society "begins with Locke, and thus transforms him, stays with Locke, by virtue of an absolute and irrational attachment it develops for him."[52] Carl Becker locates these beginnings in the nation's founding when "most Americans had absorbed Locke's works as a kind of political gospel."[53] Today, mainstream textbooks in U.S. politics tell us that Locke was "the strongest influence on Americans at the time of the revolution," and radical textbooks agree that Locke's liberalism was "implanted in the American environment by the Founding Fathers and the frontier realities of the early American experience."[54]

There is a strong sense in which Lockean liberalism was a perspective whose time had come in early America. Locke's own life was a microcosm of the forces that shaped the new nation.[55] He was a Protestant; America was settled mainly by Protestants. He opposed tyranny in the name of natural rights; so did Americans. He was something of an upwardly mobile entrepreneur; America's population consisted mainly of people seeking economic advancement. Locke's liberalism was a brilliant synthesis of these forces. His articulation of the state of nature could have been a metaphor for America. The inconveniences that drove his people into the social contract were the same ones that drove the American Founders to make a federal constitution. His government was a powerful force for conflict resolution, which was to free people to accumulate wealth, just as Madison's government became a power to put down rebellions and to free entrepreneurs to exploit the continent. Locke's marketplace was a perfect setting for Jefferson's gentleman farmer, who was religious, cultivated, and hardworking. In short, Lockean liberalism justified much of what early Americans experienced and desired.

Once implanted, Lockean liberalism branched out into every corner of American life. America's folk heroes have been archetypal Lockean figures. Poor Richard, Horatio Alger characters, and even today's Charlie Brown fit the mold. Their morality is one of individual success and failure; they accept established procedures for competition and do their best to profit by them. Whether or not they actually succeed, they take personal responsibility for the outcomes. On a grander scale, U.S. politics and political discourse also fit the Lockean mold. Lockean individualism, fairness, and acquisitiveness are Americans' major political ethic, manifest in the U.S. Constitution, state laws for chartering corporations, and local voluntary associations. Even political policies that appear to contradict this ethic are framed in Lockean terms. Thus, welfare measures are justified in terms of helping individuals to help themselves rather than in terms of social happiness or universal self-development. In the United States, those able to wear the Lockean mantle are also those usually able to capture mass political support.

Revisionist historians remind us that Lockean political culture has never fully comprehended the norms of American society.[56] Early Americans and the Founders drew on many intellectual sources, and Locke himself may have been relatively unimportant among them. The democratic norms of some American revolutionaries only partially overlapped with Lockean liberalism. The Founders preached a "republican" ideology that valued public virtue, substantive justice, and the commonweal in opposition to Locke's individualism, proceduralism, and acquisitiveness. At the very least, the intellectual foment stirred up by revolutionary pamphleteers suggests that no one moral perspective was deeply implanted here. Thus, Max Weber's claim that American Protestantism fed the American spirit of capitalism too easily ignored the Protestant groups that catered to the anticapitalist spirit of fraternity. [57] Or Louis Hartz's claim that Lockean liberalism absorbs all ideological competition ignores the persistence of competing values. Lockean liberalism, itself, never was and still is not a complete picture of what American life is all about.

American political culture is Lockean in the sense that the concepts and terms of political discourse and understanding create a climate of opinion that facilitates Lockean perceptions and militates against the expression of radical democratic or even republican norms, though those norms persist. Whether Locke's political writings were the direct inspiration for the Declaration of Independence or the U.S. Constitution, Locke's way of looking at the world was part of the early American atmosphere. It influenced the English radicals, who were widely known in the United States, and the political movements that, in Peter Laslett's words, "had their issue in the American Revolution, the French Revolution, and their parallels in southern America, in Ireland, in India—everywhere where government by consent of the governed made its impact felt." [58] Lockean discourse was in the air, and one could not avoid inhaling it. Moreover, though the Founders did preach republican virtues in opposition to democratic virtues, they did so in an atmosphere of republican disenchantment, agreeing with George Washington that "we have probably had too good an opinion of human nature." [59] In large part, both republican and democratic discourse was soon adjusted to individualism, proceduralism, and materialism, which James Madison wrote into the U.S. Constitution and his defense of it. Earl Klee calls republicanism the patrician response to U.S. history, a force of some magnitude when John Adams preached it, but a shadow of its former self when Henry Adams eulogized it in the nineteenth century. [60] The terms of democratic discourse never disappeared; they were, instead, redefined to fit better with the representative government of Lockean liberalism.

By occupying the center stage of American political life, Lockean liberalism does not eliminate the countercurrents of thought that make up American ambivalence. Rather, it dominates and shapes public discussion to the extent that the countercurrents appear as nothing other than deeply submerged undercurrents, without channels into the mainstream. One indication that Lockean liberalism still defines that mainstream is that modern antifeminism, a profoundly conservative doctrine, is now articulated and publicly legitimated in renegotiated Lockean terms. [61]

The significance of Lockean liberalism, for our purposes, is that its pervasiveness in American discourse imprints the culture

with Manichaean predispositions. Lockean moral terms are meaningful only in opposition to countervalues: individualism is freedom from
political community; procedural fairness is freedom from substantive
norms of justice; marketplace rights are freedom from state intervention. These value oppositions constitute what Michael Rogin calls an
American Gothic. Ronald Reagan appeals to the American Gothic
when he portrays life as "a titanic struggle between the forces of good
and evil, in which the world is under the devil's sway."[62] Louis
Hartz evokes the American Gothic when he speaks of the "colossal
liberal absolutism" that pervades U.S. domestic and foreign policy. [63]
If Lockean values are automatically good, then countervalues are
automatically suspected as evil; if people who propose Lockean values
are good Americans, then people who contest these values or advocate
alternatives to them are suspected of being bad Americans or even
anti-Americans. In popular translation, those who are not with us
are likely to be against us.

The dialogic ambience makes it difficult to detect the degree to
which Americans temper their Lockean liberalism with democratic
norms of community, justice, and public control over the economy.
Not only is it difficult to express these countervalues, it is also dangerous. One can easily be portrayed as on the side of evil or anti-
American, beyond the limits of tolerance, and justifiably ostracized
and repressed. As long as there is no abiding left-wing movement
that forcefully demonstrates how one can be a patriotic American and
yet support the extension of democracy beyond its present confines,
it makes a certain amount of sense for people to resolve their ambivalence in favor of Lockean norms. To the extent that people do so,
neither general appearances nor public opinion polls will show that
Americans have much stake in radical democracy.

Moreover, the American Gothic culture offers only two alternatives to the Left. First, it invites the Left to associate with "good"
if it wishes to take part in the dialogue but then exposes the Left to
the forces of assimilation to the Lockean mainstream. Second, it
warns the Left that to associate with "evil" is to suffer isolation from
the dialogue and even repression for having gone outside the limits
of Lockean tolerance. For its part, the American Left has always
had the choice of obliging these alternatives or renegotiating them.
Historically, the American Left has been more than obliging.

The most common Left strategy has been to accept the Lockean
terms of discourse and to hope to augment them. [64] Individualism can
be reconciled with some community; fair procedures can be adjusted
to some norms of justice; economic acquisitiveness can be balanced
against rights to decency. However, when it has appeared that the
radicals put too little emphasis on Lockean norms and too much emphasis on the augmenting values, radicals have often gone out of their

way to prove their American credentials. To avoid conservative back-lash, they have rededicated themselves to Lockean rationality and underplayed democracy. By so doing, they underplayed the only values that distinguished them from the mainstream, thus suffering the invisibility that comes with assimilation. Moreover, their rededi-cation to Lockean rationality has often involved their participation in a Gothic attack on socialists, Marxists, Stalinists, the USSR, the People's Republic of China, and other evil enemies. In a sense, they have become the Cold Warriors who reproduce Gothic divisions within the American Left. [65]

The second most common Left strategy has been to oppose out-right Lockean values and condemn them on the basis of revolutionary values that require a complete overhaul of U.S. institutions and life. Such outright and totalistic opposition to Lockean values has generally been unintelligible and unacceptable to the vast majority of Americans, and it clearly associates the Left with anti-Americanism. It also breeds a counter-American Gothic: anyone who vests their hopes in the mainstream is "bourgeois" and constitutes the enemy, while vir-tually everyone who contests the course of U.S. history is radical and good. [66] This partly explains how some American radicals could support Stalinism well after its terrors became apparent, see in civil liberties only a mask for "repressive tolerance," or perceive in Ho Chi Minh or Mao Tse-tung only virtues while disregarding significant faults. The counter-American Gothic declares that those who are sub-jectively pro-American are objectively anti-American, and those who are anti-American in the long run have America's best interests at heart.

Put another way, the American Left has allowed itself to be shaped by American culture and, thus, to participate in the "either/or" options afforded by the culture. It has failed to develop strategies that root it in the familiar political culture without becoming its cap-tive. It has failed to develop strategies that contest Lockean values without suffering the stigma of anti-Americanism. It has failed to practice a politics that draws on American ambivalence, makes it conspicuous, and organizes people in familiar, yet radical ways. Ul-timately, it has failed to understand that to be a liberal in the United States undermines radicalism and to be a socialist in the United States is to be a radical without effect.

Nonetheless, as will be detailed in the next chapter, the Ameri-can Left has repeatedly returned to these self-defeating strategies. Part of the reason is that the American Left has not fully appreciated that these inherited European strategies make sense in European cul-tures but not in American culture.

In Europe, Lockean values are tempered and even supplanted by other liberal ways of thinking. Utilitarianism and idealist liberalism participate in Lockean discourse but also incorporate notions of social happiness or individual self-development in ways that enhance talk about social interdependence, substantive justice, and common economic welfare. Europeans can be liberals who extract from their native cultures radical egalitarian values; Europeans can be socialists who extend liberal values to encompass public control over the means of production. One only has to consider nineteenth century England. Jeremy Bentham and the philosophical radicals founded a utilitarianism that could be extended into John Stuart Mill's social utilitarianism. Mill was able to advocate sexual equality, economic redistribution, forms of worker ownership and control, mass political participation, and even communism as ideals. [67] In turn, Mill's ideas could be extended into the radical liberalism of L. T. Hobhouse or the Fabian socialism of G. D. H. Cole. [68] This created an environment flexible enough to support the growth and development of the Labour party, which though not revolutionary, has provided an abiding focus, degree of autonomy, and base of mass influence for the English Left, something the American Left has never known. One could also argue that the liberal idealism in German and Italian cultures made for settings in which the ideas of Marx and Gramsci would be relatively meaningful and persuasive. [69] In Europe it has been possible to be liberal and radical, and it has been possible to be socialist and patriotic.

America's Gothic culture precludes these possibilities. Liberals assimilate, and their radical messages are lost; socialists are isolated as aliens whose radical messages go unheard. Nonetheless, the American Left, perhaps more enamored of its European forebears than its own experiences, has acted as if European possibilities are American possibilities. The result is that the American Left, historically, has been homeless in its own country.

THE "AMERICAN" LEFT

John Diggins points out that "most Left intellectuals and activists read Jefferson and Whitman before they read Marx, or, later, Mao, and many caught the flame of William Jennings Bryan or John Fitzgerald Kennedy before they felt the fascination of Lenin or Castro." [70] The biographies of many American radicals—perhaps most—tell of individuals born into Lockean cradles, with American Gothic rattles to teethe on, who somehow become adults with radical ideals. These are individuals who were first Americans who learned the Lockean lexicon, but who then made the transition to the American Left. This suggests to me that there must be something in American Lockean culture that can feed Left aspirations in ways that avoid assimilation and yet promote radical egalitarian meanings familiar enough to buffer against isolation. I will later suggest that Lockean political culture contains radical democratic seeds that can be cultivated by the Left.

However, when one looks to Left perceptions of the political landscape, one finds few attempts to develop an American-rooted Left. Instead, each generation of American radicals has promoted the European ideologies that fragment the American Left, involve it in vicious cycles of assimilation and isolation, and provide little guidance to activists who hope to engage the American public. In the process, America's radical ideologists have weakened the Left's democratic credentials and, thus, its most important foundation for creating an abiding role in American politics.

NOTES

1. Sheldon Wolin, "The People's Two Bodies," Democracy 1, no. 1 (January 1981): 11-12.

2. See Bernard Bailyn, The Ideological Origins of the American Revolution (Cambridge, Mass.: Harvard University Press, 1967), pp. 83-84.

3. Gordon S. Wood, The Creation of the American Republic, 1776-1787 (New York: Norton, 1969), p. 229 ff.

4. Ibid., pp. 83-90.

5. John Adams quoted in Isaac Kramnick, "Tom Paine: Radical Democrat," Democracy 1, no. 1 (January 1981): 138.

6. John P. Diggins, The American Left in the Twentieth Century (New York: Harcourt Brace Jovanovich, 1973), p. 16.

7. See Henry F. May, The Enlightenment in America (New York: Oxford University Press, 1976), pp. 229-30.

8. Ray Ginger, Eugene V. Debs: The Making of an American Radical (New York: Collier Books, 1949), p. 240.

9. Diggins, The American Left, p. 16.

10. This argument is made in detail by Louis Hartz, The Liberal Tradition in America (New York: Harcourt, Brace & World, 1955), chap. 1.

11. See Richard Sennett, Authority (New York: Knopf, 1980), chap. 2.

12. See Murray Edelman, Political Language: Words That Succeed and Policies That Fail (New York: Academic Press, 1977), chap. 3, for an extended discussion of "crises."

13. Howard Zinn, A People's History of the United States (New York: Harper & Row, 1980), chap. 10.

14. James Weinstein, Ambiguous Legacy: The Left in American Politics (New York: New Viewpoints, 1975), pp. 77-86.

15. Stanley Aronowitz, False Promises: The Shaping of American Working Class Consciousness (New York: McGraw-Hill, 1973), p. 239.

16. Jim O'Brien, "American Leninism in the 1970s," Radical America 11, no. 6/12, no. 1 (November 1977/February 1978): pp. 27-62, begins to sort out many small, isolated sects that compose a part of the American Left.

17. Harry C. Boyte, "Populism and the Left," Democracy 1, no. 2 (April 1981): 64; for a good critique of Boyte's position in the same issue of Democracy, see Jeff Lustig, "Community and Social Class," pp. 96-111.

18. Zinn, A People's History, p. 209.

19. Compare Alexis de Tocqueville, Democracy in America, ed. R. D. Heffner (New York: New American Library, 1956), p. 26; and Diggins, The American Left, p. 36.

20. Staughton Lynd's Intellectual Origins of American Radicalism (New York: Vintage, 1968) nicely captures the sense of free will and unlimited opportunities that most American radicals share with the American people.

21. I recently heard the neoconservative Michael Novak "brag" that he and most other neoconservatives were once socialists, have transcended their youthful naiveté, and now expose and oppose socialism's peril to the United States.

22. Jane Alpert quoted in "An Anti-War Bomber of the '60s Grows Up," Los Angeles Times, November 25, 1981.

23. See Christopher Lasch, The Culture of Narcissism: American Life in an Age of Diminishing Expectations (New York: Warner, 1979), pp. 43-48.

24. Philip Slater, The Pursuit of Loneliness: American Culture at the Breaking Point, rev. ed. (Boston: Beacon Press, 1976), p. 2.

25. Werner Sombart, Why Is There No Socialism in the United States?, ed. C. T. Husbands (White Plains, N.Y.: M. E. Sharpe, 1976). Writing in 1906, Sombart was referring to both social democracy and socialism. An excellent discussion of recent refinements is contained in John Laslett and Seymour Martin Lipset, eds., Failure of a Dream? (Garden City, N.Y.: Anchor, 1974).

26. See Mark E. Kann, "The Crisis of Authority in America," Humanities in Society 3, no. 2 (Spring 1980): 113-25, for a critique of this argument.

27. Diggins, The American Left, p. 9.

28. Sombart, Why Is There No Socialism?, p. 55.

29. For a discussion of the meaning of Marx's phrase, see Ralph Miliband, Marxism and Politics (Oxford: Oxford University Press, 1977), chap. 4.

30. See Leon Samson, Toward a United Front (New York: Holt, Rinehart & Winston, 1935); Michael Harrington, Socialism (New York: Bantam, 1972), p. 118; and Peter Clecak, Crooked Paths: Reflections on Socialism, Conservativism, and the Welfare State (New York: Harper & Row, 1977), pp. 52–53.

31. See Sheldon Wolin, "The Idea of the State in America," in The Problem of Authority in America, ed. John P. Diggins and Mark E. Kann (Philadelphia: Temple University Press, 1981), pp. 41–58.

32. Sombart, Why Is There No Socialism?, pp. 33, 50–51.

33. See Mark E. Kann, "Consent and Authority in America," in The Problem of Authority in America, ed. John P. Diggins and Mark E. Kann (Philadelphia: Temple University Press, 1981), pp. 59–83; see also Bailyn, The Ideological Origins.

34. Zinn's A People's History of the United States is one such book. Herbert G. Gutman's "Whatever Happened to History?", Nation, November 21, 1981, pp. 521, 553–54, is a nice discussion of the strengths and weaknesses of the new historical scholarship.

35. Max Skidmore, American Political Thought (New York: St. Martin's Press, 1978), pp. 90–93.

36. Sombart, Why Is There No Socialism?, p. 20.

37. On the "brilliance" of U.S. capitalists, compare Aronowitz, False Promises; and Harry Braverman, Labor and Monopoly Capital: The Degradation of Work in the Twentieth Century (New York: Monthly Review, 1974).

38. Sombart, Why Is There No Socialism?, p. 106.

39. Lester C. Thurow, The Zero–sum Society (New York: Penguin Books, 1981), p. 17.

40. Compare Aronowitz, False Promises; and Herbert Marcuse, One-Dimensional Man (Boston: Beacon Press, 1965).

41. The divisions between the political Left and the cultural Left during World War I are nicely outlined in Diggins, The American Left, pp. 73–106.

42. Boyte, "Populism and the Left," p. 61; James Scott applies a similar argument to peasants. In the course of defending traditions against market forces, peasants have engaged in rebellions and have sometimes been radicalized. See his "Hegemony and the Peasantry," Politics and Society 7, no. 3 (1977): 267–96; and "Revolution in the Revolution: Peasants and Commisars," Theory and Society 7 (1979): 97–134.

43. Christopher Lasch, "Mass Culture Reconsidered," Democracy 1, no. 4 (October 1981): 21.

44. See C. T. Husbands, ed., Why Is There No Socialism in the United States? (White Plains, N.Y.: M. E. Sharpe, 1976), p. xvii.

45. See Frank Parkin, Class Inequality and Political Order: Social Stratification in Capitalist and Communist Societies (New York: Praeger, 1971), chaps. 4-5.

46. See Martin Clark, Antonio Gramsci and the Revolution That Failed (New Haven, Conn.: Yale University Press, 1977), chaps. 9-10.

47. See Sombart, Why Is There No Socialism?, p. 115 ff.

48. Ibid., p. 118.

49. John Locke, Two Treatises of Government, ed. Thomas Cook (New York: Hafner, 1947), p. 138 ff.

50. George Orwell, Burmese Days (New York: New American Library, 1963).

51. William T. Bluhm, Theories of the Political System, 2d ed. (Englewood Cliffs, N.J.: Prentice-Hall, 1971), p. 391.

52. Hartz, The Liberal Tradition, p. 6.

53. Carl Becker, The Declaration of Independence (New York: Vintage, 1970), p. 27.

54. Compare Peter K. Eisenger, Dennis L. Dresang, Robert Booth Fowler, Joel B. Grossman, Burdett A. Loomis, and Richard M. Merelman, American Politics: The People and the Polity (Boston: Little, Brown, 1978), p. 29; and Edward S. Greenberg, The American Political System: A Radical Approach (Cambridge, Mass.: Winthrop, 1977), p. 25.

55. See Peter Laslett, "Introduction," in John Locke, Two Treatises of Government, ed. Peter Laslett (London: Cambridge University Press, 1963), pp. 3-113.

56. For example, see Garry Wills, Inventing America (New York: Vintage, 1978).

57. See Wilson Carey McWilliams, The Idea of Fraternity in America (Berkeley and Los Angeles: University of California Press, 1973), pp. 105, 126-27.

58. Laslett, "Introduction," pp. 3-4.

59. George Washington quoted in Wood, Creation of the American Republic, p. 472.

60. See Earl Klee, "Henry Adams and the Patrician Response to the Liberal Polity," Humanities in Society 3, no. 3 (Summer 1980): 243-63.

61. See Mark E. Kann, "Legitimation, Consent, and Antifeminism," Women and Politics, in press.

62. See Michael Rogin, "Ronald Reagan's American Gothic," Democracy 1, no. 4 (October 1981): p. 54.

63. Hartz, The Liberal Tradition, p. 285.

64. For a discussion, see Clecak, Crooked Paths, chap. 3.

65. Kirkpatrick Sale, SDS (New York: Vintage, 1974), provides detailed accounts of these verbal and organizational wars.

66. See Chapter 2 of this book for further discussion.

67. Especially see John Stuart Mill, "The Subjection of Women," in Essays on Sexual Equality, ed. Alice Rossi (Chicago: University of Chicago Press, 1970), pp. 216-42; idem, Principles of Political Economy, ed. D. Winch (Baltimore: Penguin, 1970); and idem, Socialism, ed. W. D. P. Bliss (New York: Humboldt, 1891).

68. See Michael Freeden, The New Liberalism: An Ideology of Social Reform (Oxford: Oxford University Press, 1978), chaps. 1-2.

69. An extremely good treatment of the Machiavellian/idealist basis for Antonio Gramsci's thought is Matthew Stolz, "Gramsci's Machiavelli," Humanities in Society 4, no. 1 (Winter 1981): 67-87.

70. Diggins, The American Left, p. v.

2

THE POLITICS OF
DEVALUATION

What has the American Left done to find its place in American
political competition? Very little that is effective. Mainly, it has
in each generation contributed to and compounded its own problems.
It has promoted old European ideologies, which provide little guidance
for American activists; it has practiced an activism that lacks focus
and direction. Most important, it has devalued the political potentials
of the American demos and has, therefore, created a wide gulf between itself and those people who alone could give it some leverage
in American society. This chapter is based on the premise that only
when the American Left recognizes its complicity in its failures will
it be able to recognize its potential to better its fortunes.

OLD IDEOLOGIES: RADICAL LIBERALISM

One reason why the American Left has failed to articulate a
vision that might give it cohesion beyond historical moments is that
its ideologists have advocated two antagonistic views of the political
world: radical liberalism and socialism.[1] These Left ideologies
share the idea that fundamental reconstruction of U.S. institutions
and American attitudes is necessary to create a more egalitarian
United States and a more liberated American people. However, they
are poles apart in the ways in which they blueprint the reconstruction
process.

Radical liberalism is an appreciation of "the radical implications of liberalism's very old aims and principles."[2] It transforms
American liberalism into a "truer" liberalism that delegitimates
U.S. power structures and supports a more participatory, open, and
egalitarian alternative. Both historically and today, this ideology

has taken many forms, with shifting emphases. But its core characteristic or "deep structure" is the attempt to radicalize "the consent
of the governed" as the basis for a "new politics."

From James Madison to Joseph Schumpeter, "democratic elit-
ists" have used consent of the governed to justify mass subordination.[3]
Elite power is considered legitimate if the people take an occasional
oath of allegiance, cast a symbolic vote every few years, share in
governmental benefits, or simply acquiesce to the powers that be.
"It is easy to forget," writes Joseph Tussman, "that the consent of
the governed, upon which we insist, is consent to be governed. It
is . . . an act of voluntary subordination."[4] Radical liberalism is
generally an attempt to recapture consent of the governed and recast
it in opposition to elite rule and mass subordination. Peter Bachrach
expresses the basic challenge: "The fundamental issue is not whether
the few rule in the interest of the many or in their own interest. It
is rather that they rule and thereby deprive the many of their freedom."[5] Radical liberalism is premised on the belief that the consent
of the governed is actually the consent to be self-governing. At least
at a rhetorical level, it is antielitist and prodemocratic.

Consent must be enriched. Political and civil liberties should
be extended to excluded groups and to nongovernmental arenas that
seriously affect people's daily lives. Procedures to open up and to
encourage mass participation must be defended and especially augmented. Initiative, referenda, recall, proportional representation,
equal opportunity, and affirmative action processes should be strengthened. Ombudsmen, public representatives, worker delegates, or
consumer advocates should be installed and empowered on decision-
making boards; and significant decision-making processes should be
decentralized and put within the reach of people in communities, neighborhoods, and workplaces. The greater people's access to the reigns
of power, the more meaningful their consent.

Enriched consent must be informed by open, rational dialogue
among participants. People should have at hand all information relevant to decisions; they should have the critical education and perspective necessary for intelligent discourse, rational choice, and mutual
tolerance; they need a sense of efficacy, which tells them that their
voices and actions have more than symbolic meaning and make a real
difference. The goal, according to Bruce Ackerman, is "a public
dialogue by which each person can gain social recognition as a free
and rational being."[6] Radical liberalism urges freedom of information; public access to the media; an education that encourages analysis;
and especially the First Amendment guarantees, which make open
dialogue possible and invite citizen activism.

Participatory and dialogic processes must finally be advanced
in a political atmosphere in which people have equal power to take

advantage of them. Polities that harbor economic elites with superior power support "an ongoing process of adapting men to the needs of the productive mechanism rather than vice versa."[7] Economic elites use their superior power to make their own profits a number one priority and to degrade public interests and individuals' autonomy to secondary status. These priorities must be reversed. While some radical liberals are overtly anticapitalist, most assume that "considerable economic planning on a governmental level is compatible with a capitalist structure" and yet ensures that "the privileged distribution of economic rewards is exposed to the corrective efforts of the democratic electorate."[8] In a sense, economic elites' power margin can be neutralized by a government that represents the public. John Kenneth Galbraith supports government regulation of capitalism not only to assure efficient production and fair distribution in the public interest but also to guarantee people access to the power that assures them a decent quality of life. We need to "subordinate economic to aesthetic goals."[9] These aesthetic goals include balancing property rights against rights to a safe and healthy environment, decent jobs and wages, adequate housing, and readily available health care for all Americans.

Political systems that afford maximal opportunities for mass participation, open and rational dialogue, and equal influence are ones in which the consent of the governed can be fully expressed to legitimate governments; they also obligate individuals to obey them. In The Radical Liberal, Arnold Kaufman writes, "If an individual more or less 'consents' to the existing structure of social institutions . . . then he ought to acknowledge that he has some special obligations."[10] These include a sense of patriotism and support for one's political system, concern for national interests, and especially a willingness to pursue one's own interests through established channels that make it possible for people to live together peacefully and fairly. Of course, conscientious individuals may decide that their political system invites few people to participate, to voice their views openly and intelligently, or to influence decision making; they have every right to seek rectification through dissent and guarded disobedience.

Should this ideology be considered "radical?" Most studies of the American Left do not include it. Kenneth and Patricia Dolbeare call it reform liberalism because it concerns "the realization (or modest change) of long established values, and by means which accept the procedures and affirm the validity of the established political process." They add that "except under the most extreme conditions of official obstinacy or willful disregard for established procedures, however, reform liberalism does not endorse illegal actions."[11] The most conventional argument is that what I have called radical liberalism is not radical because it is tied to old American liberal values closely associated with the mainstream and because it ultimately justifies accommodationist politics. Let me raise two problems with this perspective.

First, radical liberalism does indeed advocate a moderate revision of old values but does so in a way that constitutes a radical critique of conventional American politics and envisions a radical transformation of it. Consider this statement: "The gap between rhetoric and reality is so wide, the values actually operative so unrelated to biological, intellectual, and spiritual development in its fullest sense, that authentically human existence for most Americans is an impossibility."[12] This is no moderate critique. It suggests that American realities are inhuman, unacceptable, and in need of substantial change. As Kaufman puts it, "It is impossible for someone to be authentically liberal without turning resolutely towards radicalism."[13] This turn toward radicalism involves working for a "new" America; one with a polity devoid of elitism, framed by truly fair procedures, and founded on the equal consent of the governed; one in which major social institutions are accountable to the public interest either through government intervention or mass participation in them. This new America may be rooted in old liberal values, but it carries those values considerably beyond the imaginations of most American liberals and certainly beyond Americans' actual historical experiences. Second, radical liberalism does not necessarily justify accommodationist politics. Some radical liberals believe that the American political system provides ample opportunities for enriching consent and stand behind what Stuart Scheingold calls the politics of rights, which combines legal tactics, coalitions, and mass mobilizations.[14] But many radical liberals have questioned America's consent procedures and have opted for dissent to justify a politics of civil disobedience, passive resistance, and mass protest. We can see this in the histories of civil rights movements, unionization efforts, feminism, populism, progressivism, antinuclear mobilizations, and environmental movements. Certainly these American "rebels" have considered themselves radicals, and so have the elites who opposed them.

Radical liberalism does not fail the test of radicalism. It is an ideological perspective that can and has supported a radical critique, a radical alternative, and a radical politics. However, it does fail the test of "political adequacy."[15] That is, it does not work in the United States as a basis for transformation. It is so firmly rooted in Lockean presumptions that it must ultimately cast its lot with a reformism that leaves elite power intact and systematically devalues the abilities of Americans to be self-governing. In short, it can sustain a democratic rhetoric but not a democratic practice.

Lockean liberalism is "a philosophy of sobriety, born in fear, nourished by disenchantment, and prone to believe that the human condition was and was likely to remain one of pain and anxiety."[16] Locke's social contract was rooted in his fear that people were so bestial in nature that they would destroy one another lest they entered into a formal agreement. The Founders' conversion from republicanism to constitutionalism was based on their disenchantment with Americans' ability to respect one another's rights, particularly property rights. Though radical liberalism is an enrichment of this tradition, it continues to share a liberal sobriety that places rationality above and, at crucial moments, against democracy.

Hints of this liberal sobriety can be found in virtually all historical movements inspired or legitimated by radical liberal perspectives. Samuel Gompers's brand of trade unionism, for example, assumed that rational labor leadership and the most advanced segments of the labor movement were free to strike bargains for the mass of workers, who did not realize that a small piece of the pie was better than no piece at all. Liberal sobriety can also be detected in Kaufman's disdain for the "self-indulgence" of New Leftists, who quickly grew "impatient with calculations and compromises."[17] Kaufman wants a passionate liberalism but not too much passion by activists. Ackerman's new theory of justice opens with the line, "So long as we live, there can be no escape from the struggle for power." To make sure we get the point, he adds, "Someone, somewhere, will—if given the chance—take the food that sustains or the heart that beats within."[18] Ackerman wants a progressive liberalism but also rational recognition of the sobering limits of human possibility. In general, radical liberalism tempers radical aspirations with rationalistic limitations on reality; ultimately, it also tempers its support for democracy.

Radical liberalism can justify movements for extended individual rights. It can also justify demands for extended public control over political and social areas of life. It can also justify mass mobilizations to take advantage of existing procedures for change or to contest existing procedures as inadequate. It can justify all of this and more—but only to a particular point. That point is located at the intersection of elite tyranny and mob anarchy, the traditional liberal Scylla and Charybdis. When pressed, elites may threaten to wipe out past liberal victories by whipping up or simply abetting a conservative backlash. Mass mobilizations can generate impassioned mobs that feed the backlash and themselves threaten to undermine liberal rights (for example, by shouting down speakers with whom they disagree). At this point, liberal sobriety demands a refocus of political vision from long-range reforms to short-term defense of past gains. The best defense, as in Locke's state of nature, is to negotiate a new social contract between elites and the people.

The negotiation process generally follows a distinct pattern. Radical liberals bargain with elites, suggesting that elites not touch past gains but grant some concessions, if only to bring the mob under control and restore social order. Even if "it is not possible to compel concessions from elites that can be used as resources to sustain oppositional organizations over time," liberal sobriety dictates that reformist victories are better than no victories at all.[19] Radical liberals do not bargain with the mob, which is irrational, but they hope to organize it to accept compromises as practical necessities. Frances Fox Piven and Richard A. Cloward graphically describe the historical process in the following:

> When workers erupted in strikes, organizers collected dues cards; when tenants refused to pay rent and stood off marshals, organizers formed building committees; when people were burning and looting, organizers used that "moment of madness" to draft constitutions.[20]

The organization of mass disruption usually institutionalizes and contains conflict. Procedures for remediation are set up to replace direct demands and direct actions aimed at substantive change and redistribution of power. In the end, the new social contract is a form of pacification. Elites win social order; the masses win some concessions; but the inequalities of elite-mass relations are not disturbed. Thus, radical liberalism may work to support the reformism of concessions here and there, but it does not work to guide a transformation of unequal power relations in the United States. In this sense, it is assimilationist.

Furthermore, radical liberalism's support for democratic participation, dialogue, and equality is belied in its application. Radical liberals who bargain with elites to extract concessions thereby legitimate structures of elitism; radical liberals who advocate a rational sobriety that pits them against mass movements testify to their distrust in people's ability to represent their own interests, articulate their own demands, and exercise sovereignty on their own behalf. When radical liberals support efforts to organize the people and to institutionalize their participation, they in effect retract their invitation to become self-governing and offer instead to represent for the people their best interests. While radical liberal elites may be more benign than conventional elites, they are nonetheless elites whose very existence witnesses the paucity of democracy in the United States.

OLD IDEOLOGIES: SOCIALISM

Roughly speaking, socialism is the other ideological pole of the American Left. Since the late nineteenth century, American socialism has primarily derived its form and content from various aspects of Marxism. Even Michael Harrington's brand of democratic socialism, which the Dolbeares consider one form of reform liberalism, emerges from a Marxist theoretical tradition. [21] Though there are important exceptions and variations, which will be discussed in Part II, the Marxist cast to American socialism has meant that its primary assumptions have been economic rather than political and its prevailing and recurring strategies have focused more on revolutionism than reformism.

Each new generation of American socialists has rediscovered Marx's notion that capitalism is the historical basis for egalitarian change and the major stumbling block to it. The capitalist system of private ownership and control, accumulation, and investment for profit has generated the abundance required for an egalitarian community, access to a life of nonalienating labor, and fulfillment of shared human needs. Capitalism has also extended exchange relations that undermine religious, national, ethnic, racial, and regional cleavages, which traditionally divide people against one another. Capitalism has brought together workers in factories and offices, where they can potentially recognize their common interests as a class, organize a revolutionary movement, and usher in the socialist era of justice. Put another way, capitalism has created the objective conditions for socialism.

However, Marx was naive, uninformed, incomplete, or simply wrong about how those objective conditions would become manifest in the subjective consciousness of American workers. Competitive capitalism evolved into monopoly capitalism, which has brought relative abundance to American workers by underdeveloping the peripheral economies of the "modern world-system." [22] Monopoly capitalists have used traditional cleavages to keep the American working class quiescent and divided. A majority of American workers are not unionized or affiliated with workers' political organizations; those who are organized tend to be reformist rather than revolutionary. American socialists continue to point to "the irrationality and moral bankruptcy of modern capitalism" as an explanation for "the degradation and suffering which poison human existence," but socialists consistently add that the degraded and suffering are doing little to alter their objective situation. [23] Thus, Harry Braverman writes a book about "the working class as a class in itself, not a class for itself." [24] Conventional socialist analysis allows him no other option.

The socialist dilemma is that monopoly capitalism must be dismantled, but no social force exists in the United States to carry out the historical task. Socialists can speak of educating and organizing the working class, even marginal social groups, but they generally agree with Paul Baran and Paul Sweezy that these groups are "too heterogeneous, too scattered and fragmented, to constitute a coherent force in society."25 Socialists can also consider using the political system against monopoly capitalism. For most socialists, however, the American state is a "capitalist state."26 It is an instrument of the ruling class, a semiautonomous institution that serves the ruling class's long-term interests, or an arena of conflict that consistently favors ruling-class victories. Socialists can sometimes imagine competing in the marketplace of ideas to prepare the groundwork for future revolutions. But they usually know that ruling class hegemony means that capitalists control the social means of intellectual production and use it to their own ends.27 The most advanced capitalist system in the world, contrary to Marx, is the one least vulnerable to socialist revolution.

What is to be done? One answer is to return to the historical drawing board to find out what has gone wrong. Socialists have updated Marx's economic theories and applied them more specifically to the United States; they have revised Marxism somewhat to make it more accessible to the analyses of scholars in the social sciences, humanities, and even natural sciences; they have augmented Marxist epistemology with critical theory, structuralism, poststructuralism, deconstructionism, phenomonology, existentialism, psychoanalysis, and other European imports; and they have distilled some of their findings into Marxist textbooks, which have worked their way into college classrooms. This explosion in Marxist thought has done much to clarify problems in Marxist theory and to make conspicuous the immense barriers on the road to socialism. But, in my reading, it has failed either to reveal the immanent sources for socialist revolution in the United States or to enhance the prospects for future revolution in the United States. Much of the literature is so technical and esoteric that only the few who speak the language of "overdetermination" or who cultivate "post-Enlightenment consciousness" can grasp it. The more accessible segment of the literature, such as Michael Parenti's popular textbook, Democracy for the Few, seems to have had little effect on the college students who read it, let alone on the more general population, which does not even care or know about it. Narcissism and born-again Christianity have fared much better on and off college campuses.28

Another answer, which is really no answer at all, is for socialists to do anything that makes the idea of socialism better known to Americans, thereby preparing them for the time when revolutionary situations actually occur. For example, Bertell Ollman admits that the "revolution" is at least decades away. He suggests that "we begin preparing for it among the workers who will be around and relevant at the time."[29] Preparing for it can take on innumerable meanings. Perhaps socialists should devote energy to unions and radical caucuses within them; socialists might run candidates in primary elections "to contend for working people's sympathy";[30] socialists could use U.S. courtrooms to unmask the repressive nature of the American state;[31] socialists should support Third World liberation movements against U.S. capitalism, which will "profoundly affect the inner as well as outer course of events."[32] Recently, the writings of Antonio Gramsci have been resurrected to suggest that the "counterhegemonic" struggle for workers' hearts and minds is a long one that is a necessary prerequisite to socialist revolution.[33] However, this smorgasbord of tactics aimed at revolution is generally self-defeating. On the one hand, American socialists have extraordinarily limited resources, which are being squandered in many directions rather than being used with any sense of focus. On the other hand, how long can socialists prepare the groundwork for revolution and exhaust themselves without the stimulus of concrete victories now and then? The idea that bourgeois politics produces bourgeois results is always available to justify withdrawal from the struggle. Withdrawal is a real temptation when lovely, abstract visions of socialist society bear little relation to miserable, concrete political realities. I would not be surprised if the United States has fewer working socialists than apathetic or highly critical exsocialists.

American socialism is unquestionably a radical ideology. It goes to the root of class domination, and it offers a revolutionary alternative to U.S. power relations. It recognizes in American liberalism and consent procedures the mechanisms for elite domination and mass quiescence; it recognizes that new social contracts and reformism usually reinforce rather than undermine elitism. Milton Fisk summarizes this view, stating that "the motivation for developing a contract is to support the forces of stabilization."[34] American socialism is not taken in by bourgeois democracy or reforms. It knows that capitalism must be overthrown if more profound versions of socialist democracy—wherein people truly take control of their own histories and lives—are to become realities. It easily supports the most radical politics imaginable: revolution. The problem is that all is justified, but nothing seems to work. In part, nothing seems to work because American socialism is so firmly rooted in Marxist presumptions about the capitalist past and revolutionary future that it cedes the political terrain of the present. In the process, it systematically devalues the ability of Americans to make their own transition to a more democratic future.

American socialism is dedicated to the analysis and reanalysis of class history. Whether this is manifest in scientific socialism or less forbidding forms of historicism, it has two implications. First, it locates socialism in a world that is alien to most Americans, who, as socialists aver, have little sense of class or history. Socialists are comfortable with one set of concepts and languages, Americans with another, and never the twain shall meet. Second, socialists' class history is often a teleological history, with revolution as the end point. History must reveal a revolutionary praxis regardless of its actual content. Thus, Herbert Marcuse analyzed one-dimensional America but somehow found in marginal groups, students, and artists the revolutionary hope for tomorrow. Or, Stanley Aronowitz provides an excellent analysis of U. S. trade unionism in False Promises but ends by leaping to the conclusion that, somehow, "the infection of democratic ideology and social legitimation of erotic needs by mass culture among this generation of young workers constitute the permanent roots of revolt."[35] For a great many American socialists, "thinking the unthinkable" is to imagine that U. S. history produces no revolutionary praxis in the foreseeable future.[36] However, because socialists consistently affirm the coming of revolution, even when its coming is apparent to no one but themselves, they become guilty by association with a doctrine that few Americans accept or want to accept.

Tied to constant analysis of the past and affirmation of the revolutionary future, socialists have little to say that is relevant to the present. Most American socialists are beyond the stage of believing that history or revolution will automatically remedy all forms of exploitation and alienation. But most American socialists have had little to say about a socialist ethic or a socialist policy orientation that speaks to current issues or identifies a socialist alternative to today's politics. Why not develop a socialist theory of rights and obligations? Why not outline a socialist foreign policy for the United States, a socialist budgetary and tax policy for Americans, or a socialist crime prevention program that makes sense in light of the very real, everyday fears of American people? In short, why not confront the problems of today, the ones that occupy people day in and day out? A part of the answer relates to the Marxist roots of American socialism: ethical discourse is superstructural, while socialist policy studies outside of a socialist historical context are utopian. A more significant answer may be that such concrete discussion might force comparison with existing socialist societies that consistently fail to remedy exploitation and alienation. Consequently, it is common for socialists simply to assert that life will be better and more democratic under socialism. However, the very act of assertion suggests that many socialists are unwilling to engage in serious democratic dialogue: they have "true" consciousness, and the rest of the people do not.

The political irrelevance of socialist ideology for most Americans is especially apparent when socialists talk about revolution or preparing for it but do not even consider the preliminary steps in making it. Certainly, the acts of the handful of terrorist groups that claim Left credentials convince nò one that a real revolution is in the making; in fact, these acts alienate Americans from the Left. Other socialists who only talk about revolution or preparing for it almost never ask serious questions about real revolution. [37] How is it to be fought? With handguns? Mass defections from the military? Newsprint? How is America's modern military to be overcome? Through guerrilla tactics learned from the Vietnamese or the Sandinistas or perhaps through some variant of Ghandian passive resistance? How will the revolutionary forces by constituted, organized, and coordinated? How will a transition take place? How will the inevitable counterrevolution be confronted? If socialists' concern for revolution is more than talk, then they had better ask these questions to develop at least preliminary answers. However, the fact that socialists do not pose these questions suggests that revolution is for them more a Marxist abstraction rooted in analysis than a concrete prospect for any foreseeable American future. If socialists do not take revolution as a serious prospect, then there is no reason why Americans should take socialists' revolutionary rhetoric seriously. Of course, they do not.

Furthermore, there is a sense that socialist ideology is politically irrelevant to the activist Left itself. With very few exceptions, left-wing movements in U.S. history have not been revolutionary. They have not aimed at the overthrow of capitalism so much as the containment of capitalism as well as of particular capitalists, slumlords, or corrupt politicians. According to socialist doctrine, these movements have accommodated the bourgeoisie more than they have threatened them. As Piven and Cloward note, "The movements of the people disappoint the doctrine and so the movements are dismissed." [38] If socialists do not dismiss the movements, they often attack them as reformist. Though these attacks may be justified, they are based on such abstract analyses and such feeble commitments to concrete alternatives that they themselves are dismissed as irrelevant or counterproductive to Left politics. As long as American socialism is bogged down in eternal yesterdays and revolutionary tomorrows, playing today's occasional critic, it will mire itself in an unchanging state of isolation.

Within a U.S. context, conventional socialist ideology cannot sustain its democratic credentials, whether or not its theories of transition are democratic or vanguardist or its revolutionary visions are decentralized or state socialism. Its investment in class history and revolutionism creates a specialized, "knowing" world for the few Americans initiated into it, because they have somehow escaped the prejudices of American culture. By both implication and overt statement, conventional socialist ideology has condemned most Americans for the ignorance that is false consciousness. At present, Americans cannot be trusted either to change the world or to be self-governing. Perhaps someday, in the process of revolution or as an outcome of revolution, they can become a "class for itself," able to shape its own history. Having condemned the bourgeois democracy that Americans know about while outlining a socialist alternative that Americans do not understand, socialism is suspected of being an ideology that the few wish to impose on the many against their will. Often these suspicions are not unfounded.

THE AMERICAN LEFT GOTHIC

Taken separately, radical liberalism and socialism guide activists to reproduce and, thus, relive the Left's history of failures. One is so enmeshed in the Lockean liberal paradigm that it assimilates to the reformism that denies structural change. The other is so estranged from America's Lockean culture that it knows no passageway between historical cause and revolutionary effect. Conceivably, ideological competition or dialogue between radical liberals and socialists might produce a synthetical understanding somewhere between reformism and revolutionism, which might suggest how radicals can be engaged in politics today and yet move toward a more egalitarian tomorrow. In fact, there has been very little interchange between the ideological poles of the American Left; more often, there has been Gothic contempt.

A broad intellectual gulf separates radical liberals and socialists. At the turn of the twentieth century, liberal populists attacked the concentration of wealth, the parasites in the cities, and the socialists who wanted to subvert family and religion; in turn, socialists generally saw the concentration of wealth as a historical stepping-stone to revolution, looked to the cities as their prime basis for support, and counterattacked liberal populists as "Band-Aid" moralists whose money reforms could not root out the capitalist evils of the nation.[39] Since then, radical liberals have mainly focused their energies on the political arena, where they hoped to win procedural reforms that are winnable. Socialists have exerted their greatest energies in the economic arena, particularly the labor movement, where they hoped to organize and garner working-class support for the coming revolution. Consequently, both groups of radicals looked to a more egalitarian future, but their routes to that future differed in scope and direction.

This intellectual gulf has been deepened by the linguistic differences that prevent radical liberals and socialists from engaging one another in discourse. Radical liberals speak a distinctively Lockean tongue. They talk about moral rights and duties, political representation, accountability, toleration, the wealth of nations, and the opportunities of individuals. Their idiom is universalism, in the sense that they can debate the public interest, citizenship, or the nature of "the people" outside of particular social contexts. [40] Socialists tend to voice their perspectives either in Marxist terms or in Marxist accents. Their terminology includes historical materialism, the ruling class, dialectics, and praxis. Their idiom is the historicism that demands that talk about interests, politics, and people be organically situated on the terrain of historical classes, conjunctures, and contradictions. [41] Intellectual differences make communication between radical liberals and socialists difficult; linguistic differences make it nearly impossible. Thus, it is quite common for radical liberals and socialists to talk past one another, if they talk at all.

Finally, the gulf is widened by political rhetoric. Radical liberals are, in fact, most comfortable proposing the procedural gradualism most consistent with their sense of Lockean rationality and limits. They are least comfortable supporting dissent and disobedience, not because they oppose protest, but because they fear that mass actions may spark a cycle of elite tyranny and mob anarchy. Socialists, to the contrary, do not like to talk about procedural gradualism. They often practice it but would rather not defend it, lest they be accused of bourgeois reformism, revisionism, or other dirty words in the Marxist lexicon. [42] They prefer to talk about the revolution and preparations for it, though, as I earlier suggested, such talk often has little concrete basis. In the end, radical liberals' talk is more conservative than their ideology justifies, and socialist talk is more extremist than their ideology necessitates.

Ideological distance breeds Gothic misunderstanding and contempt. Theodore Becker is a radical liberal who appreciates the power of Marxist analysis and yet writes the following:

> Unfortunately, something occurred to American political
> thinking in the twentieth century that obscured native
> American revolutionary thinking and supplanted it with an
> alien set of notions that could not flourish in the New
> World. American political theory was buried by an ava-
> lanch of intellectuals and political theorists from Europe.

> Their major orientation, if not sole one, was the think-
> ing of Karl Marx as interpreted by regiments of apostles
> and apologists. Sad to say, American radicals and re-
> formers became mesmerized by the complexity and
> pseudo-science of this political and economic philosophy
> that is still praised and practiced abroad. [43]

Becker misses the variations and adaptations of Marxism in the United States (discussed in Part II) and, more important, condemns it as obscuring, supplanting, and alien and its advocates as apostles, apologists, and pseudo-scientists. Becker's enmity to Marxism is simply more direct than that of Arnold Kaufman, whose rationalist distinctions between radical liberalism and Marxism only partially obscure his misreadings and contempt. First, Kaufman misinterprets Marxism by arguing that its premise is that "all the chronic and remedial ills of society will disappear once the alienation of labor has ended."[44] Since the beginning of the century, very few socialists have accepted this reading. Then, Kaufman adds, "in particular, liberals are convinced that political democracy . . . is independent of alienation of labor, and just as basic to the realization of a good society."[45] By omission, he implies that Marxists have little or no interest in political democracy.

Even a careful philosopher like Bruce Ackerman cannot resist a hint of red-baiting. He writes about socialists who "typically speak as if exploited and exploiter can neatly be sorted into two grand classes containing all of humanity."[46] The hint is that socialists are simpleminded ideologues who are blind to other cleavages in social relations; Ackerman seems unaware that American socialists are typically consumed by those cleavages, because they undermine clear class distinctions. In general, radical liberals do not see the main trends in socialist thought, stereotype it somewhere between Second International orthodoxies and Stalinism, and then treat it as sheer idiocy or a malignancy on the body politic.

Of course, this misunderstanding and contempt is mutual. American socialists have developed a certain expertise in accusing radical liberals of false consciousness, reformism, or petit bourgeois idiocies; socialists have also developed intricate power elite or mass society theories, which portray radical liberal movements as objects manipulated by elites, without an independent will.[47] Socialists often assert "the behavioral and normative superiority of Marxian class analysis" and sometimes add that a "true" understanding of social forces will reveal the inner emptiness of bourgeois politics.[48] Socialists who appear to be too closely associated with radical liberal reformism are almost automatically accused by other socialists of having sold out, substituting reformism for revolutionism. This ideological atmosphere makes possible the growth of what Todd Gitlin calls weathermania.[49] Socialists make themselves vulnerable to vanguardist claims that reformism and reaction are a seamless web of social fascism. Socialists must dissociate themselves from any politics that even hints of reformism; they must instead "bring the revolution home" by associating themselves with militant minority groups, Third World revolutionaries, and underground violence. Most socialists do not follow the vanguardists underground but are sensitive enough to vanguardist claims and bravado to sever links with radical liberal politics and attack it as reactionary. By 1969 the national leadership of Students for a Democratic Society (SDS) was making unilateral decisions without consulting members. As the leadership saw it, their task was "to clarify the irreconcilable and antagonistic characteristic of differences" through action; their task "was not to vote."[50] SDS members hardly objected. They distrusted liberal reformism and procedures enough to appreciate an attack on them, but they thereby allowed vanguardists to take over their organizations and ultimately destroy them.

The impact of ideological separation and Gothic enmity on the American Left can be seen in the antiwar movement of the 1960s. The antiwar movement was an unplanned and uneasy partnership between radical liberals and socialists, who, for very different reasons, protested U.S. involvement in Vietnam. The partnership was not long sustained.

Radical liberals protested against racial inequalities in American politics and the draft; drafting minors who had no political rights; universities that undermined academic freedom by cooperating with the Central Intelligence Agency (CIA), the Federal Bureau of Investigation (FBI), or the Selective Service System but did not allow students a voice in university policy; and the centralization and bureaucratization that allowed elites to make a war without declaring it, according to constitutional guidelines. Socialist antiwar activities were only peripherally related to these procedural questions. Instead, socialists protested against the war as an extension of socioeconomic injustices at home. The roots of war were planted in the economic system; the production of war revealed the capitalist script; the selling of war followed the principles of capitalist advertising; and the prosecution of war aimed at the obliteration of a popular socialist movement in a Third World nation. While radical liberals wanted to close the gap between liberal rhetoric and illiberal reality, socialists protested against a liberal reality bent on extending ruling-class domination.

Radical liberals won some reforms. Civil rights legislation, changes in selective service requirements, and reforms in military policies equalized racial opportunities somewhat. America's 18-year-

olds got the vote. Some university connections with the war machine
were severed, and some universities invited modest forms of student
representation. "Maximum feasible participation" seemed to make
government bureaucracy more accessible, and Democratic party reforms allowed for greater representation of and participation by once
excluded groups. The unorganized were being organized, and silenced
minorities, feminists, gays, old people, and recipients of welfare
were entering into the pluralist arena. In these ways, Samuel P.
Huntington was right when he said that "the 1960s witnessed a dramatic
renewal of the democratic spirit of America."51

Consent had been enriched, not enough, but hopefully the 1970s
would show even greater progress. However, the enrichment process
was imperiled. A law and order backlash produced a Nixon-Agnew
administration, with George Wallace waiting in the wings. The backlash was fueled by urban revolts and a new socialist militancy, which
respected no one's rights. The killings at Kent State and radical in-
cendiarism brought home the realization that the intersection of elite
tyranny and mob anarchy was being approached. It was time to negotiate a new social contract, and McGovernism was to be its issue.

Radical liberals began to direct activists off of the streets and
onto the sidewalks to canvas for George McGovern. They argued
that past gains and new concessions needed to be consolidated; that
the political system was increasingly open to progressive politics;
that McGovern could win the Oval Office; and that his administration
would be the foundation for far-reaching changes that would bring the
United States to a truer liberalism. Consenting to work within the
system would pay off. Concomitantly, the socialists who stayed in
the streets to preach direct action, resistance, and revolution were
considered out of touch with American realities. Intelligent people
understood that these socialists abetted the power of the Nixons, Ag-
news, and Wallaces by making conservative hysteria seem reasonable.

When radical liberals committed themselves to the McGovern
campaign, they implicitly committed themselves to accepting the
coming Nixon landslide. Consent of the governed never guaranteed
that the governed would make good choices.52 In their more sober
moments before the 1972 election, radical liberals suspected that
Americans would not make good choices. Nixon's victory was the
proof in the pudding. However, consent of the governed did mean
that Americans would have some opportunity to rectify their errors.
It was especially bright people in government and the press who did
so by hounding Nixon out of office a year later. For the remainder
of the 1970s, radical liberals worked behind the political scenes for
reforms and won quite a few. However, one year of Reaganism testified to the fragility of reforms based more on interelite bargaining
than on mass movements.

Socialists' participation in coalitions, demonstrations, marches, sit-ins, teach-ins, civil disobedience, protests, or confrontation politics failed to stop the war or to win many recruits to socialism. The "defection" of radical liberals to Eugene McCarthy and Robert Kennedy in 1968 revealed for a moment how socialists were isolated, even during a period when they won minor acclaim. For some, it was time to escalate the revolutionary struggle. The rhetoric of black militants and the actions of Third World revolutionaries; the ideologies of Ché, Ho, and Mao; and the guerrilla warfare of the National Liberation Front (NLF) provided the models. Radical subcommunities were formed, with their own linguistic codes and special brands of radical rhetoric. Perhaps the "new working class" would be the revolutionary base; perhaps the "primary contradiction" could be found; perhaps a spark here and there could set off a revolution. Isolated in their subcommunities, these revolutionary socialists increasingly lost touch with other radicals and with the American people, who had no interest in revolution except to stop it. "There is, on the whole, " writes Richard Hamilton, "probably nothing that could more effectively limit communication between members of such a subcommunity and any segment of the larger society than the use of a language that cannot be understood by anyone outside of that community."[53] Socialist revolutionaries were like fish out of water. Not understood or appreciated by the sea of Americans, they created utopian scenarios of change out of thin air.

Other socialists decided that they had better start anew the preparations for the always-coming revolution. The New American Movement (NAM), for example, was formed to "construct a movement for democratic socialism in the United States." It would associate itself with "the revolutionary process," which would eventually "bring out the common class interests of various sectors against capital."[54] In more conventional language, it planned to educate workers and related groups to their true interests in revolutionary socialism. But revolutionary socialism was not on Americans' agenda in the 1970s. John Diggins put it well: "Once again, we have a young radical intelligentsia without a radical proletariat."[55]

The brief celebrations that followed the fall of Saigon and the rise of Ho Chi Minh City were the last gasp of the antiwar movement. Radical liberals had faded back into the mainstream and conventional reformism; socialists continued to seek the revolution or revolutionary preparations in isolation. It was almost inevitable and certainly predictable. The ideological gulf and enmity that divide radical liberals and socialists create an either/or mentality on the Left that reasserts itself to fragment the Left. Radical liberals who are not drawn to socialist analyses, indeed, who reject them, gravitate to assimilationism without a socialist counterweight to resist it; socialists who tire of radical liberal reformism and reject it sever their final links with political relevance in American politics. Left ideologies neutralize one another and, in the process, provide no sustained direction for activists.

LEFT ACTIVISM

"A major problem for the New Left," wrote Christopher Lasch in 1971, "was precisely to work out a new conception of social reconstruction" that avoided the reformism of "left-leaning liberals" and the "Third World revolutionary doctrines quite inapplicable to the U.S."[56] Left ideologists failed on this score, and the by-product of ideological failure was to cast adrift the many activists who filled the ranks of mass marches and demonstrations. In the 1970s, many ex-New Left people continued to work for egalitarian change, but they did so without any systematic direction. Without direction, small gains made on one front could easily be offset by large losses on another front.

Analysts of the New Left are often struck by its anti-ideological character.[57] Its action orientation challenged ideology; its worship of spontaneity and authenticity spilled over all ideological boundaries; and its experimentalist ethic tied to a counterculture contested all ideological authority. At once, without order or priorities, the New Left challenged corporate domination, government and bureaucracy, technology, received traditions and social cleavages, parental authority, restrictions on drugs and restricting bras and corsets, and everything that stood in the way of the liberation of the id. This was the Woodstock generation; Marx, Locke, and other ideologists had nothing to teach it. Anarchism was the rule. This characterization of the New Left captures one aspect of the radical realities of the 1960s; indeed, various forms of cultural anarchism have appeared whenever the American Left had its moments. But it mistakes a media's eye view for the total picture.

The New Left, like all American Lefts before it, was founded on an ambivalent or inarticulate base of support, which was far from anarchistic. The base was composed both of religious people and secular citizens who opposed the war on procedural and substantive grounds: Government policies should have people's consent, and people should not consent to this particular war. It was composed of people who in some senses looked forward to a new America that would contain both enriched consent and greater public control over the nation's economy. It was composed of individuals who were sensitive to the gap between liberal rhetoric and U.S. realities and supported reforms to narrow it and who were also concerned that liberal equality is incomplete without large doses of egalitarian community and social practices. In short, the New Left was implicitly founded on the activism of Americans who saw radical liberalism and social-ism as potentially complementary; but they lacked an ideology and language that identified how it was possible to occupy this ideological gulf. In many cases, their ambivalence and inarticulateness were manifest in the demands for all-around freedoms made in the counter-culture.

This posed no real problem at the height of the antiwar move-ment. Left coalitions allowed activists to work for procedural and substantive changes simultaneously. Depending on the priorities of the moment, they could always find willing allies in umbrella organi-zations. Since virtually everyone on the Left agreed that dissent and disobedience were justified while American bombs rained on Vietnam, the question of reform versus revolution was temporarily suspended. Perhaps activists were united by a core belief that opposition to the war might generate a political equality that would end the war and some general enthusiasm for the extension of democratic norms into economic and social spheres of American life. During that moment of Left unity, activists could leave ideological subtleties to Left in-tellectuals.

When the antiwar movement started to disintegrate, radical ac-tivists inherited the paradoxes of both Left ideologies. Should they follow radical liberals into the national political arena to suffer as-similation? Should they follow socialists into isolation and suffer impotence? Without a new conception of social reconstruction, they had no way to work out a relationship between enriched consent and public control; they had no way to give direction to their strategies of the coming decade. Ultimately, they had no systematic vision of a third way that might include "the pursuit of reforms of every kind—economic, social, and political—within the framework of capitalism" but does not "consider such reforms as being the ultimate purpose: these are at best steps and partial means towards a much larger pur-pose."[58] Neither radical liberalism nor socialism provided an agree-able sense of that much larger purpose.

Some radical activists resurfaced in mainstream politics during the 1970s with hybrid platforms for change. Tom Hayden dissociated himself from socialism but ran for the U.S. Senate nomination on a platform offering mildly socialist reforms.[59] Justin Ravitz became Detroit's Marxist judge, who promoted greater procedural equity in the courtroom as one basis for substantive changes in society.[60] Ac-tivists in mainstream politics organized the Conference on Alternative State and Local Policies to bring together progressive people in gov-ernment and communities to map out concrete proposals. The problem facing them is that they have no systematic vision of change that might inform those proposals. A Berkeley councilwoman said, "The war in Vietnam, as terrible as it was, did give us, in a sense, a great negative vision. We knew what we wanted to stop. . . . We need now to develop a positive vision. We need to dig in for another ten years perhaps."[61] Exactly where to dig in or how to dig in has not been obvious.

In fact, many New Left activists dug in wherever they happened to be. They became organizers in their own communities and did the difficult if not mundane job of exposing local corruption, organizing people in opposition to it, supporting local progressive efforts, and seeking ways to enhance the quality of daily life. In many cases, they were the inspiration and energy behind fights against nuclear power plants, racism and sexism, outrageous utility rates, ecological degradation, union bureaucratization, landlord domination in rental markets, redlining by banks, or discrimination against gay people. A number of New Left activists in the 1970s found their way into university and teaching jobs, social service networks, or perhaps journalism, where they could, at least minimally, combine their careers and their politics. Others took "straight" jobs to support radical life-styles. Even those who dropped out of the political contest often retained a lingering nostalgia and attachment for the New Left, which became manifest in their involvement in local cooperatives or in their occasional support for local progressive politics.

Where has this "grass rooting" of the American Left led? In one sense, it has led to an implicit breakdown in American Left ideologies. For example, one can consider environmentalism. It approaches its issue area in terms of the procedural question of political equality. Do particular interests exert undue influence over ecological policy and administration? It also approaches politics in terms of the substantive question of public control. Should citizens or communities directly control investment decisions in ways consistent with human health needs? While some environmentalists are primarily concerned with procedural questions and others are mainly focused on substantive questions, the distinctions are generally blurred. Similarly, current debates over the use and control of union or public employees' pension funds simultaneously raise interwoven procedural and substantive questions. Conceivably, these questions and debates can be the basis for "a new conception of social reconstruction" that avoids the pitfalls of radical liberalism and socialism.

In another sense, the grass rooting of the American Left has led nowhere in particular and everywhere in general. As long as the crucial decisions that affect American life are centralized in Washington conference rooms and in corporate boardrooms, local radical activism can be little more than a lone voice in the wilderness of plural-

ist politics. As long as local radical activism is ideologically inarticulate and, thus, without a unifying vision, it cannot develop the long-
term strategies and nationwide support necessary for contesting
elitism in the United States. Were nothing significant to change, we
could expect during the next moment of Left ascendancy that Left ideologists would draw activists into another oppositional movement,
only to leave them stranded in their communities without a political
compass.

The failure of Left ideologists to give suitable direction to activists and the failure of activists to articulate a more adequate vision
that draws from their own experiences are failures that oblige America's Lockean political culture. Left ideologists reproduce the Gothic
divisions that fragment radicals and facilitate their assimilation and
isolation. Left activists experience some victories in the pluralist
arena of local politics, but these do not add up to a systematic or effective challenge to U.S. elitism. Furthermore, the Left's uncertainty about the demos and how trustworthy it is has resulted in some
self-defeating organizational strategies. On the one hand, some
Left organizations do not want to be polluted by activists' and people's
misconceptions. They are composed of an encapsulated leadership,
a hierarchical organization chart, and a preconceived distancing from
constituents. On the other hand, many Left organizations do not want
to be accused of reproducing elitism in their own ranks; they become
110 percent minidemocracies. They rotate leadership and job positions as if people are interchangeable cogs in the organizational machine; they invite everyone and anyone into their organizations, including vanguardists who seek to take them over and cranks whose
fads destroy organizational cohesion. A good many of these organizations are or become so intolerant of one another that they frighten
away dedicated activists, who move on elsewhere, and potential recruits, who see nowhere to contribute their energies. [62]
These problems are symptomatic of a more basic one. The
American Left has failed to develop an outlook that is rooted in American experiences and able to draw radicals toward unity; that speaks to
the egalitarian aspects of activists' and Americans' ambivalence to
help build a base of mass support; and that guides a political and organizational strategy to winnable reforms, which both cushion the impact of inequalities and empower people to contest inequalities. The
American Left has long preached praxis in various ways; the point
is to practice it to change the world.

DEVALUATION AND REEVALUATION

The FBI recently foiled an attempted holdup of a Brinks armored truck. The suspects were identified as members or associates of the Weather Underground, the Black Liberation Army, and the May 19 Communist Action Organization. The subsequent investigation unearthed a number of "safe" houses where the suspects had made their plans, kept their records and communications, and, according to one newspaper account, "showed a fondness for photographing one another and other members of the network—often posing with guns."[63] Apparently, these "radical" thieves could not resist framing their historical moment before its inevitable passing. Whether their actions would win public support or somehow benefit the public were minor considerations when failure was at some level expected, sooner or later. In a related sense, American Left theories and practices have been poised for failures, which has compounded the Left's devaluation of the American public.

In Part I, I have tried to photograph the American Left, not to record its failures but to distinguish its contributions to them. I have not meant to discount American exceptionalism as an explanation; but I have meant to discount it as a complete explanation or as a set of historical determinants that doom the American Left to perpetual impotence. Nor have I meant to ignore variations and subtleties in Left thinking and action; but I have meant to focus on the recurring characteristics of the American Left that systematically contribute to its failures. My thesis is that the American Left must assume some responsibility for forging its own chains. Only then can it understand how it might unchain itself from its own history and freely seek new paths into the future.

I have argued that the American Left has advocated ideologies that play directly into the snares set by Lockean political culture and, in the process, devalue the intelligence and potential contributions of the American people to egalitarian change. I have argued that the American Left has created its own esoteric world of concepts, terms, rationalities, and rhetoric, which have little support in American experiences and systematically shut out Americans' daily experiences. I have argued that the American Left consistently advocates reformism and revolutionism as the only two routes to change and, thereby, has little to say to activists who are ambivalent about both routes and to Americans who do not see a solution to their frustrations in either route. It is almost as if the American Left has been posing for history before it passes away; in its passing, it has shown great disregard for the Americans who alone could prevent it.

Consider this analysis an incomplete one that is useful as a benchmark for gauging change. In the course of the twentieth century, some segments of the American Left have reevaluated Americans' potential contribution to change. They have tried to root themselves in America's democratic soil and have sought out ways to cultivate democratic commitments to procedural justice and substantive justice. As part of the process, they have revised the old ideologies to reveal the democratic terrain familiar to Americans; they have experimented with languages that are intelligible to Americans and yet convey radical meanings; and they have increasingly converged on a radical democratic politics that replaces reformism and revolutionism with reforms, which are themselves democratic and entrust people with the power to demand more extensive democracy. In Part II, I will extract and examine these trends to suggest the potentials of radical democracy, in theory and practice, to be an abiding foundation for Left unity, popularity, and influence.

NOTES

1. Obviously, there have been other ideologies that guided American Left politics. I focus on these two because they are the ones that seem to predominate among the political Left and are also able to incorporate many of the issues of the cultural Left.

2. Arnold S. Kaufman, The Radical Liberal: The New Politics, Theory and Practice (New York: Atherton, 1968), p. 2.

3. See Peter Bachrach, The Theory of Democratic Elitism: A Critique (Boston: Little, Brown, 1967).

4. Joseph Tussman, Obligation and the Body Politic (London: Oxford University Press, 1960), p. 25.

5. Peter Bachrach, "Interest, Participation, and Democratic Theory," in Participation in Politics, ed. J. Roland Pennock and John W. Chapman, Nomos 16 (New York: Lieber-Atherton, 1975), p. 39.

6. Bruce A. Ackerman, Social Justice in the Liberal State (New Haven, Conn.: Yale University Press, 1980), p. 93.

7. Kenneth M. Dolbeare and Patricia Dolbeare, American Ideologies: The Competing Political Beliefs of the 1970s (Chicago: Markham, 1971), p. 84.

8. Robert L. Heilbroner, "The Future of Capitalism," in Views on Capitalism, ed. Richard Romano and Melvin Leiman, 2d. ed. (Beverly Hills: Glencoe Press, 1975), pp. 213, 216.

9. John Kenneth Galbraith, "The New Industrial State," in Views on Capitalism, ed. Richard Romano and Melvin Leiman, 2d. ed. (Beverly Hills: Glencoe Press, 1975), p. 183; see also idem, The New Industrial State, rev. ed. (Boston: Houghton Mifflin, 1971), pp. 348–55.

10. Kaufman, Radical Liberal, p. 144.

11. Dolbeare and Dolbeare, American Ideologies, pp. 80, 86.

12. Kaufman, Radical Liberal, p. 26.

13. Ibid., p. 15.

14. See Stuart A. Scheingold, The Politics of Rights (New Haven, Conn.: Yale University Press, 1974), pp. 203-19.

15. I develop this concept in my Thinking about Politics: Two Political Sciences (St. Paul: West, 1980), chap. 9.

16. Sheldon Wolin, Politics and Vision (Boston: Little Brown, 1960), p. 294.

17. Kaufman, Radical Liberal, pp. 48-51.

18. Ackerman, Social Justice, p. 3.

19. Francis Fox Piven and Richard A. Cloward, Poor People's Movements: Why They Succeed and How They Fail (New York: Vintage, 1979), p. xxi.

20. Ibid., p. xxii.

21. Compare Dolbeare and Dolbeare, American Ideologies, pp. 96-102; and Michael Harrington, Socialism (New York: Bantam, 1972), chaps. 1-5.

22. See Immanuel Wallerstein, The Modern World-System: Capitalist Agriculture and the Origins of the European World-Economy in the Sixteenth Century, text ed. (New York: Academic, 1976).

23. Paul A. Baran and Paul M. Sweezy, Monopoly Capital: An Essay on the American Economic and Social Order (New York: Monthly Review, 1966), p. 363.

24. Harry Braverman, Labor and Monopoly Capital: The Degradation of Work in the Twentieth Century (New York: Monthly Review, 1974), p. 27.

25. Baran and Sweezy, Monopoly Capital, p. 364.

26. For a good summary, see Albert Szymanski, The Capitalist State and the Politics of Class (Cambridge, Mass.: Winthrop, 1978), chap. 1.

27. For example, see Alan Wolfe, The Seamy Side of Democracy (New York: McKay, 1973), chaps. 5-6.

28. See Michael Parenti, Democracy for the Few (New York: St. Martin's, 1974); Christopher Lasch, The Culture of Narcissism (New York: Warner, 1979); and Mark E. Kann, "The Crisis of Authority in America," Humanities in Society 3, no. 2 (Spring 1980): 124.

29. Bertell Ollman, "Toward Class Consciousness Next Time: Marx and the Working Class," in The Politics and Society Reader, ed. Ira Katznelson, Gordon Adams, Philip Brenner, and Alan Wolfe (New York: McKay, 1974), p. 328.

30. G. William Domhoff, "Blueprints for a New Society," in Is America Necessary?, ed. Henry Etzkowitz and Peter Schwab (St. Paul: West, 1976), p. 600.

31. See United States vs. Bob Avakian and the Mao Tse-tung Defendants, a publication of the Committee to Free the Mao Tse-tung Defendants, 1981.

32. Baran and Sweezy, Monopoly Capital, p. 366.

33. See Mark E. Kann, "Antonio Gramsci and Modern Marxism," Studies in Comparative Communism 13, nos. 2-3 (Summer-Autumn 1980), pp. 250-66.

34. Milton Fisk, "History and Reason in Rawls' Moral Theory," in Reading Rawls, ed. Norman Daniels (New York: Basic Books, 1975), p. 79.

35. Stanley Aronowitz, False Promises: The Shaping of American Working Class Consciousness (New York: McGraw-Hill, 1973), p. 423.

36. Some socialists do not use the word revolution, but they generally adhere to its underlying meaning. Thus, Howard Zinn speaks of the need "to dismantle that system while creating a new one." See his A People's History of the United States (New York: Harper & Row, 1980), p. 582.

37. See Richard F. Hamilton, Class and Politics in the United States (New York: Wiley & Sons, 1972), pp. 545-46.

38. Piven and Cloward, Poor People's Movements, p. xi.

39. For a brief discussion, see John P. Diggins, The American Left in the Twentieth Century (New York: Harcourt Brace Jovanovich, 1973), pp. 40-49.

40. For example, see Jessie Bernard, Women and the Public Interest: An Essay on Policy and Protest (Chicago: Aldine, 1971), chap. 1.

41. Virtually any issue of the journal Telos is certain to support this point.

42. Hamilton, Class and Politics, p. 551.

43. Ted Becker, Paul Szep, and Dwight Ritter, Un-Vote for a New America (Boston: Allyn & Bacon, 1976), p. 144.

44. Kaufman, Radical Liberal, p. 5.

45. Ibid.

46. Ackerman, Social Justice, p. 244.

47. See Hamilton, Class and Politics, chaps. 2, 12.

48. Compare Isaac Balbus, "The Concept of Interest in Pluralist and Marxian Analysis," in The Politics and Society Reader, ed. Ira Katznelson (New York: McKay, 1974), p. 303; and Bertell Ollman, "On Teaching Marxism," in Studies in Socialist Pedagogy, ed. Theodore Mills Norton and Bertell Ollman (New York: Monthly Review, 1978), pp. 215-53. For a good critique, see Martin Sklar, "Some Remarks on Ollman's 'On Teaching Marxism,'" in Studies in Socialist Pedagogy, ed. Theodore Mills Norton and Bertell Ollman (New York: Monthly Review, 1978), pp. 261-72.

49. See Todd Gitlin, "Weathermania: White Heat Underground," Nation, December 19, 1981, pp. 657, 669-74.

50. See Kirkpatrick Sale, SDS (New York: Vintage, 1974), p. 572.

51. Samuel P. Huntington, "The United States," in The Crisis of Democracy, ed. Michel Crozier, Samuel P. Huntington, and Joji Watanuki (New York: New York University Press, 1975), p. 59.

52. An interesting attempt to link consent of the governed to good choices is contained in Alan Gewirth, "Political Justice," in Social Justice, ed. R. B. Brandt (Englewood Cliffs, N.J.: Prentice-Hall, 1962), p. 160.

53. Hamilton, Class and Politics, p. 550.

54. NAM: The Political Perspective, a publication of the New American Movement, 1972, pp. 1, 21.

55. Diggins, The American Left, p. 194.

56. Christopher Lasch, "The Disintegration of the New Left," in Political Ideologies, ed. James A. Gould and Willis H. Truitt (New York: Macmillan, 1973), p. 337.

57. Compare Diggins, The American Left, chap. 6; and Lyman Tower Sargent, Contemporary Political Ideologies, rev. ed. (Homewood, Ill.: Dorsey, 1972), chap. 7.

58. See Ralph Miliband, Marxism and Politics (Oxford: Oxford University Press, 1977), pp. 157-58.

59. See Tom Hayden, Make the Future Ours, a Tom Hayden for U.S. Senate campaign document, Los Angeles, 1976.

60. See Dan Georgakas and Marvin Surkin, Detroit, I Do Mind Dying: A Study in Urban Revolution (New York: St. Martin's, 1975), especially the section called "Mr. Justin Ravitz: Marxist Judge of Recorder's Court," pp. 211-25.

61. Loni Hancock quoted in Ellen Hume, "60's Radicals Change System from Within," Los Angeles Times, June 21, 1976.

62. See Hamilton, Class and Politics, p. 548.

63. John Goldman and Doyle McManus, "50 Radicals May Be Linked to Brink's Heist, FBI Says," Los Angeles Times, December 24, 1981.

PART II

RADICAL DEMOCRACY

INTRODUCTION TO PART II

> Democracy means the power and the freedom of those
> controlled by law to change the law, according to agreed
> upon rules—and even to change these rules; but more
> than that, it means some kind of collective self-control
> over the structural mechanics of history itself.
>
> C. Wright Mills

The most admirable aspects of radical liberalism and socialism
are summarized in the term <u>radical democracy</u>. It is a theory, a
politics, and a way of social life where enriched consent and public
control overlap. It has roots in America's Lockean political culture
but potentially branches out to a more egalitarian future. It is a basis
for opposing elitism and a vision that may be attractive to different
segments of the American Left and significant numbers of Americans.
In Part II, I will extract from the American Left's twentieth century
experiences the tendencies that favor radical democracy and, ultimately, greater Left unity, popular support, and influence.

Chapter 3 points out the radical democratic terrain where
Lockean liberalism and Marxism sometimes overlap. The former
ideological tradition has been flexible enough to admit into American
dialogue the idea of democratic political control over social life. The
latter tradition can and has been reinterpreted in ways to highlight the
importance of the democratic socialization of the political system. In
different ways, the once antagonistic theoretical foundations of the
American Left are now conceptually complementary. This staking
out of radical democratic terrain conceivably can provide an identity
for radical activists that outlives past moments of Left influence.

Chapter 4 examines the language in which radical democracy
can and has been communicated to the American people. Early
American socialists, like Eugene V. Debs and Morris Hillquit, show
how radical democratic messages within the Marxist world can be
translated into the American vernacular in ways that can be transmitted to public audiences without losing their radical meanings.
Recent "economic democrats" show how the Lockean vernacular can
be radicalized and democratized in ways that cue Americans to resolve their ambivalence in favor of egalitarian alternatives. These
are examples of how the American Left has sometimes found a voice
that opens up rather than closes dialogue with the American people.

Chapter 5 traces the political changes undergone by the American Left in the last two decades. It suggests that some radical liberals have forsaken their sobriety and have developed political strategies based on trusting the American public; it also suggests that
some socialists have converged on political strategies that are neither

reformist nor revolutionist but that aim to enhance people's power today so that people themselves may extend democracy tomorrow. Conceivably, this is a politics that takes advantage of common Left concerns, strengthens the Left's democratic credentials, and at least hints at a means by which the Left can garner political influence.

There are indications that the American Left has begun to recast its thought, talk, and politics in ways that militate against the Left reproducing its own history of failures. In Part III, I will consider if these radical democratic tendencies are likely to facilitate American Left fortunes. Do they make elite vulnerabilities conspicuous? Do they legitimate Left values? Do they inform a politics able to undermine elite power and to defend and extend democratic terrain in modern America?

3

WHERE LOCKE AND MARX MEET

America's Lockean culture is a hospitable environment for elites. It is a world of meanings that enables elites to legitimate their power through consent and to wield their power over a relatively quiescent population. It is also a Gothic world that insulates elites from the radical challenges that historically run aground on the shores of assimilation and isolation. In short, it is a powerful source of elite hegemony.

This chapter investigates if Lockean culture and liberalism are flexible enough to encompass values that go beyond radical liberalism and overlap with important aspects of socialism. These values may provide the American Left with the basis for an identity that is more than oppositional, articulates the ambivalent concerns of radical activists, and provides avenues of communication to Americans. I suggest that where Locke and Marx meet is on the terrain of radical democracy.

LOCKEAN LIBERALISM AND ELITISM

The problem for U.S. elites, suggests Sheldon Wolin, is "to secure a steady and continuous flow of legitimacy <u>from</u> the people without promoting steady and continuous interference <u>by</u> the people."[1] During the American Revolution, colonial elites recognized that any new political order would have to be founded on popular consent if it was to survive. They also knew that governments based on popular control endangered their own power and wealth. Somehow, popular consent and popular control would have to be divorced. "The solution," continues Wolin, "was provided by the political theory of John Locke, worked out in practice in the British House of Commons, and perfected later in the American system."[2] Locke's liberalism contains the key strategies for founding a United States based on the appearance of political equality to attract popular consent and the reality of elitism that denies popular control.

Locke's theory is an attack on paternalistic political power. His alternative rests on divine natural law, which declares all individuals are born "free and equal" to one another.[3] In a state of nature—that is, outside of history—individuals share natural rights to life, liberty, and property; they also enjoy a mutual respect for their neighbors' rights. Individuals can live in relative harmony, peace, and prosperity. Unfortunately, this Edenic garden contains a snake or two. It has a few "dangerous and noxious creatures" who live by "no rule but that of force and violence."[4] It is populated by individuals who, when push comes to shove, defend their own rights at their neighbors' expense.[5] Those who feast at the tree of knowledge understand that a state of war always threatens civilized life.

How can individuals protect their natural rights? Rational people understand that they have an interest in drawing up and consenting to a social contract. Each person must "resign" his "natural power" to enforce his own rights and cede it to an impartial or neutral government that "umpires" social relations.[6] This government is to defend individual rights and arbitrate disputed rights; it is to monopolize the means of coercion to deter and punish private violence. Government is legitimate because individuals consent to it; individuals consent to it because it provides equal and maximal protection of their natural rights.

Like any umpire, government is subject to bribery and corruption and must be appropriately limited. Locke institutionalizes the limits in his plan for mixed, representative government.[7] State power must be mixed among several branches of government and the people to avoid concentrating it in the hands of officials who might abuse it without being checked. Officials must be representatives whose tenure depends on periodic elections, which provide people with regular opportunities for dismissing and replacing them. If government mechanisms are precisely engineered, political attempts to deny rather than defend individual rights will automatically set in motion powerful forces to ensure their failure.

A government that administers individual rights is the superstructure for a free society. Individuals are free to practice the religion of their choice without fear of repression; they can participate in electoral politics to protect their own interests, without denying others the same opportunities; they can strive to accumulate wealth, knowing they will receive the fruits of their labor, their contracts will be enforced, and their disputes will be settled peacefully and fairly. The abiding ethic that emerges, stated in John Rawls's contemporary terms, is "justice as fairness" or "the principles that free and rational persons would accept in an initial position of equality as defining the fundamental terms of their association."[8]

Thus described, Lockean liberalism appears to play an important role in what Alexis de Tocqueville called the gradual development of the principle of equality.[9] Individuals have equal rights; government protects those rights equally; and such protection provides individuals with an equal opportunity to pursue their goals in life. The theory is tailored to attract the consent of those who have suffered from religious intolerance, political tyranny, or aristocratic economic restrictions (that is, it is tailored to fit the mood of the Europeans who colonized the United States). However, it is also tailored to foster a culture that distances people from centers of power and encourages the discontented to vote or migrate rather than revolt, that easily accommodates elitism rather than contests it, and that legitimates a capitalist economy that breeds mass dependence.

Lockean liberalism rests on a natural law foundation that serves as a depository for prejudices that silence democratic discourse. Locke, for example, assumes men are "naturally" superior to women. Carole Pateman's analysis suggests that "a man must learn to interpret women's 'consent' when, as in Locke's civil society, there are no obvious expressions of it."[10] There are no obvious expressions of it because women are "naturally" isolated in their families, or, as Lorenne M. G. Clark states:

> Locke's argument is basically very simple. The role of women is to bear men's children; the price of bearing children is loss of autonomy with respect to acquisition, ownership, and control of property. Thus, women who bear children are and must be dependent on men for their survival and for the survival of their children.[11]

To the degree that patriarchy is taken as natural, Locke's liberalism implicitly condemns egalitarian alternatives as unnatural. Thus, William Ellery Channing could support Mary Wollstonecraft's human rights doctrine as "noble, generous, and sublime" but could not imagine the application of the doctrine to women and their families as anything other than unnatural.[12] Similarly, if white racial superiority or heterosexuality are taken as natural, then full equality for blacks or gay people must be considered unnatural and, by extension, illegitimate.

In addition, Lockean natural law petrifies individual rights by making them indisputable. People who consent to a government that administers Lockean rights to life, liberty, and property may justly claim that God and nature sanctify their choice. However, people who consent to a government, for example, that denies private property rights have made an unnatural and immoral choice; such a government is no more legitimate than the Nazi government chosen by a plurality of German voters in the 1930s.[13] This is precisely the line of reasoning Noah Webster had in mind when he condemned the redistributive policies of state legislatures during the Articles of Confederation period. "So many legal infractions of sacred right—so many public invasions of private property—so many wanton abuses of legislative powers!"[14] This is also the line of reasoning that allows federal courts to declare as void local control over property relations.

Once embedded in the culture, Lockean natural law establishes the limits of tolerance to spawn American Gothic predispositions. People who accept these limits are free to engage in public discourse, but people who contest the limits are seditious. Women who have protested their subordinate status have been labeled agents of the devil, witches, or insane; blacks who have protested have been labeled barbarians or "bad niggers"; gays who have protested have been labeled queers and perverts out to destroy the family; and radicals who have protested have been labeled atheists or seditious aliens. The labeling process condemns protesters as treasonous, justifies a suspension of what rights they have, and legitimates state repression against them.[15] It also provides ambivalent Americans with a strong motive for quiescence or migration. On the one hand, the ambivalent may avoid the stigma of being considered unnatural or un-American by reaffirming their belief in acceptable ideas. Tocqueville writes, "I know of no country in which there is so little independence of mind and real freedom of discussion as in America."[16] On the other hand, the social stigma may be avoided by migrating West, to places like San Francisco, where the limits of tolerance are sometimes more flexible. The overall result is that democratic discourse is silenced and protest is both defused and diffused.

Lockean liberalism prescribes a combination of rights and politics that is useful to elites, who wish to justify their power and distance people from it. Lockean rights are procedural rights that free individuals to pursue the sustenance necessary for life, the personal values and interests that constitute liberty, and the unlimited wealth symbolized by property. They are rights to compete, without undue interference, in the moral, political, and economic marketplaces. However, they are not rights that guarantee individuals certain access to the resources necessary for competing effectively. They do not entitle individuals to the communication skills and expertise needed to place their values on the public agenda; they do not entitle individuals to the material resources required for political influence; and they do not entitle individuals to access or control over the means of production, which would make them viable economic competitors. Both in logic and in history, the poor and downtrodden have always lacked the requisite resources for taking full advantage of procedural rights, and the powerful and wealthy have always had resources enough to monopolize public marketplaces.[17] Equal procedural rights in class societies generate greater power and wealth for those who already have it.

A major contribution of Lockean liberalism is to sanitize the whole process. Lockean rights are rights outside of history. They are not linked to the force and violence that is the historical basis for the original accumulation of power and wealth and, therefore, the superior means to take advantage of rights.[18] Lockean rights launder this history by making sacred the right to inheritance, which transforms the ill-gotten gains of yesterday into legitimate private property today. How many Americans remember or even care that John D. Rockefeller's corrupt and criminal practices were the source of the contemporary Rockefeller empire?[19] America's premiere Lockean liberal of our time, Robert Nozick, speaks of rectifying past injustices but does not take rectification seriously enough to consider a redistribution of ill-gotten wealth.[20] As long as redistribution is out of the question, elites will be free to use and abuse procedural rights to their own advantage. Furthermore, Lockean rights are linked to a Protestant ethic, which encourages the belief that any individual, howsoever situated in society, can take advantage of one's rights, if only one works hard enough. The cultural implication is that people who fail in the marketplace must blame only themselves for not having put forth adequate effort. This predisposition to self-blame motivates ambivalent Americans to strive to become better competitors rather than to question the foundation of competition itself.[21]

Lockean politics is an ideal mechanism for washing away any traces of residual unfairness. Locke himself gives prominence to the legislature, elected by a majority of voters, to safeguard rights, because he foresees the electorate will consist mainly or exclusively of propertyholders who benefit by these rights.[22] Nonetheless, Locke checks the legislature with executive prerogative to invoke natural law against the legislature and with a constitutional prohibition against the legislature asserting power over "the whole or any part of a subject's property without the owner's consent."[23] Under the guise of a mixed, representative government, private wealth that can be converted into superior political power is well protected. The Founders and their heirs "improve" Lockean politics by advocating a "science of politics" that is "avowedly antidemocratic."[24] Fearful that an electoral majority might contest private property rights, James Madison dilutes legislative powers through a mechanistic system of checks and balances. Alexander Hamilton's contribution was to locate significant powers in the executive and judicial branches, where public accountability is minimal. Herein lies the historical foundation for an American politics now characterized by an impotent Congress, a president with freedom to catalyze the rationalization of the domestic and international economy, and a Supreme Court that extends individual rights to corporations.[25] Individuals still have the Lockean rights to voice their views, vote, and even petition their legislators; but these rights do not provide individuals with either access to or influence in the centers of decision-making power.

Lockean liberalism stands ready to ease any public anxieties that arise from the distance between centers of control and the American people. The existential bottom line is that life concerns itself mainly with the practice of one's God-given rights in the individual, private realm. Politics is simply an administrative realm, and administration is best left to the experts—those whom Locke characterizes as "a few good men . . . of understanding, diligence, and disinterestedness."[26] Certainly administrative abuses that harm people are possible, but people need not be overly concerned; mechanistic checks and balances will minimize potential damage, and upcoming elections will eliminate it. Citizenship is primarily a matter of an occasional vote; it is basically a waste of dear human time to discuss the issues, participate in their resolution, or get emotionally involved in political contests.[27] Once mass apathy becomes habitual, Locke suggests, "great mistakes in the ruling part, many wrong and inconvenient laws, and all the slips of human frailty will be borne by the people without mutiny or murmur."[28] A silenced majority is one that will not challenge elite power except under the most extraordinary conditions.

In the social sphere, Lockean liberalism promotes an ethic of sacrifice, what Sheldon Wolin calls voluntary self-mutilation, which ultimately profits elites and pacifies majorities.[29] Lockean rationality is the ability to sacrifice pleasures today in order to accumulate greater pleasures tomorrow. Good Protestants sacrifice the pleasures associated with sin to attain eternal bliss in the next world. More to the present point, rational economic beings sacrifice the pleasures of idleness and immediate consumption, work hard and long, save and invest, and eventually experience the pleasures of material security, enhanced productivity, and potentially unlimited profits.[30] Of course, this is the ethic that predominates in the myth of early U.S. capitalism.

Locke's political theory assumes that all people are born with a capacity to think and act rationally; but his more influential empirical theory suggests that only a few people are situated to develop that capacity into an actual ability.[31] This gap is a function of social differences.

Individuals are always tempted to give in to the impulse of immediate satisfaction. They must be educated properly to learn why
they should resist such impulses and to acquire the habit of obeying
their reason. This education must begin at an early age because "he
that is not used to submit his will to the reason of others, when he is
young, will scarce hearken or submit to his own reason, when he is
of an age to make use of it."[32] As a matter of historical course,
Locke assumes that only the wealthy and leisured can afford to provide their children with a proper education; indeed, only the upper
classes have that "large, sound, round-about sense" that makes them
understand the importance of such an education.[33] Locke's linkage
between class and education, and thus, rationality, is questioned but
generally accepted by the Founders. Thomas Jefferson and James
Madison agreed that there is no necessary connection between riches
and reason, but, in the aggregate, they considered property the best
indicator of intellectual ability.[34] "Jefferson's aristoi, Hamilton's
men of 'strong minds and merit,' and Adams's 'natural aristocracy
of talent'" were theoretically classless but historically leaders who
spoke in upper-class accents.[35]

The flip side of the Lockean coin is the assumption that the bulk
of humanity is governed by passions and superstitions. Locke puts
it quite simply in the following:

> The ordinary necessities of our lives fill a great part of
> them with uneasinesses of hunger, thirst, heat, cold,
> weariness, with labour, and sleepiness in their constant
> returns. To which if we add fantastical uneasiness (as
> an itch after honour, power, or riches) which acquired
> habits, by fashion, example, and education, have settled
> in us . . . we shall find that a very little part of our life
> is so vacant from these uneasinesses, as to leave us
> free to the attraction of remoter absent good.[36]

Those whom Locke labels the vulgar and the mass or the laboring and
the illiterate are engaged in an animal struggle for survival. They
have neither the wealth that would allow them to sacrifice appropriately
for their children's education nor the inclination to do so. Instead,
they practice "barbarous habits" and "evil customs," which condemn
them to reproduce impoverished lives in each generation.[37] While
Locke's American heirs have rarely been as open and direct in their
portraits of mass irrationality, certainly their estimations of mass
society paint as bleak a picture. The children of Locke cannot
imagine entrusting significant power to the American masses.

Intelligence is for the few; ignorance is for the many. On this
foundation, Locke erects a two-tiered edifice of sacrifice. The top

tier is occupied by the sober and industrious, by "those, me thinks, who by the industry and part of their ancestors, have been set free from a constant drudgery to their bellies."[38] These are men of property and intelligence who must be free to sacrifice some of their wealth to the investments that bring greater productivity and wealth. Locke anticipates later trickle-down theories. "The king of a large and fruitful territory," he writes, "feeds, lodges, and is clad worse than a day-labourer in England."[39] The message is that entrepreneurs must be free in the marketplace to produce the wealth of nations, which trickles down even as far as the "day-laborer." In a sense, even the least well-off in a free economy are better off than otherwise.[40] Locke's bottom tier is occupied by most of humanity, by people who still drudge for their bellies and have no surplus wealth for investments. They are to make two kinds of sacrifices. First, they must sacrifice political and economic control to rational elites, who alone can produce trickle-down benefits. Second, they can make small sacrifices at their disposal—work harder and longer, budget and save, or find some way to educate their children—to move up the social ladder. A few of them even make it.

Possibly, those on the bottom tier are not even rational enough to recognize their own interest in ceding control or working harder. Locke's fallback position is to school them in the Gospels, which teach obedience as the human lot.[41] His American heirs are slightly more sophisticated. They translate the ethic of sacrifice into the norm of desert.[42] The "deserving" poor are those without resources who stand ready to make sacrifices for self-improvement. They are to be helped, through private charity or public largesse, to help themselves. The "undeserving" poor are stigmatized as ne'er-do-wells and are the object of the following city manager's attack:

> We challenged the right of social parasites to breed illegitimate children at the taxpayer's expense. We challenged the right of moral chiselers and loafers to squat on the relief rolls forever. We challenged the right of cheaters to make more on relief than when working. . . . We challenged the right of people to quit jobs at will and go on relief like spoiled children.[43]

The scorn that Lockean culture attaches to those who refuse to make the rational sacrifices required on the bottom tier is often enough to cue ambivalent Americans to resolve their uncertainties in favor of the capitalist economy rather than suffer guilt by association with parasites, chiselers, loafers, cheaters, and spoiled children who "squat" on America.

These are some of the ideas that wed Lockean liberalism to U.S. elitism and divorce popular consent from popular control. In my estimation, Lockean liberalism and the culture it informs may be the most powerful sources of elite hegemony anywhere in the world. Nevertheless, they are not perfected sources of elite hegemony; they are ideas, myths, and symbols that are always at odds with Americans' daily experiences. Today, millions of gay people, blacks, and women do not consider their claims to equality unnatural; millions of voters and nonvoters recognize that the ballot box does not provide much political influence and are bothered by that fact; millions of employed, underemployed, and unemployed Americans realize that the ethic of sacrifice is failing to bear economic fruits for them. When the conventional Lockean way of understanding conflicts with everyday experience, mass ambivalence results. People may still wear Lockean lenses to perceive their dilemmas, but at some level they "know" that the actual organization of power in the United States is harming their interests. Even if people resolve their ambivalence in favor of quiescence, the sources of ambivalence persist. Conceivably, the American Left can extract from the familiar Lockean world some ideas that are more attuned to people's frustrations, re-evoke popular ambivalence, and suggest the possibility of uniting popular consent and popular control.

BEYOND RADICAL LIBERALISM

Richard Ashcraft recently highlighted some of the radical features of Locke's Second Treatise. Ashcraft builds a case for understanding Locke's work as "a political declaration for a revolutionary movement" (misnamed the Rye House Plot). The document was designed "to urge radicals to unite, through revolutionary actions" and was directed at the "brewers, tailors, silk dyers, weavers, and carpenters" who would make the revolution.[44] If Lockean liberalism was founded not to justify the exchange of elites in 1688 but to help create a revolution from below years earlier, then it may contain ideas suitable to radical democratic movements. Mary Lyndon Shanley recently pointed out that Locke radicalized classical notions of consent in the marriage contract. Whereas consent to marriage once meant consent to preconceived, elitist terms of marriage, "John Locke suggested that if marriage were a 'contractual' relationship, the terms of the contract as well as whether or not to enter into the relationship were negotiable."[45] If Lockean liberalism could justify a renegotiation of the terms of the marriage contract, then why not the social contract? Conceivably, it opens the door to democratizing social relationships.

Whatever flexibility exists within Lockean liberalism, even more flexibility exists within a Lockean political culture. Locke's theory is somewhat rigid, because it complies with the canons of logic and exposition; but Lockean culture, like all culture, contains many subworlds. Beliefs, demands, and attitudes fluctuate, regularly appear in contradictory combinations, and adjust and readjust to differing patterns of experience. Let me suggest that America's Lockean political culture is pliant enough to provide a foothold for radicals who wish to bring out its more radical and democratic meanings.

Lockean natural law has always been open to renegotiation.[46] The religious Left in U.S. history, from the abolitionists and early feminists to Martin Luther King, Jr., Malcolm X, or today's Sojourners, have promoted reinterpretations of God's law that demand greater democracy. God has given humankind the rights, called self-evident in the Declaration of Independence, that should be extended to all people. God has commanded the human race to care for one another and to ensure that people's needs are equally respected. The secular Left has sometimes laid claim to natural law. The ecology movement, for example, extracts from nature people's rights to survive, work, and live in healthy environments; it sometimes suggests that it is natural for people to control their environment in order to safeguard their rights. Implicitly, other activists have used natural truths to legitimate people's rights to decent housing, fulfilling jobs, adequate health care, or, in the case of women, control over their own bodies. Rather than directly attack natural law as reactionary or ahistorical, these activists have contested some of the antidemocratic prejudices in it and have sought to substitute more egalitarian content. One might say that they have found immanent in natural law the core of a liberation theology and a radical democratic ethics.[47]

Lockean rights have also been renegotiated, redefined, and reweighted in ways more consistent with human equality. If Lockean rights are indisputable in the United States, perhaps they can be given new meanings. The right to life can be construed as the right to guaranteed subsistence for all people, including people in the Third World exploited by the likes of the Nestlé Corporation.[48] The right to liberty can be redefined as a right to individual autonomy, which contests elite hegemony and demands that people take collective control over their lives. Perhaps the rights to life and liberty should be more important than property rights; or perhaps property rights in the United States should be reexamined. In what sense do Americans have property in their labor or their goods when economic elites control the labor market and monopolize land and capital? In what sense is corporate property "private" if the state defines the rights and terms of incorporation? These questions do not directly attack the right to property so much as suggest that it is negotiable and subject to democratic dialogue. Recently, a California governor's task force made the "radical" proposal that public employees who own their retirement funds should also be able to control their retirement funds in the public interest and, thus, be able to underwrite loans to build low-cost housing but not provide capital to nuclear power interests, firms with discriminatory hiring policies, or corporations that invest in apartheid in South Africa.[49]

Three potential payoffs are to be had from this renegotiation process. First, it is a familiar form of Lockean dialogue that promises to expand the American limits of tolerance and to admit into public debate elements of democratic discourse. Second, it is one means of breaking down the elitist distinction between procedural right and substantive justice. To redefine the right to life as the right to guaranteed subsistence at some level of decency is to legitimate demands for fairer processes of acquiring wealth and a more just distribution of wealth. Third, it provides the Left with new avenues of communication to the American people. Arthur Allen Leff's statement about modern moralists applies equally well to most Left ideologists. "Very rarely do modern moralists actually give the ethical positions of the people on the Clapham Omnibus equal weight. Notably preferred by them are the people in the professorial Volvo, ostensibly because they do not have just any old view of an ethical question but a 'considered' view."[50] Radical liberals in particular are rationalists who do not like to talk about natural law or dispute natural rights. They fear such a talk is an invitation to involve the masses in a dialogue for which they are unprepared and in which groups like the Moral Majority will reap the greatest benefits. However, radical activists have better understood that talk about religion and truth, good and evil, is an important line of communication to Americans, who temper their rationalism with the religious and secular verities that are a part of their everyday lives. Indeed, such talk provides a source of inspired commitment that rationalism does not. The point is not to eliminate rationalism but to augment it with the moral talk necessary for contesting elitist Lockean terrain; the point is to allow radicals to say, "Napalming babies is bad. Starving the poor is wicked. Buying and selling each other is depraved."[51] If the Left is really concerned about democratic dialogue, it must speak about the moral issues with which ordinary Americans are both familiar and concerned.

Lockean politics is not democratic, but it does have a democratic facet that can be used for radical ends. In particular, Lockean values, like equal liberty and majoritarianism, can be used to claim that the state is an instrument for extending democratic rights and a forum for articulating a collective will regarding the direction of social life. Despite the fact that the state is not neutral, according to Philip Green, "there is no institutional tool for change that can equal the agencies of government in scope and impact."[52] Criticisms of the welfare state notwithstanding, minorities and women especially have found that government can be a useful tool for winning some public control over society.

Equal liberty is assumed in Locke's state of nature and, more recently, is John Rawls's first principle of justice. Rawls's Left critics have faulted his priorities, but Norman Daniels points out that equal liberty, in fact, is the principle that "carries the egalitarian punch."[53] One can ask under what social conditions people are situated so that they can take full advantage of equal liberty. Most Americans understand from their own experiences, for example, that poor schooling deprives children of the intellectual resources necessary for being free to compete equally in the nation's marketplaces. This understanding can be extended in three ways. First, variants of affirmative action—in education or hiring—could be justified as required bases for equalizing people's freedom to compete. Second, it can be argued that equalized freedom cannot be sustained in a competitive marketplace, which produces winners and losers with unequal abilities to take advantage of liberty.[54] Third, equal liberty can be a foundation upon which to build the notion that people, individually and collectively, must have equal access to the economic institutions and resources so important for exercising political and civil rights. From this, one can use Locke to valorize either a Jeffersonian one-class society or a democratic socialist society.

Majoritarianism is a Lockean value that can be enriched to justify popular movements aimed at using government as an instrument for promoting democratic dialogue, mass participation, and public control over aspects of society. On the one hand, majoritarianism locates popular sovereignty in the demos and is a basis for arguing for democratic control over elite-dominated political and social institutions. The experts and bureaucrats who monopolize public discourse, the checks and balances that shield political elites, and the privileges of property that empower economic elites can be contested as means that facilitate elite rule in opposition to majoritarian sovereignty. On the other hand, majoritarianism is a serviceable value for vocalizing and politicizing silenced citizens. It invites people to play a role in the discourse that shapes the majoritarian will; it legitimates popular participation in the exercise of power; and it ennobles discourse and participation, with the expectation that the majoritarian will should be the fount of the public policy that shapes Americans' social life together. It is a value that may spark what Cloward and Piven call the politics of turmoil, whereby people give up habitual quiescence and demand to be heard, empowered, and in control of their government as an instrument for meeting their common needs.[55]

This distended version of Lockean politics goes beyond radical liberalism in several ways. It systematically links liberty with the reconstruction of social power and, thereby, prefigures a breakdown in conventional distinctions between private and public realms of life. It also introduces into public dialogue the idea that democratic collective control over politics and society is a possible meaning for popular sovereignty. Perhaps most important, it catalyzes a mass politicization that contravenes the quiescence elites desire as well as the sobriety radical liberals prefer. This politicization means that people who one day support a progressive like Dennis Kuchinich of Cleveland may the next day support a conservative like Congressman Jack Kemp; it means that people may engage in a degree of social turmoil that both makes it difficult for elites to rule and makes possible a conservative backlash against democratic rights. "Connecting authority and disorder is not arcane," writes Richard Sennett, "it is simply taking seriously the ideal of democracy."[56] Perhaps an elitist order can only be weakened by the popular disorder that follows no ideological guidelines but that does allow people to articulate for themselves the kinds of rights and needs that ought to be taken seriously.

Finally, the Lockean liberalism that erects the two-tiered edifice of sacrifice implicitly contains blueprints for the egalitarian renovation of economic life. Let us first assume that the American people are as irrational as most Lockean liberals believe. Let us assume that the masses harbor undemocratic attitudes, little respect for one another's rights, and impulses toward immediate gratifications that undermine peace and fairness. Why are the American people so irrational? According to Lockean logic, one reasonable answer is that they are engaged in an animal struggle for survival (at some level of decency) and lack the time and resources necessary for developing their rational capacities into effective abilities. But rather than using this insight to justify elite rule and mass obedience, one can raise a prior question. Why do most people lack the time and resources necessary for developing their rational capacities? A historical answer may be to resurrect the injustices of original entitlements, which provide the few with leisure and wealth and the many with perpetual want. For example, if economic elites' power stems from the accumulations made possible by slavery, then, as the Black Economic Development Conference suggested in 1969, slaves' contemporary heirs should receive reparations, which would constitute an egalitarian redistribution of power and wealth.[57] A political answer may suggest that today's socioeconomic conditions deprive a majority of Americans of the power and wealth necessary for developing their rational capacities. Perhaps those socioeconomic conditions must be restructured along egalitarian lines to enable all citizens to develop the rationality necessary for consent, full citizenship, and productive lives.

Let us next consider the counterassumption that Americans are not as irrational as most Lockean liberals assume. Compared with Locke's own era, our era is one where wealth is abundant and public education is open to all. Conceivably, all Americans have leisure and wealth enough to develop their rational capacities. A number of empirical studies suggest, in fact, that elites do not have a corner on democratic attitudes, respect for rights, or deliberativeness.[58] Furthermore, studies like Thomas Kuhn's The Structure of Scientific Revolutions and Barry Commoner's The Poverty of Power bring home the point that "experts" are no less ideological than other Americans, despite claims of objectivity.[59] If these arguments can be made persuasively, then the old justification for elite decision making in the polity and economy is weakened considerably, while the basis for demanding public control over decision making is strengthened. The people are reasonable enough to be self-governing in the community and the workplace.

These arguments use familiar notions of Lockean rationalism to replace trickle-down thinking with both redistributive justifications and public control mechanisms. While the arguments may be used to justify extraordinary measures aimed at some form of economic equality, at the very least, they can be used to suggest that all residual economic inequalities in society that, as Rawls puts it, "are reasonably expected to be to everyone's advantage" should be decided not by elites but by the people.[60] In addition, these arguments make possible a public dialogue that questions the permanence of the division of society between the rational few and the irrational many and opens to discussion the democratization of scientific priorities, administrative practices, or family relationships based on unequal endowments of reason. Whereas Locke envisioned a society organized from the top down, his own logic in the contemporary American context can be used to legitimate a vision of society structured from the bottom up.

I have purposely stretched Lockean liberalism out of conventional shape to identify the ways in which it can, and sometimes has, been used to challenge elitism and promote radical meanings. Values like natural law and rights, equal liberty and majoritarianism, and rational decision making have historically been used to legitimate elite rule, but they are negotiable enough to challenge elite hegemony; open up discussion about the terms of Americans' social contract; and underwrite rights and processes based on common human needs, the redistribution of power and wealth, and public control over government decisions and social policies in everyday life. To the extent that these values go beyond radical liberalism in ways that prefigure the breakdown of distinctions between procedural rights and substantive outcomes, private and public spheres of action, and expert and mass rationality, they abut on and even overlap with significant aspects of American socialists' Marxism.

THE FRONTIERS OF MARXISM

Marxism has long been considered the most powerful and prominent critique of Lockean liberalism. Marxism reveals Lockean liberalism as the rationalization for bourgeois hegemony, class rule, and private ownership of the means of production; it reveals Lockean liberalism as the true consciousness of the capitalist class and the false consciousness of the working class. Recently, however, Marxism has been reevaluated as something more than a critique of Lockean liberalism; it is sometimes considered its errant stepchild, too. For example, Martin Sklar suggests that "bourgeois modes of consciousness are also, historically linked to Marx's thought. They are the key condition of its emergence and maturation, and more broadly, of the socialist outlook. . . . Concrete elements of bourgeois ideology . . . for example, flow into the socialist (and Marx's) outlook."[61] Studies that focus on the early writings of Marx bring out his concerns with human nature and morality, which show sustained traces of liberal influences. Studies that focus on Marx's political writings highlight, to a degree, his debt to and investment in liberal political emancipation. When Marx writes that he is not a Marxist, he invites people to go beyond the particular socialist orthodoxies of the moment and to exhibit some flexibility in interpretation and outlook. In this section, I want to accept his invitation in order to distinguish the terrain where Lockean liberalism and Marxism overlap.

"Species-being" is a concept Marx takes from Feuerbach and augments with an action orientation. "Man is a species-being, not only because in practice and in theory he adopts the species as his object . . . but—and this is only another way of expressing it—also because he treats himself as the actual, living species; because he treats himself as 'universal' and therefore a free being."[62] Marx's species-being taps what is natural or essential to human life. The truth of human existence is that people are organically bound to one another as members of a common species, as people with common species-needs and aspirations. However, historically people often think and act in ways alien to their essential nature. "Men," writes Marx, "who do not feel themselves to be men grow up for their masters like a breed of slaves."[63] In other words, there is a historical gap between people's capacity to be fully human and their ability to live fully human lives beyond the animal struggle for survival. Marx's concern with alienation, which links his 1844 Manuscripts to Capital, is one basis for explaining and narrowing this gap. Using Hegelian terminology, Marx partly reproduces the Lockean distinction between people's rational capacities to be free human beings and their irrational abilities, which make them slaves to their bellies.

Marx's baseline explanation for alienation is found in Capital, where he writes, "In fact, the realm of freedom actually begins only where labour which is determined by necessity and mundane considerations ceases; thus in the very nature of things it lies beyond material production."[64] The daily struggle for material goods, either for subsistence or some socially acceptable standard of decent living, makes people dependent both on the largesse of nature and the class that controls the means of producing wealth. It also makes it extraordinarily difficult, if not impossible, for most people to strive for the spiritual goods essential to species development and, thus, to enter into the realm of freedom, where individual self-development and collective control over history can be practiced. In this sense, both Marx and Locke agree that abundance and leisure are prerequisites for full human development. Both also explain human underdevelopment (alienation or irrationality) as a product of people's historical inability to share in abundance and leisure.

What Marx means by human development is expressed by Eugene Kamenka in his analysis of Marx's ethics. "The 'presumption' and the true 'end' of ethics, of philosophy, of all human activities, is the free, truly human man. Man is potentially the only 'subject' in a world of objects, and anything that turns him into an object, subordinates him to powers outside himself, is inhuman."[65] Man as a species-being is man as a radically free person who lives within a social context of production, abundance, and leisure, which enables him to develop his natural capacities in harmony with others and to control the world of objects. He is free to become the hunter, fisherman, and critic; he is free to fulfill his physiological, psychological, and social needs with others. Man as a historical being, however, is the object of social forces that control him and, therefore, alienate him from others and from his humanity. One reading of Marx's corpus is that it is primarily an effort to understand and change the social forces that objectify people. This reading is quite consistent with a renegotiated natural law and rights that emphasize human needs and cooperative public control over society.

Marx's notion of "praxis" is a concept that relates the problem of human alienation to the historical possibilities for eliminating it. Shlomo Avineri provides a working definition. " 'Praxis' means for Marx both a tool for changing the course of history and a criterion for historical evaluation. 'Praxis' means man's conscious shaping

of the changing historical conditions."[66] Praxis is historical theory
that organizes thought in ways that make conspicuous how structures
of power fuel human alienation and objectify people. Thus, Marx tells
us, wage laborers in capitalist societies are free from feudal forms
of domination but are as yet unfree to decide whether or not to sell
their labor power. Praxis is also thought and action aimed at revealing the forces of change that drive people to overcome alienation and
objectification. Thus, Marx sees in capitalism the contradictions that
urge workers to unite as a class in itself and for itself and to overthrow the bourgeoisie. Though Marx's own praxis focuses mainly on
the economic sphere, it also finds useful employment in the political
sphere of human life.

Marx sees the rise of the liberal state as a form of progress.
Political emancipation frees people from feudalism's rigid blend of
social and political inequality. It nourishes the French revolutionaries' vision of liberty, equality, and fraternity. Historically, it is
one of the preconditions for fuller human emancipation, which comes
with socialism and communism. Of course, political emancipation
is a step and not an end in itself. In practice, it is an instrument of
capitalist elites; it legitimates values that are not practiced; and it is
a mechanism of social control that inhibits further progress. Put
another way, the liberal state and political emancipation reproduce
the contradictions of capitalism in the political realm. It is both an
arena for class conflict and an instrument for class rule.

Marx suggests that capitalists' attachment to the liberal state
and the norms of political emancipation last only as long as they are
useful to bourgeois rule. When people begin to capture political
power through mass suffrage and mass movements, capitalists must
repudiate their "bourgeois constitution" and announce the following:
"Our dictatorship has hitherto existed by the will of the people; it
must now be consolidated against the will of the people."[67] At least
one aspect of Marx's praxis concerns the thought and action of a politicized people, who demand control over the public arena.

Marx rarely underestimates the limits of political action. "To
be represented," he writes, for example, "is in general something
to be suffered." Universal suffrage mainly symbolizes a right to decide "once in three or six years which member of the ruling class
was to misrepresent the people in parliament."[68] Neither does Marx
underestimate the potentials of political action. He supports the more
equal liberty that will result from a ten-hour bill limiting the exploitation of labor; and he supports universal suffrage and majority rule as
instruments that may facilitate popular victories in the political arena.
He recommends that workers organize and join political parties that
promote "the rule of the working class against the rule of the bourgeoisie" as well as establish "their own revolutionary workers' gov-

ernments, whether in the form of municipal committees or in the form of workers' clubs or workers' committees. "[69] He sometimes promotes forms of direct democracy, where officials are "elective, responsible, and revocable" and mass politicization forces officials to defend workers' interests. [70] Marx, in short, rarely shies away from demands for equal liberty, majority rule, and mass participation within the context of the capitalist state; he supports political engagement as part of the struggle to transform society. In part, then, Marx's political praxis is consistent with a renegotiated Lockean politics of mass politicization and struggle in the governmental arena.

Furthermore, Marx's political praxis justifies an infusion of political struggle into social life. Marx often supports rights to a free press or free assembly, which make possible the growth of cooperative and trade union movements. He speaks highly of mass organizations that exert great pressure on elites, for example, through the "great extra-parliamentary demonstrations" that he witnessed in his own era. [71] He stands behind workers' organizations that foster mass participation, educate workers to understand and act on their own interests, and organize together to defend and extend their political rights and historical options. Such social groups not only clarify the lines of class conflict, they also provide workers with experiences in self-government, which are invaluable for controlling their own histories. [72] Marx has no systematic political theory, in my reading, but does implicitly advocate a political praxis consistent with popular sovereignty and mass activism, even turmoil, which can be extracted from Lockean liberalism.

Marx argues that the state will lose its historical function of serving as an instrument for class domination, when capitalist abundance births socialist society. "The working class, in the course of its development will substitute for the old civil society an association that will exclude classes and their antagonism, and there will be no more political power properly so-called, since political power is precisely the official expression of antagonism in civil society. "[73] Marx outlines the nature of this new association by using a metaphor relating an orchestra conductor to the orchestra. He says that all associations require

> a directing authority, in order to secure the harmonious working of individual activities, and to perform general functions that have their origin in the action of the combined organism, as distinguished from the actions of its separate organs. A single violin player is his own conductor; an orchestra requires a separate one. [74]

Marx indicates that the authority of the conductor is noncoercive. His role mainly is to articulate the needs and desires of the collectivity of musicians. Mainly, he is an administrator who performs "simple administrative functions" but who does not exercise political power over others. [75]

In a special sense, Marx's directing authority can be considered a representative of the people. Young Marx articulates what the older Marx implies.

> The legislative is a representation in the same sense
> which every function is representative. For example,
> the shoemaker is my representative insofar as he ful-
> fills a social need, just as every definitive social ac-
> tivity, because it is a species-activity, represents only
> the species; that is to say, it represents a determina-
> tion of my own essence the way every other man is rep-
> resentative of the other. [76]

Restated according to an admittedly flexible Lockean translation, Marx is saying that individuals are not obligated to obey a directing authority simply because they have participated in procedures for choosing that authority. Their obligation is also a function of the fact that the directing authority represents what is essential to human life and its administration. From this, we can derive a construction of reality that posits a society organized to fulfill essential human needs and to empower people in general to define those needs. Put another way, we can extract a social construction of reality that is consistent with eliminating distinctions between the rational few and the irrational many, between experts and the people, and with justifying the democratization of social life.

This reading can lead to some interesting reinterpretations of Marxian socialism. Certainly, it can be used to justify community control and worker control of production in the name of fulfilling common needs. But it can also be used to legitimate a political authority with the obligation to enact "a variety of redistributive policies stipulated by egalitarian values." Conceivably, if workers agree and use authority as a mechanism to implement their agreement, these policies might include a regulated marketplace, whereby "inegalitarian tendencies inherent in an unmitigated market distribution will be offset by the redistributional activity of the state." [77] The point here is not to defend such reinterpretations but to suggest that Marxism is flexible enough to admit them and, thus, to encompass the concerns of radicals from the Lockean tradition, who would rather restructure the economic marketplace than eliminate it. The foundation for any such discussion is that some form of democratic control from below is the source for economic transformation, whatever form it takes.

To summarize, Lockean liberalism and culture have generally been interpreted in ways that limit political power and, thus, insulate elites from demands for public control. However, a renegotiated version of Lockean norms can be used to justify democratic political control over social life. Marxism has usually been interpreted as an economic theory that limits politics to the superstructure. However, a flexible interpretation of Marxist analysis can be used to justify democratic struggles in the political arena. I have consciously emphasized these possibilities to point out that these ideologies, which continue to inform the American Left, share some common ground as critiques of elitism and, more important, as the basis for an American radical vision. Both can support an ethics that gives precedence to people's basic needs and development; a politics clothed in familiar terms of equal liberty, majoritarianism, and political activism; and a notion of social life characterized by diverse possibilities for public control and economic redistribution. The best way to characterize this intermediate world, which goes beyond radical liberalism and crosses the frontiers of Marxist socialism, is "radical democracy."

THE TERRAIN OF RADICAL DEMOCRACY

I will defer a fuller discussion of radical democracy to Chapter 7 but would like to outline its contours as an indication of its location and relationship to the American Left. Vaguely defined, radical democracy occupies the terrain where radical liberalism and Marxist socialism overlap and, as suggested in the previous chapter, where a great many Left activists have discovered the values most meaningful to them. It certainly includes concern for egalitarian processes in politics, processes that facilitate open discourse, mass participation, and forms of public control; it also includes concerns for fulfilling common human needs and for organizing society in ways that facilitate the fulfillment of those needs. It is liberal and socialist in what I consider the best senses of both traditions. However, radical democracy is not an ideology, like liberalism or Marxism, in the sense that it leaves unanswered many questions on which both liberalism and Marxism traditionally demand closure. Let me conclude this chapter by suggesting that the closure of the old ideologies on such questions has been one vice of the Left that can be rectified by the openness of radical democracy.

Does the gap between people's natural capacities and historical abilities (that is, the gap that issues forth in human underdevelopment or alienation) require a special vision or strategy for its elim-

ination? Radical liberals generally look to intellectuals or experts
to close the gap by educating people and, in the meantime, by acting
for people. In fact, U.S. education, often linked to social reforms,
has not closed the gap but has tainted radical liberalism with a de-
served elitist ambiance. Socialists generally assume that the resolution of objective class conflict will do the trick. But Americans have
shown little interest in class warfare, and let us remember that the
creation of socialist societies has not eliminated the sources or manifestations of alienation there. As a theory without an audience, socialism, too, is tainted by suspicions of an elitist agenda. Radical
feminist Nancy Hartsock suggests a different approach more consistent
with radical democracy. She argues that "theory is the articulation
of what our practical activity has already appropriated in reality. In
theorizing, we examine what we find in ourselves; we attempt to clarify for ourselves and others what we already, at some level know."[78]

Theory, as a democratic enterprise, must be flexible if it is
to articulate experiences and to highlight possibilities for change. It
is, in a sense, an examination not of abstract idea systems inherited
from the past but of experiences lived over time. When American
radicals examine themselves, as they do all too rarely, they generally
discover that neither radical liberalism nor Marxist socialism is able
to articulate their own experiences and, yes, ambivalence. It is very
hard to be a consistent radical liberal having experienced the persistent class differences that impoverish the lives of millions; it is
equally difficult to be a consistent Marxist socialist having learned
to take for granted the political liberty and opportunities, limited as
they may be, that exist in the United States and in all too few other
places on the globe. The traditional ideologies make it difficult to
conceptualize and talk about these experiences; they tend to eliminate
democratic dialogue over basic assumptions. Such rigidity is not
only foolish, it is also antidemocratic and certain to alienate potential
public support.

What is the nature of the struggle to overcome inequalities?
Must it be the reformism of radical liberals, who are haunted by the
everpresent specter of elite tyranny and mob anarchy? Or must it
be the revolutionism of socialists, who all too often imagine that sud-
den and dramatic change is the key to human control of history? Of
course, both reformism and revolutionism have done little to eke out
an abiding role for the American Left and its egalitarian values, but
the rhetoric attached to such strategies has succeeded in distancing
the Left from the American people. Again, Hartsock provides what
may be the basis for a radical democratic alternative when she asks,
"How, for example, can support for the Equal Rights Amendment
lead women to take power in such a way that the structures of social
relations as they are at present constituted cannot survive?"[79] The

question of reformism versus revolutionism is a theoretical abstraction in the modern United States. The question of how concrete reforms can empower people to command greater control over their own lives is one of interest both to radical activists and to Americans who see a need for change.

What kind of society should the Left strive to create? Should it be the modern-day Jeffersonianism preferred by radical liberals or the brands of collectivism that emanate from Marxism? Or are both visions based on an anachronistic Lockean and Marxian assumption of material abundance, which is increasingly denied in our own era of limits? Perhaps radicals need to readjust their ideas in ways consistent with the persistence of the realm of necessity and begin to talk about the processes and outcomes for distributing material sacrifices. "Change," writes Hartsock, "is the process of creating new problems out of our solutions to earlier problems."[80] For the American Left, earlier problems include disunity, lack of direction, and the invisibility that comes without a distinct identity and social basis of support. Perhaps the most sensible thing radicals can say about the future organization of society is that it should be guided by a democratic ethic of experimentation, which will allow people to shape it in ways they see fit. Solving the problem of elitism means freeing people to confront other problems.

American feminists are uniquely placed, because, in a sense, they have been the victims of the old ideologies. They have experienced how radical liberal or socialist ideas often give birth to a politics that does not respect the equality of women. They are especially sensitive to the ways in which feminists themselves tend to reproduce the old forms of inequality. Charlotte Bunch says that she is "disturbed that many socialist feminists are demanding once more that independent, nonaligned feminists curtail their political explorations . . . by declaring socialism is THE WAY, just as other feminists are demanding that we renounce socialism or embrace spirituality as THE WAY."[81] If THE WAY exists, be it radical liberalism or socialism, then those who advocate it have no firm basis for identifying with democracy; they leave no room for the demos itself to create its own future. What I have suggested in this chapter is that a flexible treatment of the old ideologies helps to identify the radical democratic terrain that vests authority in the demos to choose its own way, again and again.

NOTES

1. Sheldon Wolin, "The Idea of the State in America," in The Problem of Authority in America, ed. John P. Diggins and Mark E. Kann (Philadelphia: Temple University Press, 1981), p. 46.

2. Ibid.

3. John Locke, Two Treatises of Government, ed. Thomas Cook (New York: Hafner, 1947), p. 122.

4. Ibid., p. 129.

5. Ibid., pp. 130-31.

6. Ibid., p. 163.

7. Ibid., bk. 2, chaps. 11-14.

8. John Rawls, A Theory of Justice (Cambridge, Mass.: Harvard University Press, 1971), p. 11.

9. Alexis de Tocqueville, Democracy in America, ed. Richard Heffner (New York: New American Library, 1956), p. 29.

10. Carole Pateman, "Women and Consent," Political Theory 8 (May 1980): 155.

11. Lorenne M. G. Clark, "Women and Locke: Who Owns the Apples in the Garden of Eden," in The Sexism of Social and Political Theory, ed. Lorenne M. G. Clark and Lynda Lange (Toronto: University of Toronto Press, 1979), p. 37.

12. Henry F. May, The Enlightenment in America (Oxford: Oxford University Press, 1976), pp. 225-26.

13. For a good analysis of how Locke relates natural law to consent, see Patrick Riley, "On Finding an Equilibrium between Consent and Natural Law in Locke's Political Philosophy," Political Studies 22 (December 1974): 436; see also Hanna Pitkin, "Obligation and Consent—I," American Political Science Review 59 (December 1965): 990-99.

14. Noah Webster quoted in Gordon S. Wood, The Creation of The American Republic, 1776-1787 (New York: Norton, 1969), p. 411.

15. See Murray Edelman, Political Language: Words That Succeed and Policies That Fail (New York: Academic, 1977), for a good analysis of the dynamics and effects of the labeling process.

16. Tocqueville, Democracy in America, p. 117.

17. Two good analyses of the logic of Lockean proceduralism are C. B. Macpherson, The Political Theory of Possessive Individualism (London: Oxford University Press, 1962), pt. 5; and Garry Wills, Nixon Agonistes (New York: New American Library, 1970).

18. Both David Hume and Jean-Jacques Rousseau pointed this out centuries ago.

19. See G. David Garson, Power and Politics in the United States (Lexington, Mass.: D. C. Heath, 1977), chap. 9.

20. See Robert Nozick, Anarchy, State, and Utopia (New York: Basic Books, 1974), pp. 230-31.

21. See Richard Sennett and Jonathan Cobb, The Hidden Injuries of Class (New York: Vintage, 1972).

22. See Macpherson, Political Theory, pt. 5; see also Peter Laslett, The World We Have Lost (New York: Charles Scribner's Sons, 1971), p. 193.

23. See Locke, Two Treatises, pp. 191-93, 202-3.

24. Wolin, "Idea of the State," p. 47.

25. See Alan Wolfe, "Presidential Power and the Crisis of Modernization," Democracy 1, no. 2 (April 1981): 19-32; see also Jim Mann, "Corporations: A New Voice in Elections," Los Angeles Times, June 29, 1980.

26. John Locke, "Journals," quoted in Lord King, The Life of John Locke (London: Henry Coburn, 1829), p. 119.

27. This, of course, was the conclusion drawn by many mainstream political scientists in the 1950s and resurrected by some, like Samuel P. Huntington, in the 1970s.

28. Locke, Two Treatises, p. 235; see also pp. 234, 247.

29. See Sheldon Wolin, Politics and Vision (Boston: Little Brown, 1960), chap. 9.

30. See John Locke, An Essay concerning Human Understanding, 2 vols., ed. Alexander Fraser (New York: Dover, 1959), 1: 313-14, 331, 345.

31. See Garry Wills, Inventing America: Jefferson's Declaration of Independence (New York: Vintage, 1978), pp. 95-97, for a view that recognizes the extent and limits of Locke's empiricist impact in the United States.

32. John Locke, "Some Thoughts concerning Education," in The Educational Writings of John Locke, ed. James Axtell (London: Cambridge University Press, 1968), pp. 140, 152 ff.

33. See John Locke, On the Conduct of Understanding (London: Bowdery and Kerby, 1829), pp. 5, 23-25; see also idem, "Some Thoughts concerning Education," pp. 170-71.

34. See Wood, Creation of the American Republic, p. 218.

35. Sheldon Wolin, "Higher Education and the Politics of Knowledge," Democracy 1, no. 2 (April 1981): 40-41.

36. Locke, An Essay concerning Human Understanding, 1:343; see also 2:447.

37. Ibid., 1:87, 343, 479; 2:443-44, 447; and John Locke, On the Reasonableness of Christianity, ed. George Ewing (Chicago: Regnery, 1965), pp. 170, 193.

38. Locke, On the Conduct of Understanding, p. 24.

39. Locke, Two Treatises, p. 141.

40. Herein is the Lockean basis for Rawls's second principle of justice, which reads, "Social and economic inequalities are to be arranged so that they are both (a) reasonably expected to be to everyone's advantage, and (b) attached to positions and offices open to all." See Rawls, A Theory of Justice, p. 60.

41. See Locke, On the Reasonableness of Christianity, pp. 170-71.

42. See Edelman, Political Language, chap. 4.

43. Joseph Mitchell quoted in Joe R. Feagin, Subordinating the Poor: Welfare and American Beliefs (Englewood Cliffs, N.J.: Prentice-Hall, 1975), p. 3.

44. See Richard Ashcraft, "Revolutionary Politics and Locke's Two Treatises of Government: Radicalism and Lockean Political Theory," Political Theory 8, no. 4 (November 1980): 429-86.

45. See Mary Lyndon Shanley, "Marriage Contract and Social Contract in Seventeenth Century English Political Thought," Western Political Quarterly 32, no. 1 (March 1979): 79-91.

46. Further consideration of specific renegotiations of natural law and rights is found in Chapter 5 of this book.

47. This idea was suggested to me by Elizabeth Rapoport and is manifest in William Appleman Williams's discussion of Mormonism as a basis for regional opposition to the MX missile. See his "Backyard Autonomy," Nation, September 5, 1981, pp. 161, 178-79.

48. See Emily Albrink Fowler, "Skepticism in Statis," Humanities in Society 4, no. 1 (Winter 1981): 57-68.

49. See Martin Baron, "Pension Shifts," Los Angeles Times, November 23, 1981. An extended discussion of the potential of public investment as a source of control over corporate policies is contained in Maurice Zeitlin, "The American Crisis: An Analysis and Modest Proposal," in The Future of American Democracy: Views from the Left, ed. Mark E. Kann (Philadelphia: Temple University Press, 1983), chap. 5.

50. Arthur Allen Leff, "Unspeakable Ethics, Unnatural Law," Duke Law Journal, December 1979, pp. 1229 ff.

51. Ibid., p. 1249.

52. Philip Green, "Redeeming Government," Nation, December 12, 1981, p. 625.

53. Norman Daniels, "Equal Liberty and Unequal Worth," in Reading Rawls, ed. Norman Daniels (New York: Basic Books, 1975), p. 280.

54. Wills, Nixon Agonistes, p. 224.

55. See Richard A. Cloward and Frances Fox Piven, The Politics of Turmoil (New York: Pantheon, 1974).

56. Richard Sennett, Authority (New York: Knopf, 1980), p. 168.

57. See Dan Georgakas and Marvin Surkin, Detroit, I Do Mind Dying: A Study in Urban Revolution (New York: St. Martin's, 1975), pp. 94-99.

58. Compare Richard F. Hamilton, Class and Politics in the United States (New York: Wiley, 1972); and Albert Szymanski, The Capitalist State and the Politics of Class (Cambridge, Mass.: Winthrop, 1978).

59. See my Thinking about Politics: Two Political Sciences (St. Paul: West, 1980), chap. 8; see also Donna Haraway, "The Contest for Primate Nature: Daughters of Man-the-Hunter in the Field, 1960-1980," and Charles Schwartz, "Atoms for War," in The Future of American Democracy: Views from the Left, ed. Mark E. Kann (Philadelphia: Temple University Press, 1983), chaps. 7, 8.

60. See Rawls, A Theory of Justice, p. 60.

61. Martin Sklar, "Some Remarks on Ollman's 'On Teaching Marxism,'" in Studies in Socialist Pedagogy, ed. Theodore Mills Norton and Bertell Ollman (New York: Monthly Review, 1978), pp. 268-69.

62. Karl Marx, The Economic and Philosophic Manuscripts of 1844, ed. D. Struik, trans. M. Milligan (New York: International, 1964), p. 112; see also Ludwig Feuerbach, The Essence of Christianity, trans. G. Eliot (New York: Harper & Row, 1957), pp. 1-2.

63. Karl Marx, Early Texts, ed. and trans. David McLellan (Oxford: Basil Blackwell, 1971), p. 75.

64. Karl Marx, Capital, ed. Friederich Engels, trans. S. Moore and E. Aveling, 3 vols. (New York: International, 1967), 3:820.

65. Eugene Kamenka, Marxism and Ethics (New York: St. Martin's, 1969), p. 11; see also James J. O'Rourke, The Problem of Freedom in Marxist Thought (Boston: D. Reidel, 1974), p. 11.

66. Shlomo Avineri, The Social and Political Thought of Karl Marx (London: Cambridge University Press, 1968), p. 138.

67. Karl Marx, On Revolution, ed. and trans. Saul K. Padover (New York: McGraw-Hill, 1971), pp. 229-30.

68. Ibid., p. 351.

69. Ibid., pp. 34, 116-17.

70. Ibid., pp. 343, 350.

71. Ibid., p. 235; see also Karl Marx, On the First International, ed. and trans. Saul K. Padover (New York: McGraw-Hill, 1973), pp. 10-11, 164; idem, The Poverty of Philosophy (New York: International, 1963), p. 172; and Karl Marx and Friederich Engels, The Civil War in the U.S. (New York: International, 1961), pp. 139-40.

72. To some extent, I am imposing a Gramscian interpretation on Marx's politics. See my "Political Education and Equality: Gramsci against 'False Consciousness,'" Teaching Political Science 8 no. 4 (July 1981): 423-45.

73. Marx, Poverty of Philosophy, p. 174.

74. Marx, Capital, 1:330-31.

75. Marx, On the First International, p. 222.

76. Karl Marx, Critique of Hegel's "Philosophy of Right", trans. A. Jolin and J. O'Malley (London: Cambridge University Press, 1970), pp. 29-30, 119-20.

77. See Arthur DiQuattro, "Alienation and Justice in the Market," American Political Science Review 72, no. 3 (September 1978): 878-79.

78. Nancy Hartsock, "Fundamental Feminism: Process and Perspective," in Building Feminist Theory, ed. Charlotte Bunch et al. (New York: Longman, 1981), p. 39.

79. Nancy Hartsock, "Political Change: Two Perspectives on Power," in Building Feminist Theory, ed. Charlotte Bunch et al. (New York: Longman, 1981), p. 17.

80. Ibid., p. 7.

81. Charlotte Bunch, "Beyond Either/Or: Feminist Options," in Building Feminist Theory, ed. Charlotte Bunch et al. (New York: Longman, 1981), p. 52.

4

THE MEANS OF COMMUNICATION

Political discourse in the United States is carried on in a Lockean language. Elites use this language to legitimate their rule by public argument and by broadcasting symbolic cues that evoke mass support. Left thinkers rarely appreciate the importance of language. Radical liberals generally take the Lockean tongue for granted, only to compromise their radical messages; socialists often speak their own technical language, which requires endless translations and evokes little more than mass hostility. If the Left is to develop mass support in the United States, it must develop a means of communication both familiar to Americans and able to convey radical meanings.

In this chapter, I will suggest that the American Left can find its voice only if it adapts Lockean language to radical democratic content. To a degree, the groundwork already exists. Early American socialists, like Eugene V. Debs and Morris Hillquit, were able to translate their democratic Marxist vision into conventional Lockean terms intelligible to American audiences. The modern language of economic democracy infuses the Lockean vernacular with mistakably radical accents. In short, it is possible for the American Left to contest ownership of the means of communication in political dialogue.

A section of this chapter is adapted from "Challenging Lockean Liberalism in America: The Case of Debs and Hillquit," by Mark E. Kann, reprinted from Political Theory 8 (May 1980): 203-22, with permission of the publisher, Sage Publications, Beverly Hills and London.

AMBIVALENCE AND LANGUAGE

One persistent strain of mass ambivalence in the United States is people's mixed attitudes toward the idea of equality. In prerevolutionary Boston, for example, mass demands for economic equality took the form of mob action against the homes of rich people. However, these demands were organized and tempered by men like Samuel Adams and James Otis, who argued that the pro-British rich "entirely owe their grandeur and honor to grinding the faces of the poor," while the pronationalist rich implicitly earn their wealth by "labour" and "sweat."[1] The ambiguous idea that economic equality is good and economic inequality based on labor and sweat is also good captures the ambivalence of a Protestant people caught between older communitarian norms and emerging possessive individualism. Similarly, Tocqueville's Democracy in America taps the ambivalence of a Jacksonian era, when Americans opposed to traditional aristocracy demanded "equality of condition" and yet harbored "a love of money," which reproduces all forms of inequality.[2] Such ambivalence takes many forms today, ranging from demands for political equality, which are compromised by attachments to economic inequality, to radicals' affirmation of egalitarian ends by way of elitist means.

The sources of this ambivalence are complex and changing. American Protestantism and cultural antagonism to privilege support "ascriptive" equality and "achieved" inequality. The U. S. political system is structured on the appearance of equality and multiple realities of inequality. It may be that the American working class has an objective interest in opposing economic inequality, but particular individuals in the working class may find subjective opportunities to benefit by it. One might note that ambivalence is structured into bureaucratic organizations, which subject most members to an alienating domination from above but make them complicit in the subordination of those below. One might also locate sources of ambivalence in the ethical dilemmas and strategies of people who believe in equality but experience daily life as a choice between different versions of inequality. On the one hand, women with some feminist consciousness may recognize men as their oppressors but also live with and love men. On the other hand, men with some feminist consciousness may take class issues as primary and temporarily treat female subordination as secondary. Whatever the sources or their historical combinations, the reality is that perhaps most Americans simultaneously affirm and reject equality in the course of their everyday lives.

In a society of ambivalence, language and symbols are potent instruments for shaping people's perceptions and cuing them to resolve their ambivalence in particular ways. Elites who dominate the means of communication, for example, promote the perception that property rights are sacred, or natural, or normal and, thereby, cue people to resolve their ambivalence in favor of unequal economic outcomes. Today's New Right suggests that homosexuality is sinful, unnatural, and abnormal and, thus, cues Americans to resolve any ambivalence about gay rights in favor of restriction. The dynamics of the cuing process were perhaps best articulated by E. L. Bernays, the founder of the modern public relations industry. How appropriate!

Bernays was interested in "the engineering of consent" well before Antonio Gramsci's related idea of hegemony was adopted by American radicals.[3] Bernays wanted to understand how a public relations expert could persuade consumers to buy their particular product when consumers were ambivalent about making the purchase. A particular product might be attractive to consumers but could also have some negative aspects that alienate consumers. On the other hand, the product might be attractive but no more so than similar or related products offered in the marketplace. Bernays understood that long-winded descriptions of one's product or systematic comparisons of it with competing products was not a very useful sales technique. Instead, Bernays's strategy was to "find out which words, pictures, and actions will intensify favorable attitudes, which ones may convert people to one's point of view and may help to negate distorted or prejudiced viewpoints."[4] Language and symbols communicated to mass audiences were considered subtle and effective cues to "intensify favorable attitudes" as a resolution of ambivalence. Among the more famous and effective examples was the advertising campaign that created the Marlboro man, whose masculinity and ruggedness intensified favorable attitudes to a particular brand of cigarettes.

Bernays's insights have long been adapted by U.S. elites interested in engineering the consent of the governed. U.S. elites rarely engage in long-winded arguments to legitimate their rule. Instead, they typically use Lockean language and symbols as cues aimed at intensifying Americans' feelings about support or quiescence to inequality and at negating distorted or prejudiced viewpoints that might support radical democratic forms of equality. While the language and symbols associated with patriotism and anticommunism are the most obvious examples, less conspicuous examples are readily available.

First, U.S. elites underwrite an "academic and foundation world" that lays claim to individual research, objective and neutral scholarship, and the free market of ideas. The words are cues that evoke support for research findings and conclusions that usually support elite rule.[5] The words work as symbols, in large part, because they recall a Lockean world where individual liberty, fairness, and reason prevail. Second, U.S. elites present their foreign policies to the public in a language that arouses and then assuages mass anxieties. Elites invoke national security crises, justify huge defense expenditures as rational and effective responses to the crises, and claim that public opinion legitimates their responses.[6] The words evoke a familiar Lockean logic: a peaceful state of nature is one on the brink of war, which can be averted by a rational agreement whereby government protects individual rights and citizens consent to abide by government policies. In both examples, elites use language and symbols to associate their dominance and policies with familiar cultural meanings in ways that help people to live with continued elite rule.

Murray Edelman argues that symbolic cues "go far toward defining the geography and typography of everyone's political world." However, "symbolic cues are not omnipotent."[7] In part, their effectiveness depends on their cultural familiarity. Lockean words and symbols are effective in the United States only because Americans participate in a Lockean culture. Those able to harness these words and symbols to their own interests are likely to win mass support among ambivalent people. To the degree that elites have monopolized the Lockean means of communication, they have been able to sustain consistent public support, even under adverse circumstances. A crisis like the Great Depression or an oil shortage can be interpreted as a cause for national unity and rededication to the social contract rather than as a reason for dissent.[8]

In part, the effectiveness of symbolic cues depends on particular audiences. Lockean cues are most effective when directed at Americans who experience individualism as rewarding, perceive government as at least partially responsive to their interests, and have known the reality of upward social mobility. The cues intensify their favorable attitudes. Lockean cues are least effective when aimed at Americans who have experienced satisfying forms of community life, confront government as an alien force, and are somehow involved in vicious cycles of poverty. For these people, the cues contradict daily experiences and, at best, evoke rather than resolve ambivalence. Historically, the Lockean cuing process helps elites to garner the support of middle-class and upwardly mobile working-class Americans and perhaps the quiescence of lower-class and minority Americans paralyzed temporarily by ambivalence.[9]

Relatedly, Lockean cues work best when they tap issues totally outside of the everyday experiences of particular audiences. Elites have usually had an easier time amassing support for foreign policies that do not directly impinge on citizens' daily lives than for tax policies that directly affect people's paychecks and spending power. Elites usually have an easier time convincing middle-class Americans that equal opportunity exists despite the persistence of poverty than convincing lower-class Americans who live with that poverty.[10] People in the middle class who have no direct experience with poverty have an interest in believing that they have had no advantages in attaining their status; people in the lower class know from experience that special barriers to mobility hinder them.

In part, finally, the cuing process depends on the times and on the symbolic competition. During major historical crises, people may reject conventional cues, attain a renewed consciousness of their ambivalence, and search for new ways to resolve it. For example, major economic crises not only frustrate the expectations of those affected; they also uproot people from their habitual attitudes and ways of life. People may be forced to leave the communities that structure their daily lives, change their routines, and reconstruct their social interactions. "The sheer scale of these dislocations," write Piven and Cloward, helps "to mute the sense of self-blame, predisposing men and women to view their plight as a collective one, and to blame their rulers for the destitution and disorganization they experience."[11] Of course, the relocation of blame from self to rulers does not necessarily work against inequality. That depends on the symbolic competition. Murray Edelman writes that "anxious people reliant on dubious and conflicting cues can choose from <u>available</u> public messages the ones that support a policy consistent with their economic interests and ideological bent (emphasis added)."[12] If the only available public messages in the marketplace either root people's problems in individual rulers who are corrupt or incompetent, or suggest solutions that require alternative modes of elitist rule, then people are likely to reconstruct their symbolic worlds in ways consistent with continued inequality.

Consider the crisis of the welfare state today. On the whole, liberals cue people to believe that individuals (like Ronald Reagan) must be replaced and government must be made more efficient (through more expertise). Rarely do they cue people to perceive the structured inequalities that are part of the welfare state. The only other available public messages in the marketplace are those now broadcast by conservatives. The New Right preaches a natural and divine morality, which cues Americans to solve their problems in terms of social hierarchies (for example, the patriarchal family); neoconservatives cue Americans to see the solution in a more limited government, which defends rather than abuses individual rights; and supply-siders cue Americans to seek solutions in a renewed free market, which restores fair competition and productivity to defeat inflation and unemployment.[13] Conservative cues have been relatively effective because they use Lockean terms and symbols, speak to the experiences of people suffering dislocations, and appear to be a real alternative to discredited welfare state liberalism. Their relative effectiveness means, however, that people are likely to resolve their ambivalence in favor of systematic inequality.

The American Left has failed to make available symbolic cues that might intensify people's feelings toward equality and might urge them to resolve their ambivalence in favor of radical changes. Radical liberals adopt the language of Lockean rationalism, which makes them indistinguishable from discredited welfare-state liberals and ultimately compromises their own radical values. Radical liberals may want an enriched consent, but it must consist of rational participation, dialogue, and equality rather than self-indulgent, impatient, or irrational mob action. [14]

This linguistic division of society into rational and irrational people has two consequences. First, it provides no terms for ambivalence. It condemns mass movements or mass disruptions as irrational, without recognizing the possibility that people are acting out or coming to terms with their mixed feelings and loyalties. When radical liberals advocate organizing the people according to some logic, they implicitly cue people to deny their ambivalence and to reconcile themselves with reformist sorts of inequality. Second, this linguistic division positively fosters radical liberal complicity in some forms of elitism. If the masses are irrational, then they must be educated. This usually implies support for the helping professions, like teaching, psychiatry, and social work. The helping professions have their own technical and scientific languages, which make inconspicuous the reproduction of elitism as expertise. What educators call pedagogy might otherwise be construed as social control; what psychiatrists call therapy may in some cases be considered forms of sadism; what social workers call aid should sometimes be labeled subordination. [15] The language of Lockean rationalism, even if intended otherwise, usually functions to cue people to acquiesce to expertise rather than question or define for themselves the terms of expertise.

American socialists generally speak a Hegelian-Marxist language unfamiliar and unintelligible to most Americans. Terms like historical materialism, dialectics, or class warfare, not to mention bourgeoisie and proletariat, may be useful for historical analysis but mean almost nothing to people steeped in Lockean lore. The technical language of Marxist economic theory, including terms like surplus value, organic composition of capital, or falling rate of profit, cannot be communicated to Americans without long-winded explanations, which most people have neither the time nor interest to follow. Nonetheless, it is not unusual for socialists to use such terminology before audiences who are mystified and alienated by it. The sheer linguistic difference between socialists and Americans reinforces the tendency to divide society into those with true consciousness (usually assumed rather than stated outright) and those with false consciousness (usually stated outright). Other conventional socialist distinctions between

vanguardism and spontaneism or reformism and revolutionism not
only provide no terms for articulating mass ambivalence; they often
provide no space, for example, for feminists, who believe that patriarchy is a form of domination that cannot be subsumed by economic
categories or conventional socialist strategies. Thus, it is easy for
socialists to reproduce among themselves traditional forms of male
elitism.[16]

American Left ideologists have not developed a language or set
of symbols that might effectively cue Americans to recognize and resolve their ambivalence in favor of egalitarian alternatives. They
have yet to find a vernacular that is familiar to Americans and yet
intensifies mass attachments to equality. However, American Left
activists have been more flexible and experimental in their language.
At times, they have developed expedient terminologies, means of
communication and cuing, that are rooted in familiar Lockean language
but that successfully convey radical democratic values. They have
done this both from the perspective of Marxist socialism and radical
liberalism.

LOCKEAN LANGUAGE AND MARXIST MEANINGS

Perhaps the most creative theorist among early American socialists was Daniel De Leon, whose vision of worker control influenced,
among others, Antonio Gramsci.[17] But creative theory and political
success are quite different. De Leon's Socialist Labor party never
attracted more than a handful of followers, in part, because De Leon
spoke in a Marxist idiom few Americans could understand. When he
did speak the vernacular, his message went directly against the Lockean grain.

> In all revolutionary movements, as in the storming of
> fortresses, the thing depends on the head of the column—
> on the minority that is so intense in its convictions, so
> soundly based in its principles, so determined in its ac-
> tions, that it carries the masses with it, storms the
> breastworks and captures the fort.[18]

Such outright vanguardism was alien to American audiences, and its
expression did little more than alienate them. Eugene V. Debs and
Morris Hillquit of the Socialist party were not sophisticated theorists;
they are better described as activists intent on building a mass socialist movement. Their relative success over several decades can,
in part, be attributed to their ability to use Lockean language to win
support for Marxist ideas.

Like De Leon, Debs was associated with the left wing of the socialist movement and cofounded the revolutionary Industrial Workers of the World (IWW). Debs learned his Marxism through Kautsky and the Second Internationalists. He believed in historical materialism, class struggle, and revolution; he disagreed with socialists who thought that the interests of capitalists and workers could be magically harmonized or that the road to socialism lay on political and economic reformism.[19] Debs was, according to David Shannon, "American enough for the most prejudiced cultural nationalist and as red as flame."[20] His Americanism was partly constituted by experiences shaped in the U.S. labor movement and partly manifest in his ability to make use of the American Lockean vernacular. Hillquit was less well known but was a better representative of the central tendencies of early American socialism. He, too, was an avowed Marxist, and he, too, made good use of the Lockean vernacular. As we will see below, Debs's and Hillquit's use of Lockean words and symbols did not so much compromise their Marxist views as align them with radical democratic norms.

Debs and Hillquit believed that capitalism produced the economic progress and the contradictions that readied the world for revolutionary socialism, especially in the United States. America's vast wealth and territory, when combined with its hardworking population, had advanced the nation into the "front rank of industrial nations." Class domination and poverty were now "entirely artificial and wholly unnecessary."[21] The United States had reached an objective historical plateau on which socialism would become the workers' obvious choice for the future. Debs wrote, "The only reason that all workingmen are not socialists is that they do not know what it means."[22] History had set the stage, and the immediate political challenge was less to review that history than to cue the actors to their roles. In large part, Debs and Hillquit did so in familiar Lockean terms.

Debs told his audiences, "Socialism is the spontaneous expression of human nature." Hillquit added, "The real incentive moving all men to bring forth the best that is in them is just that best that is in them; their desire to excel and to earn the recognition of their fellow men."[23] People could become conscious of their human nature or the best within them by consulting their conscience and reason. "The higher law of righteousness," said Debs, "is a law . . . written upon the tablets of every man's heart and conscience."[24] Hillquit repeatedly stressed that workers should improve their intellectual level to better understand and analyze their moral options.[25] Debs and Hillquit were Marxist historicists, and yet they spoke in the universalist Lockean idiom of human nature, conscience, and reason.

Locke believed that people who uncovered their nature or developed their reason would discover timeless, godly truths, like natural rights to life, liberty, and property. But Debs and Hillquit believed that the historical relations of production had created a setting in which people who search for their true nature and reason would discover socialist truths whose time had come. At the very least, the moral journey would distance them from their everyday attachments to the structures and temptations of social inequalities.

Debs and Hillquit also held the Marxist belief that America's economic "tendency towards the socialization of industries" had reached a stage that urged workers to take control of their economic destinies. [26] Class conflict was immanent and imminent. The expedient challenge was to provide workers with as much space as possible for taking control. Thus, Debs and Hillquit defended workers' freedom of choice in language that recalls Locke's Second Treatise.

Hillquit preached the moral right of a citizenry to choose its own government, while Debs glowingly praised the broadening of suffrage. Their support for popular sovereignty and universal suffrage was linked to their defense of "free speech, a free press, and the right of free assemblage"—rights of "everlasting benefit to mankind."[27] In the social contract tradition, Debs and Hillquit related these rights to moral duties and obligations. Debs condemned capitalists and governors who defied "the legally expressed will of the people," and Hillquit noted that elected officials "assume certain moral obligations towards . . . voters."[28] This was not language for public consumption alone, for it was also used in reference to socialist politics. Debs reasoned that his voluntary consent to join the Socialist party incurred for him an "obligation" and "duty to obey" party directives; Hillquit said that party members "subscribe, in their application, to the ordinary, ever natural—ever implied—obligation to live up to the constitution and principles of the party."[29] Even Locke's idea of tacit consent was incorporated into the socialists' language.

Certainly, Debs and Hillquit defended public space and consent of the governed, with the expectation that this political atmosphere would allow workers to recognize their historical class destiny. Their immediate goal was not to deposit true consciousness in workers' memory banks; rather it was to nurture an appreciation for workers' common interests, which could grow only in an atmosphere of tolerance. Debs defended industrial unionism not as a historical necessity but as a product of workers' "identity of interest," a matter of "fact, cold and impassive as the granite foundations of a skyscraper." This matter of fact could be discovered by people "with open minds and in a spirit of tolerance," where free discussion allowed workers to articulate their experiences and arrive at a socialist consensus on that basis. Hillquit insisted that strong differences of opinion existed among workers, which could be resolved only by a "self-criticism . . . [that] results in a process of purification and

improvement."[30] Debs and Hillquit could speak the Lockean language
of suffrage and rights, consent and obligations, interests and tolerance, because their reading of American praxis assured them that a
free people would opt for socialism. Thus, they condemned "heresy
hunting" inside and outside of the party because, ultimately, "the fact
of the identity of interests of all workers remains."[31]

These early American socialists also communicated a Marxist
vision of politics and society in the familiar language of the American
culture. They delighted in introducing themselves as the defenders
of the "true" principles of the Founding Fathers. Debs wrote that
socialism "makes its appeal to the American people as the defender
and preserver of the idea of liberty and self-government in which the
nation was born." Hillquit portrayed socialist goals in a Jeffersonian
light, suggesting that "the present system . . . has become destructive of the very ends proclaimed as inalienable rights in our Declaration of Independence."[32] Establishing themselves as defenders of
cherished American traditions, with equality stressed as their core,
Debs and Hillquit then attempted to turn those traditions to socialist
ends. Debs simultaneously supported majoritarianism and the individual's right "to face that beast called the Majority and tell him the
truth to his teeth!" Hillquit emphasized the moral imperative that
"the minority must always submit to the concrete enactment of the
majority without necessarily approving it."[33] This was not a theoretical exercise to balance majority and minority rights; rather it
was a way of conveying the Marxist message that the majority rule
of the working class would mean each individual's ability to develop
his or her human capacities in harmony with others.

For all of their optimism, the American socialists were not so
naive as to believe that history would automatically issue forth in socialism. "Socialists," wrote Hillquit, "realize that the mere maturity
of a country for a socialist regime will not produce socialism without
conscious, planned, and deliberate action."[34] He and Debs hoped to
persuade American workers to take part in this action by convincing
them that socialism is natural and good; that it is conceivable only if
workers voluntarily choose it on the basis of an understanding of their
common interests; and that, in the end, it will mean an extension of
democratic norms beyond politics to the social realm of production.
These American socialists found it was expedient to use Lockean
language and symbols to cue their audiences to resolve their ambivalence in favor of the greater equality promised by socialism. There
is no empirical method able to prove that their use of the vernacular
accounts for their ability to have won the support of millions of Americans over two decades. But we do know that American socialists who
have adhered to Hegelian-Marxist terms have been unable to communicate with more than a few Americans or even approximate the relative popularity of the early socialists.

In fact, Debs's and Hillquit's usage of the vernacular was more than expedient. It also represented an adaptation of Marxism to specific U.S. historical conditions. Both believed that history was on the side of socialism; both knew, however, that historical trends manifest themselves in different ways; and both sought out the words and meanings that were most appropriate to the particular challenges faced by socialists in the United States.

History was ultimately on the side of the working class, but it also produced in the United States a capitalist class powerful enough to dissuade even committed radicals from opposing it. Debs and Hillquit exhorted workers to be courageous, to strengthen their will and determination, and to follow the exemplary "heroism and sublime sacrifice" of John Brown, Mother Jones, and John Swinton. [35] This focus on individual will and commitment placed Debs and Hillquit at the center of the American radical tradition, which, in Staughton Lynd's analysis, "has been based on a philosophy of free will." [36] They emphasized the faith that people could overcome the obstacles in their historical paths; they did not dwell on mass irrationality or false consciousness. Part of this faith was that individuals can sacrifice immediate goods to secure social progress. Too often, they argued, labor leaders give in to temptation and "feather their nests" at the expense of other workers. But people who look to their "enlightened self-interest" can transcend such egotism and act in harmony with their long-term interests. [37]

Certainly they believed that workers' long-term interests were class interests, but they avoided opposing a narrow version of the bourgeoisie to an equally rigid version of the proletariat that might have made little sense in the United States. Debs and Hillquit (like Marx, Lenin, and Mao) often labeled the opposition to capitalism as "the people," though they held that the proletariat would grow through the "absorption of that class of all other classes." [38] They often spoke of the common material and moral interests of workers, farmers, small businessmen, intellectuals, and middle-class Americans. Hillquit even speculated that the latter groups would "voluntarily abandon the individual form of production" when they realized that their economic interest and social ideals ultimately lay with the workers. [39] In both form and content, the American socialists articulated class and class struggle in inclusive rather than exclusive terms. They were aiming to build a mass movement.

Given the right conditions, people could educate themselves to understand this inclusive interest. Debs and Hillquit agreed that people needed time away from alienating labor to cultivate the leisure required for self-consciousness and self-development. "If only humanity could respond to the higher influences," Debs said, "and it would if it only had the time." [40] In the process of self-education, people were sure to make mistakes; that comes with the socialist turf. Hillquit argued that "the socialist program is . . . primarily one of economic reform," which left considerable room for social dispute and dialogue. Debs said that "social relations will be free to regulate themselves. Like religion, this will be an individual matter."[41] Individuals should be free to decide such matters on the basis of their needs and experience and not abstractions. Socialists should certainly point out what they consider to be erroneous choices and make a case against them. Thus, Hillquit blamed the American Federation of Labor (AFL) membership for acquiescing to their leaders' mistakes, and Debs pinpointed the blame for one governor's actions on the workers who "elected him to office."[42] People must be free to learn from their own experiences, and they also must be held responsible for their actions.

While the ultimate cause of an emerging socialist consciousness would be rooted in economic contradictions, its immediate formulation would be a product of morality and politics. The American socialists first cheered the Bolshevik Revolution in Russia and then learned from it: socialization of the means of production does not automatically or necessarily carry with it political or social justice. Debs once cabled Lenin, "I protest with all civilized people, in the name of our common humanity, against the execution of the Social Revolutionaries or the unjust denial of their liberty."[43] Hillquit summed up what became the prevailing view among American socialists: "Political institutions are after all primarily deliberate products of the conscious mind, even though they are bound to adjust themselves in the longrun to the existing material situation."[44] The disjunctions between the political and economic spheres, even if temporary, make politics a crucial concern for socialists.

Debs viewed politics primarily as an arena of class conflict. He praised the courage of individual dissenters, in and out of the socialist movement, who politicized important issues and made them the object of public debate.[45] He always took seriously the significance of political participation and action, especially when coordinated with economic activity, as a means of mass self-education. Hillquit's attachment to politics was even stronger. He believed that the political arena should be the focus for reform efforts, which simultaneously facilitate the growth of class consciousness and the easing of the worker's lot. At the same time, he feared the state under capitalism and socialism as a perpetual threat to individuals and minorities, who always need some protection against political abuses.[46] While Hillquit believed this protection could be minimal under socialism, he retained a Lockean distrust for potentially corrupt authority.

The socialists' concern for individual courage, will, and sacrifice; leisure and self-education for the people; and politics as im-

portant public terrain was at least partly a conscious adaptation of
Marxism to American culture. Debs put it this way: "The workers
of a certain country must of necessity adapt themselves to the methods
and manners of the country, and out of their own national psychology
build toward an international purpose."[47] In the process of adapting
Marxism to a Lockean United States, Debs and Hillquit extracted the
more democratic messages of both traditions. On the one hand, they
may have believed that American workers suffer some sort of "false
consciousness," but they also believed not in vanguards but in the
people's ability to educate themselves and to appreciate their own
long-term interests in equality. On the other hand, their emphasis
on people's shared experiences and destinies; voluntarism; and the
politics of debate, participation, and self-governance suggested that
the American masses were not irrational but complex, not justifiably
manipulated for their own good but justifiably freed so they may determine their own good. Thus, one reason why Debs and Hillquit could
translate their Marxism into Lockean terms is that they extracted
from both traditions a radical democratic core that placed ultimate
faith in the demos.

There is a point at which translation and adaptation of Marxism transcend the boundaries of the intellectual tradition. Debs and
Hillquit were not technicians. They placed their own peculiar marks
on American socialism. Let me suggest that the main effect of their
peculiarities was to enrich American socialist dialogue in ways that
we can best appreciate with some historical retrospection. This is
particularly apparent in their disagreements over leadership, organization, and strategies and tactics.

Debs viewed leadership as a necessary evil, and he played the
role of leader with great reservations. Occasionally, Debs talked
about leaders as if they were Rousseauian Great Legislators who articulated mass experiences and pointed out ways of building and sustaining mass movements. More often, he disdained the idea of leadership as inherently elitist. "Too long have the workers of the world
waited for some Moses to lead them out of bondage. He has not come;
he will never come. I would not lead you out if I could; for if you
could be led out, you could be led back in again."[48] More important
than leaders was the development of workers' organizations. For
Debs, industrial unions would be an effective form of self-defense
under capitalism, a good experience in self-management that prefigures socialism, and a stimulus to the class unity and action that
would bring about the transition. These organizations were "of far
greater importance than increasing the vote of the Socialist Party"
because active participation in the face of intimidation indicates a
far greater commitment to socialism than a passive vote here and
there.[49]

Debs believed that "the American workers are law-abiding and no amount of sneering or derision will alter that fact."[50] Socialist strategies and tactics would have to take this into account. At his trial for seditious speech, Debs defended himself in terms of his "right to do so under the laws of the land."[51] While he never denied the Marxist idea that the laws of the land reflect class biases and, ultimately, would have to be altered, he did not automatically or simplistically reject those laws as bourgeois. From his socialist perspective, some of those laws were good laws; from his strategic perspective, defending those good laws against capitalist abuses was a promising way to link socialism to the concrete perceptions and struggles of Americans. In the end, mass organizations and the people themselves would determine how those laws would have to be changed.

Hillquit's views on these matters were considerably different. He supported the role of leader for two reasons. First, he discriminated between different strata of the working class, arguing that "the better situated, better trained, and more intelligent workers" had the clearest socialist vision and were best placed to educate their less fortunate brothers and sisters. Second, Hillquit believed that leaders play a crucial role in guiding social movements. He wrote, for example, "At a time when a young movement has reached a critical point . . . and the masses are uneducated, inexperienced, and easily led in any direction, the loss of a clear-minded, energetic, and honest leader becomes a great blow."[52] Hillquit wanted to build a socialist leadership and situate it in the Socialist party, which would guide mass actions. Initially, he supported the Bolshevik party as founded on the "consent" of a majority of Russian people, manifest in their "aquiescent acceptance of its political rule." He felt that socialists would win power in the United States with a political majority willing "to cast their fortunes with the socialist movement."[53] Unlike Debs, Hillquit assumed that most Americans would not become active socialist participants so much as friendly supporters of particular socialist reforms, policies, and plans.

On the basis of this assumption, Hillquit argued that the transition to socialism was a matter of "a series of gradual and successive, but systematic and interrupted measures."[54] Hillquit's gradualism was an affirmation of a reform strategy. He praised the litigious person as a promoter of progress through law; he suggested, in fact, that "the higher plan of civilization" is based on law or "definite rules of conduct" in all matters pertaining to common welfare.[55] Thus, his scenario for change involved a party of leaders that would elicit the mass support necessary to use the legal system to enact reforms, which would move the nation a step closer to socialism. In this view, the need for revolution is underplayed if not denied.

It would be easy but inaccurate to explain the differences between Debs and Hillquit in conventional Marxist terms. One could classify Debs in the same tradition as Rosa Luxemburg or Antonio Gramsci—Marxists whose egalitarianism has an anarchistic bent based on a populist faith in mass spontaneism. One could place Hillquit in the tradition of LaSalle and Bernstein (or now, Michael Harrington), who accepted the constraints of the capitalist state, sought progressive changes within its context, and assumed that these changes would make for a gradual transition to socialism. Conventionally, Debs could be considered the revolutionist and Hillquit the reformist or revisionist. Though this classification is partly justifiable, it ignores the rich and uniquely American texture of the debate.

The leadership question posed the problem of authority and democracy. Debs's disdain for leadership meant that he absented himself from serving as a unifying force in the face of continuing socialist fragmentation; Hillquit's support for leadership meant that socialists would reproduce forms of hierarchy in the process of trying to eliminate them. The organization question posed the problem of the locus and meaning of democracy. Debs hoped to build socialism out of the activities of decentralized workers' organizations, which partly bound him to a localism that ceded the national arena; Hillquit's investment in the party and reforms bound him mainly to the national arena, where few opportunities for direct democratic participation existed. The strategy question ultimately posed the problem of adjusting democratic means and ends. While Debs may have been a democratic revolutionist and Hillquit a democratic reformist, they shared a sense that some sort of open mass movement would be both the foundation for change and the beneficiary of change. Above all else, this generated a receptiveness to mass experiences and demands, which allowed these early socialists to adjust their theories to American practices rather than save their theories by distorting or ignoring the complexities of daily social life in the United States.

In summary, Debs and Hillquit translated Marxist ideas into the Lockean vernacular and, thereby, enhanced their ability to communicate radical ideas to American audiences. In the process, they adapted their Marxist ideas to American culture in a way that extracted democratic lessons from both traditions. These lessons are most apparent in their shared affirmation of democratic means to change and their openness to problems that all democratic movements must confront and, as we will see in the next chapter, that have become a central focus of American socialists in recent years.

LOCKEAN LANGUAGE AND RADICAL MEANINGS

If Debs and Hillquit translated and adapted Marxist meanings to familiar Lockean terms, today's advocates of economic democracy

take familiar Lockean terms and adapt them to radical meanings.
Martin Carnoy and Derek Shearer see economic democracy rooted
"in the American radical tradition of populism, whose primary value
was always democracy," and they hope to reroot it "permanently in
American communities and American experience" as a substitute for
"the needs or perceptions of foreign 'revolutionary' parties or ideologies," which so often occupy the American Left.[56] Unlike Marxism,
economic democracy is not a comprehensive theory, but it is a way
of speaking that transfers Lockean political terminology to the economic realm.

The founding statement of Tom Hayden's Campaign for Economic
Democracy is implicitly based on the need for a new social contract
in U.S. economic life. The economic democrats oppose the tyranny
of "an unchosen corporate elite" that makes arbitrary demands on
people's lives. The U.S. marketplace is, in a sense, an economic
state of nature in which individuals' economic rights to work, health,
decent housing, education, safety, and ecological sanity are imperiled.
It is both moral and rational for people to construct "an evolving system in which economic decisions are made with the involvement and
consent of the people affected." Centralized decision making in the
governance of the economy must be limited or eliminated in order to
subject the economic state to the sovereignty of the majority of "workers, small businesses, and consumers." This should be done by de-
centralizing economic power to the workplace and community. The
issue of this social contract should be an economy that is productive
in eliminating waste and in enhancing efficiency as well as an economy
that is consistent with democratic norms.[57]

Economic democrats who adopt this Lockean terminology simultaneously transform conventional Lockean meanings. Economic rights
bespeak more of human needs than of procedures. Participation and
consent are less means of accountability than of direct public control
of power and resources. Economic productivity is not judged by exchange values so much as by use values. Here, then, is one example
of how Lockean language can be used as an invitation to Americans
to talk about values that clearly overlap with the more democratic
aspects of Marxist socialism. This may be a major reason why, in
fact, radical liberals and socialists in recent years have been able
to recognize some common terrain for cooperation.

Both the weaknesses and strengths of economic democracy as
a language stem from its lack of theoretical grounding. It is founded
on the idea that political democracy is incomplete or impossible without the "democratization of the economy from the bottom up, starting
with the work place and the community."[58] Real political equality
cannot exist as long as people with concentrated wealth or monopolistic control over the means of production exert more than equal influ-

ence in government circles; real political equality is impossible as long as the few have the effective power to make decisions that shape the lives of the many. In my reading, the theoretical grounding of economic democracy does not go much beyond this. Lacking is a systematic, historical explanation of the genesis of such inequalities and a structured sensitivity to the ways in which these inequalities reproduce themselves throughout American society. The self-proclaimed identification—economic democracy—gives primacy to one obviously important realm, but, thereby, devalues the significance of the demands for equality made by feminists, minorities, gays, the handicapped, the aged, and others; their concerns are economic and more. In substance, economic democracy is a limited language.

Yet, the lack of theoretical grounding for this language means that it can be used with great flexibility. In particular, it has been used as a language for policy analysis. It does not demand nationalization of the means of production as an article of faith. Instead, it is used to support an analysis of past policies, which allow for some public ownership and, more important, for some public control over resources in ways that go well beyond welfare-state regulations. The assumption is that radicals can build on old policies to encourage new ones that point to significantly greater degrees of public leverage over the economy. Carnoy and Shearer write the following:

> We believe that, under certain political circumstances, it is possible in a politically democratic country like the United States to win significant structural changes in capitalist society. . . . What is important and key is that the nonreformist reforms lead in the direction of a more democratic and more equal society, and they help to build a popular movement whose long-range goal is the construction of such a society. [59]

Economic democrats speak a language that allows them to investigate the strengths and weaknesses of old, familiar policies; extract from them some democratic content; and build on that content by offering up concrete policy alternatives, which are winnable now and become the basis for more democracy tomorrow. In the process, they cue ambivalent Americans to both the means by which they can enter into today's contest for democracy and the ways in which they can "redefine what is possible" for a more democratic future. [60]

It is important to add that economic democracy is a language founded on an optimism that evokes the traditional hopes that Americans have had in their national experiment. The founding statement of the Campaign for Economic Democracy concludes on this note: "We believe the human spirit can overcome any obstacle to its free-

dom. In our time it must. And it will."[61] Carnoy and Shearer put
it in the following way:

> Ideas have a power that can free untapped hope and en-
> ergy in a people. The democratic idea of America has
> been and can again be a powerful weapon. It is a living
> heritage which we can apply to the economic system in
> which we live, and with it we can build a new reality.[62]

Certainly it is questionable that ideas can change the world. But even
Marx believed that ideas can become material forces in history. The
one idea that is a necessary material force for the American Left is
the idea that radical change is possible.

In this sense, economic democrats are "born-again" radicals.
They constantly talk about renewed vision, overcoming obstacles, and
building new realities. They often understand the limits of ideological rationalism; in virtually every historical situation, a cost-benefit
analysis of radicalism will suggest huge costs and, at best, highly
uncertain benefits. Elites always have the advantages in terms of
military power, resources, organization, communication, and established influence. People need something more than ideological
calculations to attract them to radical messages and actions; they
also need a certain amount of faith that radical messages and actions
offer the best defense for what they value and for what they hope to
attain. Tom Hayden understands this when he tries to revive the spirit
of the American frontier, now turned inward to quality-of-life issues,
in the hope of recapturing what Antonio Gramsci called optimism of
the will in an age that Christopher Lasch and others characterize as
one of "diminishing expectations."[63] In part, it is this optimism
that early American socialists extracted from historical analysis and
that economic democrats discover in new public policy options, which
allows for Left experimentation with new ideas, new means of communicating with Americans, and new political strategies. This Left
experimentation testifies to some distancing from the old ideologies
and to a more distinctive identification with American democracy as
a radically incomplete reality.

FORM AND CONTENT

Historically, American radicals have always been at a disad-
vantage in the contest for public support. Conservatives, like Ronald
Reagan, and liberals, like Jimmy Carter, and the interests they
represent do not simply dominate the airwaves, newspapers, magazines, and other sources of mass communication in the United States.

Historically, this has been the case in many nations, where, nonetheless, the Left has made its mark. More important, U.S. elites
"own" the language of communication and, thus, shape the options
put before the American people. Elites have virtually uncontested
control over the words and symbols familiar to Americans, used to
evoke support for competing forms of inequality. In these circumstances, even if radicals had their own New York Times or national
television news network, it is not obvious that they would be able to
win significantly more public support—that is, unless they attempted
to lay claim to the vernacular and transform its meanings simultaneously.

The examples of Debs and Hillquit and the economic democrats
provide a few lessons. First, the relative success of the early socialists in winning mass audiences and what appears to be some local
success by economic democrats to build community movements highlight the importance of finding a public voice that speaks intelligibly
and persuasively to living human beings. Marxists must, at the very
least, integrate their technical language with a more flexible, Amer-
icanized mode of discourse. I do not suggest heresy. While Marx
may have written Capital for a highly select, intellectual audience,
he also wrote Wage Labor and Capital in a language meant for and
accessible to a working-class audience. The alternative is continued
isolation. Furthermore, radical liberals must experiment with extended versions of Lockean language that distinguish them from the
Lockean mainstream. This might mean extending the metaphor of
contract and consent to the economy, the university, the family, and
beyond. Again, there is precedent. Jefferson's formal presentation
in Notes on the State of Virginia was framed in exceedingly dry, scientific, and cautious language; but many of his public writings,
speeches, and letters were transmitted in popular terms that begged
radical meanings. The alternative for radical liberals, as I see it,
is continued assimilation.

Second, these examples suggest that the translation and adaptation of words and symbols also involve some changes in content. A
Marxism that is adapted to America's Lockean culture will, for example, dilute the technical integrity of class by placing it within the
broader category of "the people." The radicalization of Lockean
language carries with it a diminished trust in expertise and an enhanced faith in popular self-governance. If the American Left is
primarily interested in ideological rigor and integrity, such changes
in content may be unacceptable. However, if the American Left is
more concerned with identifying itself with people's democratic
struggles, with winning public support, and with gaining real political
leverage for change, then these changes in content are desirable.
They democratize the ideologies and align them more closely with

the activities of working radicals and with the frustrations of millions of Americans. Indeed, I argue in the next chapter that a significant segment of the American Left has recently and self-consciously re-adjusted its ideological lenses and focused its politics toward radical democracy.

NOTES

1. James Otis quoted in Howard Zinn, A People's History of the United States (New York: Harper & Row, 1980), p. 61.
2. Alexis de Tocqueville, Democracy in America, ed. R. D. Heffner (New York: New American Library, 1956), pp. 26, 52.
3. See Edward L. Bernays, ed., The Engineering of Consent (Norman: University of Oklahoma Press, 1955).
4. Edward L. Bernays, "Theory and Practice of Public Relations: A Résumé," in The Engineering of Consent, ed. Edward L. Bernays (Norman: University of Oklahoma Press, 1955), p. 12.
5. See Thomas Ferguson and Joel Rogers, "Oligopoly in the Idea Market," Nation, October 3, 1981, pp. 303-8.
6. See Murray Edelman, Political Language: Words That Succeed and Policies That Fail (New York: Academic, 1977), chap. 3.
7. Ibid., p. 41; see also Antonio Gramsci, "Problems of Marxism," in Selections from the Prison Notebooks of Antonio Gramsci, ed. and trans. Quintin Hoare and Geoffrey Nowell Smith (New York: International, 1971), p. 423.
8. See Mark E. Kann, "Consent and Authority in America," in The Problem of Authority in America, ed. John P. Diggins and Mark E. Kann (Philadelphia: Temple University Press, 1981), pp. 69-70, 77-78. One might also note that the ordinary language analysis of the "later" Wittgenstein suggests that the intelligibility of abstract concepts and cues depends on their use in specific social contexts. See Hanna Pitkin, Wittgenstein and Justice (Berkeley: University of California Press, 1972), chap. 4.
9. See Edelman, Political Language, pp. 150-51.
10. See Murray Edelman, Politics as Symbolic Action: Mass Arousal and Quiescence (Chicago: Markham, 1971), pp. 50-52.
11. Frances Fox Piven and Richard A. Cloward, Poor People's Movements: Why They Succeed and How They Fail (New York: Vintage, 1979), p. 12.
12. Edelman, Political Language, p. 30.
13. See M. Stanton Evans, Clear and Present Dangers: A Conservative View of America's Government (New York: Harcourt Brace Jovanovich, 1975) for an exposition that taps into virtually every Lockean myth available.

14. Refer back to Chapter 2 of this book.

15. See Edelman, Political Language, chap. 4.

16. See Jane Flax, "Do Feminists Need Marxism?" in Building Feminist Theory: Essays from "Quest", ed. Charlotte Bunch et al. (New York: Longman, 1981), pp. 174-85.

17. See Antonio Gramsci, Selections from Political Writings, 1910-1920, ed. Quintin Hoare, trans. John Mathews (New York: International, 1977), p. 296.

18. Daniel De Leon, Socialist Landmarks (New York: New York Labor News, 1952), pp. 57-58.

19. For a brief review of Debs's adherence to "radical" Marxism, see James P. Cannon, "Introduction: Eugene V. Debs, The Socialist Movement of His Time—Its Meaning for Today," in Eugene V. Debs Speaks, ed. Jean Y. Tussey (New York: Pathfinder, 1970), pp. 9-39.

20. David Shannon, The Socialist Party of America (Chicago: Quadrangle, 1967), p. 12; see also Ira Kipnis, The American Socialist Movement, 1897-1912 (New York: Monthly Review, 1972), p. 107.

21. Morris Hillquit, History of Socialism in the United States (New York: Dover, 1971), p. 137; and idem, Socialism Summed Up (New York: H. K. Fly, 1913), p. 22.

22. Eugene V. Debs, Writings and Speeches of Eugene V. Debs, ed. Arthur Schlesinger, Jr. (New York: Hermitage, 1948), pp. 114, 122; see also Hillquit, Socialism Summed Up, p. 45.

23. Eugene V Debs, Walls and Bars (Chicago: C. H. Kerr, 1973), p. 230; Morris Hillquit, Socialism in Theory and Practice (New York: Macmillan, 1909), p. 125.

24. Debs, Writings, p. 33; see also Hillquit quoted in A. Fried, ed., Socialism in America (Garden City, N.Y.: Doubleday, 1970), p. xiii; and idem, Socialism on Trial (New York: B. W. Huebsch, 1920), p. 13.

25. Hillquit, Socialism Summed Up, pp. 53-54; see also Eugene V. Debs, Debs Magazine 2 (March 1923): 2.

26. Hillquit, History of Socialism, p. 20; see also Debs, Writings, p. 239.

27. Debs, Writings, pp. 111, 436; Hillquit, Socialism in Theory and Practice, pp. 14, 24; see also idem, Socialism on Trial, p. 66, where he extends this line of argument to include all nations, especially Russia.

28. Debs, Writings, p. 270; Hillquit, Socialism in Theory and Practice, p. 177; Socialism on Trial, p. 50.

29. Debs, Writings, pp. 294, 396; Hillquit, Socialism on Trial, p. 46.

30. Debs, Writings, pp. 102, 174-75, 350, 366, 372; Hillquit, Socialism in Theory and Practice, pp. 153-54; see also idem, The Double Edge of Labor's Sword, with Samuel Gompers and Max Hayes

(New York: Arno and the New York Times, 1971), pp. 62, 79; and idem, From Marx to Lenin (New York: Hanford, 1921), p. 7.

31. Debs, Writings, p. 291; idem, Debs Magazine 1 (May 1922): 3, 8.

32. Debs quoted in Kipnis, The American Socialist Movement, p. 159; Hillquit, Socialism on Trial, p. 32.

33. Debs, Writings, pp. 111, 270, 297; Hillquit, Socialism on Trial, p. 53.

34. Hillquit, Socialism Summed Up, p. 44.

35. See Debs, Writings, pp. 281, 286, 417; idem, Walls and Bars, pp. 70, 103; Hillquit, History of Socialism, p. 20; idem, Socialism in Theory and Practice, pp. 57-58, 313.

36. Staughton Lynd, Intellectual Origins of American Radicalism (New York: Random House, 1969), pp. 168-69.

37. Hillquit, History of Socialism, p. 348; idem, "Socialist Task and Outlook," in Socialism in America, ed. A. Fried (Garden City, N. Y.: Doubleday, 1970), p. 551; idem, Double Edge of Labor's Sword, p. 22; Debs, Writings, pp. 184, 209, 304.

38. Debs, Writings, pp. 262, 290, 303-5, 323; idem, Debs Magazine 1 (February 1922): 9.

39. Hillquit, From Marx to Lenin, p. 44; idem, Socialism in Theory and Practice, pp. 160-61; and idem, Socialism Summed Up, pp. 20, 91.

40. Debs, Writings, pp. 32, 241, 309; compare Hillquit, Socialism in Theory and Practice, pp. 214-15; and John Locke, An Essay concerning Human Understanding, 2 vols., ed. A. Fraser (New York: Dover, 1959), 1:343, 2:447.

41. Morris Hillquit, Present-day Socialism (New York: Rand School of Social Science, 1920), p. 27; Debs, Writings, p. 72.

42. Eugene V. Debs, Debs Magazine 1 (July 1922): 4; idem, Writings, pp. 16, 365, 436, 442; Hillquit, Double Edge of Labor's Sword, pp. 46-47; idem, Socialism in Theory and Practice, p. 280; idem, Socialism on Trial, pp. 53-55.

43. Debs, Debs Magazine 1 (August 1922): 13.

44. Hillquit, From Marx to Lenin, p. 36.

45. Debs, Writings, pp. 310, 355; idem, Eugene V. Debs Speaks, ed. Jean Y. Tussey (New York: Pathfinder, 1970), pp. 365-66.

46. Hillquit, Socialism in Theory and Practice, pp. 23, 34, 59, 94, 99-103; idem, From Marx to Lenin, pp. 53, 107.

47. Eugene V. Debs, Debs Magazine 1 (July 1922): 12.

48. Debs, Writings, p. 225; see also pp. 109, 163, 183, 198, 215, 343.

49. Debs, Eugene V. Debs Speaks, ed. Jean Y. Tussey (New York: Pathfinder, 1970), p. 144; idem, Writings, pp. 38-39, 129, 335-36, 343.

50. Debs, Writings, p. 353.

51. Ibid., p. 435.

52. Hillquit, History of Socialism, p. 172; see also idem, Socialism Summed Up, p. 53; idem, Double Edge of Labor's Sword, pp. 26-27.

53. Hillquit, Socialism Summed Up, p. 46; idem, Present-day Socialism, p. 73; idem, Socialism in Theory and Practice, pp. 102-3; idem, Double Edge of Labor's Sword, p. 77.

54. Hillquit, Socialism in Theory and Practice, p. 203; compare with Debs, Writings, p. 341.

55. Hillquit, Socialism in Theory and Practice, pp. 67, 72, 81.

56. Martin Carnoy and Derek Shearer, Economic Democracy: The Challenge of the 1980s (White Plains, N.Y.: M. E. Sharpe, 1980), pp. 375, 403.

57. See "Founding Statement of the Campaign for Economic Democracy, 1977," in Tom Hayden, The American Future: New Visions beyond Old Frontiers (Boston: South End, 1980), pp. 303-10.

58. Carnoy and Shearer, Economic Democracy, p. 375.

59. Ibid., pp. 18-19.

60. Ibid., p. 384.

61. "Founding Statement," p. 310.

62. Carnoy and Shearer, Economic Democracy, p. 403.

63. Compare Hayden, The American Future, chap. 1; Antonio Gramsci, Letters from Prison, ed. and trans. Lynne Lawner (New York: Harper & Row, 1975), pp. 102, 159-60; and Christopher Lasch, The Culture of Narcissism: American Life in an Age of Diminishing Expectations (New York: Warner, 1979).

5

THE POLITICIZED
LEFT

The American Left has often treated politics as an instrument
for achieving "higher" ends. For radical liberals, politics has been
a tool for protecting and extending people's individual freedoms; the
public realm has been important only insofar as it makes possible
the private realm. Socialists have usually devalued politics as simply a lever for class domination in capitalist society or as an implement for administering socialist society; politics has been less important than the mode of production or economic exploitation and
alienation.

This historical predisposition against politics has made it easy
for radicals to skirt democratic terrain. The state itself, mass participation, and public discourse have rarely been treated as bases for
egalitarian association between people. They have rarely been considered ongoing ways in which process and substance overlap as a
people works out for itself what kind of community it shall be or what
kind of needs it shall strive to fulfill. Politics hints of subjectivity
and, thus, undermines the old attachments to Enlightenment rationalism or socialist objectivism. Consequently, democratic politics
could easily be ignored or deferred to uncertain tomorrows in the
name of idealized justice, particularly in the material realm.

However, one can extract from the history and legacy of the
New Left a new appreciation for democratic politics. For significant
segments of the American Left today, the old ideologies are being
adjusted to include democratic politics as an essential part of radical
visions. Left language increasingly betrays familiar democratic accents. Left political strategies more often are premised on the notion that radical democratic means are the most justifiable and expedient ways to attain influence. The thesis of this chapter is that
the American Left is becoming a politicized Left that abides on radical
democratic terrain.

THE LEFT AND AMERICAN POLITICS

The end of World War II also marked the end of liberals' limited state. Long in the making, the welfare state was now entrenched; political centralization, bureaucracy and hierarchy, militarism, and the integration of government and big business were its by-products. Clearly, the U.S. government was something other than an instrument for protecting people's rights. It was both a benefactor of the people who received entitlements and a power that fostered mass dependence. Tens of millions of Americans were its employees, recipients, and more or less willing partners.

The postwar integration of American state and American society destroyed the viability of distinguishing the public and private spheres of life. State authority grew and pervaded private life. Some of it was parceled out to semiautonomous or private policy-making groups, which could have an immense impact on people's lives without being accountable to people. New groups won access to state authority, to be sure, but soon discovered that access did not give them power over public policy. The development of what Alan Wolfe calls the Franchise State involved the following paradox:

> It renders civic life both more democratic and more
> elitist at the same time. On the one hand, more groups
> are brought into the affairs of state for the first time.
> . . . But at the same time, the price paid is that deci-
> sions come increasingly to be made in a semi-secret,
> informal manner with all the important details being
> worked out by similar-minded elites. [1]

Americans could now participate in politics and yet remain powerless and dependent. This was a reality that forced radical liberals to come to terms with a more-than-minimal state that was clearly a less-than-neutral instrument for protecting people's rights.

Concurrently, the growth of state authority slowly undermined the conventional socialist view of the state as simply an instrument of the ruling class. The state now seemed to have some semiautonomous power of its own. World events after World War II demonstrated once and for all that socialization of the means of production does not necessarily end class politics or mass alienation. De-Stalinization notwithstanding, what Milovan Djilas called the new class of party and state elites in Soviet bloc countries wielded concentrated power. Statism was a reality manifest in newly emergent socialist regimes, where political elites had the authority to dictate the terms of economic transformation. Socialist workers and peasants still had little control over their own lives or little ability to create their own history. Within this historical context, many American socialists began to reevaluate politics as an arena of action that is more than epiphenomenal.

The 1960s was a decade in which statism was attacked throughout the world. The New Left challenged concentrated political power, bureaucratism, centralized technologies, and the integration of state and society as independent sources of alienation in the West. Marxist Humanism (or "Marxism with a human face") emerged in Eastern Europe and the USSR as a protest against political elites who promised liberation but dictated social policy. Red Guards in the People's Republic of China (PRC) and national liberation movements in the Third World fought against colonial and state elites, who denied people control over their own communities. These attacks on statism took many forms and carried a host of ideological labels; but their shared content was the legitimation of political decentralization, community and worker control, and the extension of the public space, which afford people a role in scripting their common future.

American Left thinking began to catch up with such practices in the 1970s. John Rawls's A Theory of Justice deemphasized political control and stability and instead highlighted the importance of political discourse and participation.[2] Rawls gave primacy to open discussion as the basis for justice and the surest manifestation of it. He focused discourse on once submerged issues, like social equality, citizenship, and civil disobedience. He overtly acknowledged that political justice and economic justice come in a single package. Though his theory was not especially radical, its focus on the state as a democratic basis for human association was taken up by radical liberals, like Herbert Gans, who saw in Rawls's principles a justification for "more equality."[3] Rawls's principles were also reflected in works by Sanford Lakoff and Mark Nadel, who studied private governments to suggest how corporations could be subjected to "public accountability."[4] Increasingly, radical liberals committed themselves to viewing politics as a way of life that extends beyond government and into society, where democratic norms should rule.

American socialists also began to develop a noninstrumental view of politics. Translations of Selections from the Prison Notebooks of Antonio Gramsci and Jurgen Habermas's works, particularly his Legitimation Crisis, provided Americans some theoretical grounding for a political Marxism.[5] Gramsci gave credence to the state as a significant hegemonic force, with authority somewhat free from economic determinants; he also legitimated a counterhegemonic politics based on decentralized worker organizations and mass partisanship. Habermas's second generation of Critical Theory exposed the importance of political space and justified concern for the "ideal speech situations" characterized by democratic dialogue. Soon, American socialists began to construct their own understandings of the state and politics, often underscoring the importance of democratic participation and politics as means and ends of socialism. [6] Many looked at politics less as a mirror of production and more as a realm in which significant battles for community would occur.

The politicized Left is now emerging as the most prominent segment of the American Left. Certainly, the old forces of radical liberal reformism and socialist revolutionism persist to reproduce historical patterns of Left failures. But the old forces seem to be on the defensive as the politicized Left begins to outline and practice strategies that, in the long run, promise to enhance American Left fortunes.

RADICAL LIBERAL TRANSFORMATION

Radical liberals—as early populists and progressives—articulated the popular demands that were ultimately processed into the modern welfare state. [7] Though radical liberals had little impact on the shaping of the welfare state, they generally favored its growth and entrenchment in American life as realistic progress. They preferred concentrated political power in the federal government, where it might be used in behalf of consenting majorities rather than to diffuse power among the individual states, where rural conservatives would use it for reactionary ends. Radical liberals often looked to the federal government to organize the intelligence and expertise necessary for administering welfare programs, in part, because they feared incompetence, corruption, and prejudice at local levels of government. Radical liberals also accepted the assumption that the federal government was the only national power able to oversee the nation's economic health; they also relied on private groups like organized labor to ensure government oversight in the public interest. For most of the twentieth century, radical liberals considered the welfare state a realistic and rational instrument for protecting and extending people's rights in the private realm. However, radical liberals have begun to reconsider.

In the last few decades, radical liberals have been comparing the familiar benefits to the increasingly salient costs of the welfare state. Concentrated political power may allow the federal government to rule against school segregation and even to send in troops to enforce the ruling; but it also distances people from decision makers and provides people little recourse when illiberal rulings come out of Washington. Bureaucratic politics may be a way of organizing knowledge in the public interest, but it is also the basis for government growth and power, which work against public demands for local autonomy in the form of Black Power, community control over police and schools, or client influence in bureaucratic policies. A questionable declaration of war in Vietnam and systematic lying concerning that war, the Watergate scandal and other political corruption, and revelations about the illegal activities of intelligence agencies and quasi-governmental agencies continually highlighted the danger that concentrated political power, though sometimes benign, is ultimately a malignant foundation for political tyranny.[8] Meanwhile, "the best and the brightest," who constituted governmental expertise and staffed its bureaucracies, failed to solve pressing social problems but did succeed in creating what Sheldon Wolin calls dependent man as the archetype of modern American citizenship.

> The main characteristic of dependent man is not simply that he lacks autonomy but that he is demoralized. . . . Demoralization stands for living continuously and hopelessly in circumstances where one is assailed endlessly by forces that one cannot understand, much less control, but that others seemingly do know about and do control.[9]

For all of its virtues, the welfare state did not eliminate Michael Harrington's "Other America"; nor did it prevent the growth of anxieties associated with war, ecological damage, toxic wastes, nuclear holocaust, crime, child abuse, or wife beating. At best, its therapeutic efforts helped Americans to live with emerging crises; at worst, it metaphorically transformed rights-bearing citizens into numbers registered on computer cards.

The last few decades also witnessed the sensitization of radical liberals to the partnership between the welfare state and the giant multinational corporations that grew up in the postwar period. President Eisenhower himself warned of a growing "military-industrial complex," which C. Wright Mills and other power elite analysts documented. Academics and journalists added to the documentation, while minority groups, feminists, and other forgotten Americans entered into the pluralist arena to remind us that the welfare state was primarily concerned with the welfare of the rich rather than the interests of others.[10] Two major gasoline shortages in the 1970s amidst record oil company profits reinforced suspicions that our government was more democratic in word than in deed. Many radical liberals were forced to rethink the instrumentality of the welfare state.

If one traces John Kenneth Galbraith's line of thinking from the 1950s to the 1970s, one sees a "coming to consciousness" that the welfare state is mainly a service agency for big business.11 An even more rapid shift occurred in the writings of Theodore Lowi. His 1969 The End of Liberalism proposed a rationalization of the welfare state; his 1971 The Politics of Disorder concluded that "chaos is better than a bad program" to support a mass spontaneity inimical to the welfare state. 12 What were radical liberals to do once the welfare state was discredited? Many hoped to recapture the welfare state from elites through enriched consent and reforms consistent with Rawlsian principles. But some radical liberals felt that it was time to sever their attachments to the welfare state and strike out in radical democratic directions.

In 1970, for example, Lewis Lipsitz called for a reevaluation of American politics in terms of consent. "The problem of consent, like a huge tree trunk floating in the air, needs to put down serious roots; spread out, crack the facade of established institutions, and throw off at least a few useful apples."13 Consent is not serious if the state shapes people's lives rather than being shaped by people's choices. Freedom is not serious if economic elites rather than in-dividuals control "their destinies in the day-to-day issues of the job." Ultimately, the welfare state does not recognize "the main issues of today," which are not reforms from above but are "social and eco-nomic equality." If necessary, established institutions must be challenged, their facades cracked, and politics relocated in people's everyday "lives and worlds, expectations and disappointments, rages and hopes."14

By 1976, Theodore Becker was not alone when he called for an "All-American Revolution" and a "Constitutional Revolution."15 Rev-olution was justified against the welfare state because corporate elites had broken the American social contract.

> The American form of government, "contracted" for by
> the American people sprung from their revolution in the
> late eighteenth century and was based on many excellent
> values, including that "we, the people" should govern
> our own destiny. . . . Political institutions have ceased
> to work according to contractual specifications during
> the twentieth century, but more so recently. In other
> words, "there's been a breach of contract" and govern-
> ment "of the people, by the people, and for the people"
> has become, obviously, one "of the few, by the very
> few, for even fewer."16

Becker wanted a new constitutional convention that would significantly restructure the U.S. political system. His new politics would include the expansion of public control over the nation's economic life, for example, by underwriting an extensive public sector, which would compete with private corporations rather than enrich them at the public's expense. This, he said, would make for a truly "mixed economy."[17]

Radical liberals like Galbraith, Lowi, Lipsitz, and Becker were implicitly transforming the notion of realism in ways that aligned it with radical democratic politics. They affirmed the political arena as a place where people define for themselves their national identity, wield authority enough to reshape social life, and play a direct role in rule making. Realism was now based on shifted scales of trust: less for the good-intentioned elites, who sometimes staffed the welfare state, and more for the people, even when they practice "the politics of disorder." More than playing it safe by advocating incremental changes, they began to speak about radical restructuring of U.S. institutions and even of revolution. To an extent, they were laying the foundations of a new radical liberalism, still rooted in Lockean concepts, but far more radical than enriched consent. Equally important, they spawned and lent credibility to theories of "participatory democracy" and "the New Populism," which blurred some of the distinctions between them and democratic socialists.

Theories of participatory democracy are, in part, attempts to recall the communal autonomy of America's revolutionary past and to recapture some of the more radical ideas of Thomas Jefferson, who, according to C. B. Macpherson, "treated the common people as trustworthy to an extent unusual."[18] These theories were also, in part, attempts to defend geographical, functional, and minority communities against what the New Left called the Establishment as well as to articulate the experiences of radicals who had discovered the pleasures—and the pains—of face-to-face politics in the civil rights, antiwar, and counterculture movements. These theories usually share three characteristics: support for political decentralization, the politicization of social life, and mass participation as a form of mass power.[19] They are at once critiques of the welfare state and legitimations of radical democratic alternatives to the welfare state.

Popular books, like E. F. Schumacher's Small Is Beautiful or Ernest Callenbach's Ecotopia, were premised on a belief overtly stated by Lawrence Goodwyn.

Given the historical evidence that human beings have accumulated, at great cost, in the twentieth century, it now seems possible to offer a direct counterpremise to the idea of progress: societies based on large-unit production have a verifiable tendency to become increasingly hierarchical over time. Supporting evidence is so pervasive that this may now be taken as a law.[20]

The welfare state is based on large-unit production and generates not social progress but social hierarchy. It is inherently antidemocratic. Participatory democrats want to decentralize political power in order to enrich democracy. They are not new federalists, who want some federal power doled out to state governments, where it would remain beyond the control of citizens. Instead, they insist that political power be located in cities, towns, and neighborhoods, where people can learn to trust one another, openly discuss policies, hammer out decisions they will have to live with, reevaluate and test those decisions, and ultimately revise them, if necessary. The demos may make mistakes, but it will be in a position to recognize and correct them. While few participatory democrats foresee the elimination of national or regional governments, they want these distant centers of political power to be rebuilt from the bottom up. Political initiatives must come from the communities, be legitimated by the communities, and ultimately be revocable by the communities. [21] This "guild liberalism" is an attack on welfare statism and the beginning of an alternative to it.

Furthermore, participatory democrats argue that American society as a whole is based on large-unit production, which functions to reproduce hierarchy throughout American life. Elites who monopolize the media, technology, expertise, and wealth have the concentrated power to subordinate communities and individuals to their will. The democratic remedy is to politicize these social institutions, decentralize them, and subject them to popular control. [22] Cable television offers opportunities for communities to win back the airwaves from the major networks. Solar technology is a viable means of democratizing energy resources. Experiments in worker control, consumer representation, tenants' rights, and student power offer examples of how private sources of power can be politicized and controlled by relevant publics. [23] This logic can be extended indefinitely to justify community control over local crime prevention or democracy in family life. [24] Put slightly differently, participatory democracy can be seen as a defense of a one-class society, where diverse members come together to work out their form of mutual association; rarely is participatory democracy a vision of a classless society, where politics somehow becomes unnecessary. [25]

Can average citizens, political amateurs, be trusted with such political and social power? Some participatory democrats simply say yes; such trust comes with the democratic turf. Others say yes, given that the alternative is entrusting power to elites, who have consistently proven their disdain for democracy. However, most participatory democrats provide a more qualified answer. Americans have been victimized by the welfare state to become habituated to dependence and passivity; they have been victimized by a corporate economy that rewards cutthroat competition for individuals rather than humane cooperation among individuals. The victims need to be transformed into independent, active, and cooperative people. The agency of transformation is not some elite-inspired education but the self-education that comes with participatory experiences.

For Peter Bachrach, "participation plays a dual role: it not only catalyzes opinion but also creates it."26 People who participate to shape their own lives learn to articulate their values, subject them to the test of experience, and recognize their common lot with their neighbors. For Carole Pateman, participation is "educative in the widest sense, including both the psychological aspect and the gaining of practice in democratic skills and procedures."27 Participation is both a means and an end. It teaches people to assume leadership roles, develop and share requisite skills, and work toward common goals; it is a process that births egalitarian substance in community relations. It is both a political instrument for defending, extending, and practicing democratic rights and a form of association that enriches community and individual life.

Theories of participatory democracy lend themselves to a politics that is neither reformist nor revolutionary. Certainly, they can be used to justify symbolic reforms, like "maximum feasible participation" or token shop floor participation, which do not challenge elite supremacy; and they can be used to justify revolution in the name of real participation. But, they are generally used to legitimate an experimental politics aimed at displacing elite power.28 They are the theoretical basis for producer and consumer cooperatives, women's banks and poor people's health centers, neighborhood crime prevention programs, alternative day-care, and newspaper and journal collectives. These institutions generally invite mass participation, provide experience and training in organizing and self-management, and sometimes produce the resource base necessary for broader democratic struggles. Situated within a hierarchal society, these institutions often suffer a good deal of internal and external conflict, which, from the perspective of politicizing silenced issues, may be a good thing. Just as Jefferson saw some utility in Shays's Rebellion, participatory democrats sometimes want conflict to surface. S. M. Shumer provides one possible explanation in the following:

> By an overemphasis on the need to restrain and repress
> the political ambitions and violence of men, we are
> likely to miss the positive role that conflict and even
> violence play in keeping liberty alive, in keeping the po-
> litical arena truly open to citizens, in keeping it ex-
> citing and challenging and thus eliciting the best of cit-
> izens' abilities as well as their positive loyalties and

commitments. Perhaps, ironically, it is the freedom given to conflict and its expression which can form the very basis of attachment to common institutions and common life of the polity that, in turn, can be called upon politically to contain that conflict.[29]

Implicitly, participatory democracy supports a politics that opens up exploration of what liberals call the tensions and Marxists call the dialectic between consensus and conflict, community and individualism.

The distinctions between participatory democracy and the new populism are vague owing to considerable overlap and variations among the exponents of both. Nonetheless, it is fair to say that the new populism focuses more on national politics; it is Whitmanesque rather than Jeffersonian. The new populists are concerned with a great national unity made up of people from all walks of life; they are the supporters of "the little man," who already possesses the Protestant virtues, allegiance to individual rights, and desire for independence and autonomy that characterize populist democracy. The new populists want to combine national patriotism and individualism based on an appreciation of the American savvy, apparent in Studs Terkel's Working, where "the people" speak for themselves and reveal their heroic attempts to cope with the problems of our times. Populist political goals are sometimes cast in religious language; indeed, populists themselves claim serious religious concerns often. In general, these goals include helping people to appreciate their democratic heritage, enriching it by recapturing government on a majoritarian basis, and using political authority to redistribute social power in ways that restore individual autonomy. Fred Harris puts it quite simply, "Up with those who are down!"[30]

I take the core axiom of the new populism to be that the people is not an abstraction but a historical and cultural reality. From Shays's Rebellion to the old populist uprisings of the 1880s and 1890s and into recent environmental, public interest, and consumer movements, part of being American has been a willingness to define one's prerogatives and rights in mass actions. These mass actions have been the wavelike source of a collective experience that enhances people's shared visions and values of egalitarian life and heightens their awareness of the "unjust features of the received hierarchical order," which denies egalitarian life.[31] Between cresting populist waves, Americans attest to their democratic identity in a culture built on hatred of bureaucracy and impersonality, on love of voluntarism and mutual aid. The very notion of a welfare state is nourished by this culture, but the reality of the welfare state contradicts the cultural identity. The new populists are quite good at making arguments and amassing statistics that show that the welfare state and Wall Street-Madison Avenue capitalism foster injustices that harm the vast majority of the people—including white-collar workers and blue-collar workers; men and women; whites and minorities; the aged and the poor; Northerners, Southerners, and Westerners; independent businessmen and consumers; the old and the young.[32] History, culture, and the majority or public interest define and unite the people.

The new populists are interested in leading the American people in rebellion, not revolution. They urge people to overcome passivity and fatalism, to assert and defend their democratic identity, and most important, to recapture the political system as a servant of the people. As in most rebellions, political strategy is open and expedient. It includes heroes and heroines, like Ralph Nader, Saul Alinsky, Cesar Chavez, or Gale Cincotta; and groups, like Common Cause, or National People's Action, or the National Welfare Rights Organization. It includes conventional political efforts, like Fred Harris's run for a presidential nomination; Democratic Party reforms; and mass-based petitioning, referenda, initiative, and recall actions; and it also includes unconventional political efforts, like mass civil disobedience and disruption at the site of nuclear power plants or neighborhood actions to prevent marshals from carrying out unjust evictions. One might say that the new populism offers not a political strategy per se but a strategic ethic aimed at enriching political life: people should get involved, fight for their rights, uncover political and social injustices, and support attempts to unseat the powerful and replace them with the as yet powerless. Power to the people.[33] The common thread of understanding is that mass movements can win state power and then use it to transform social life according to egalitarian norms.

Once people reassume their sovereignty and install their own leaders into political authority, two kinds of change will occur. First, the populists believe that the people will attack concentrated power not accountable to the public interest. Those who monopolize the marketplaces of ideas, politics, and the economy will be subject to trust-busting and real regulation as well as to affirmative action on behalf of majorities. The strong shall fall and the weak shall rise, the result being a renewed competition in which everyone is represented and positioned to win, based not on privilege but on skill and support. Second, the people and their leaders will have the historical hindsight that alerts them to the perilous forces that transform open competition back into monopoly. Through government, these forces will be countered and neutralized. The national tax structure could be altered to equalize incomes and ensure that no one becomes wealthy enough to dominate others and that everyone has enough political and economic power to resist domination.[34] Government economic policy could be redirected toward nationalizing natural monopolies, facilitating the growth of public corporations to keep private ones honest, installing public representatives on private decision-making boards, subsidizing businesses responsive to the public interest or willing to experiment with worker control, guaranteeing decent employment for all Americans, and more. [35] In the name of restoring competition and autonomy, the new populists take a few major steps toward affirming the public realm as both a manifestation of national unity and a source for redistributing power and wealth to equalize opportunities and to fulfill people's basic needs.

Though populism can and sometimes has been the basis for racist and sexist prejudices, its recent incarnation is rarely reactionary or reformist. First, its immense faith in an inclusive understanding of the people, its support for mass participation and rebellion, and its attachment to egalitarian streams of American life add up to a clear, antielitist stance. It opposes welfare-state rationalism from above; it rejects the concentrated power of monopolies; it supports a mass spontaneism inconsistent with elite planning and social control. Second, though the new populism's primary values suggest a return to the nineteenth-century marketplace and Lincolnian America, it plots a political path through the democratization of the state, enhanced public control over social life, and even some public ownership of the means of production. To a degree, it crosses territory once occupied only by socialists.

The transformation of radical liberalism manifest in theories of participatory democracy and the new populism represents a blurring of traditional Left distinctions. Participatory democracy has attracted the support of democratic socialists, feminists, and religious radicals. It criticizes the elitism structured into American life but does not reproduce the statism that plagues both capitalist and socialist societies today. For many feminists, it is an expression of their ongoing politics, which combines building nonrepressive organizations at local levels and using those organizations as the basis for personal change and for empowering women. Some religious radicals conceive of participatory democracy as the current expression of religious communitarian traditions practiced by Anabaptists, Mennonites, and Quakers, as well as a politics that offers alternatives and suggests how "to live those alternatives."[36] To a degree, the new populism has attracted socialist interest and even support. "Its preeminent desire for a firm footing in American realities" and its attempt "to reclaim . . . our nation's civic idealism" sometimes seem to socialists as a lesson on how to build on American egalitarian traditions rather than attack those traditions, therefore, suffer more isolation.[37] Finally, both theoretical perspectives offer some con-

crete guidance to Left activists by suggesting some middle ground between reformism and revolutionism. They provide concepts and languages that can be useful in community organizing or national organizing of mass movements; they focus activist opposition against increasingly visible U.S. elites and offer a democratic alternative to
that elitism; they justify winnable reforms today, which empower
people to win more extensive changes tomorrow. Ultimately, these
theories begin to stake out the radical democratic space where individualism and community, politics and society, and private initiative
and public control can be contested and potentially made to complement one another.

SOCIALIST TRANSFORMATION

The welfare state has often been the object of an important dispute within the American socialist camp. Some socialists have seen
it as a potentially useful instrument. It was built on working-class
support; it is a mechanism for rational economic planning; and it is
also a concentration of power that can be used to transform society.
Though a creature of capitalism, the welfare state is a means for
bringing about socialism. Other socialists have viewed the welfare
state simply as the latest instrument of capitalist domination. It is
a mechanism for concentrating and rationalizing capitalist power and
a tool for co-opting the working class. Along with capitalism, the
welfare state must be destroyed in order to bring about socialism.
At times, these opposing socialist perspectives have generated Gothic
antagonisms between different socialist groups. While those times
are not past, however, significant segments of American socialism
have redefined the nature and terms of debate over the state.

Both viewpoints on the welfare state were attacked in the 1960s
and 1970s. Socialist reformism was too closely associated with the
welfare state and suffered a guilt by association with its statist tendencies, which were challenged by the New Left. Socialist revolutionism, more recently, has been condemned as a form of vanguardism
that offers a revolution from above, which omens social fascism or
anarchist terrorism rather than working-class liberation.[38] Though
such attacks on the Old Left have often been short-lived, especially
when the New Left itself reproduced the old debate, increasing numbers of socialists have shown a willingness to explore democratic
alternatives to statist, instrumentalist politics.
This willingness is nicely captured by Alan Wolfe, who argues
that "the most striking political fact about late capitalism is the absence of politics," or put differently, the growth of "alienated poli-

tics."[39] Politics increasingly is viewed as the locus of significant decisions made outside of the public sphere. Bureaucratic experts are seen as claimants to a specialized authority that silences public discourse. Conventional forms of political participation, from party politics to interest-group competition, no longer appear to be arenas of real struggle so much as ritualized expressions of mass subordination. American socialists are not unconcerned with economic conditions and contradictions; but they increasingly focus their analysis on the political realm, hoping to uncover "new sources of political energy" with which people can gain control over the resources necessary for fulfilling their needs and also express their basic human need for egalitarian community life.[40]

The politicization of American socialists is manifest in the progressively open-ended nature of socialist analysis today. They are more and more sensitive to the multiple determinants of consciousness and class; they now appreciate the unconscious psychologies and the conscious ideologies that shape people's perceptions and actions; they sometimes see in technology, the minute division of labor, and the ascendancy of expertise the wellsprings of mass quiescence; they occasionally displace causality from the realm of production to the realm of consumption that compensates people for their obedience; they usually recognize that racism and sexism are important forces that predate capitalism and that usually resurface in socialist societies.[41] While historical materialism remains the primary tion for socialist understandings, socialists increasingly take historical materialism for granted and focus their efforts on the noneconomic bases of exploitation and alienation, which, at least partially, are amenable to political discourse and decision making.

The growth of epistemological pluralism gives rise to diffuse notions of class, which, in turn, offer inclusive understandings of the potential social base for change. Who is the working class in the modern United States? Is it white-collar workers and blue-collar workers, who are wage laborers? But not upper-level managers, who are also wage laborers? Does it include professionals, middle management, bureaucrats, and technicians? Is it an all-inclusive new working class? Is the proper basis for distinguishing the working class its lack of ownership of the means of production, its lack of control, or some combination of both? Or perhaps, is it occupation, salary, education level, job autonomy, or a host of other factors? Furthermore, just how important is the working class in terms of change? Is it still more important than feminist, minority, gay, or populist movements against exploitation and alienation? Is it somehow organically linked to the elderly, the unemployed, the underemployed? Does it have common interests with self-employed businessmen and farmers, who also suffer under monopoly capitalism? Socialists have discussed these questions and others but have engineered no consensus on the answers. The openness of the debate suggests that significant numbers of socialists are seriously considering as acceptable comprehensive notions of class and social change that bear less relationship to Marx's category than to the new populists' conception of the people. Ben Agger makes this explicit when he suggests that "a dose of populism" would be healthy for American Marxism. [42]

These transformations in socialist thought were first articulated by people like Erich Fromm, who argued that changes "occur as an expression of not only new productive forces, but also of the repressed part of human nature, and they are successful only when the two conditions are combined."[43] Recalling early Marx, Fromm and others sought to moralize, psychologize, and humanize American Marxism. But the new humanism lacked specificity and was mostly displaced when American socialists adopted Gramsci's notion of hegemony. John Cammet imported it and then defined it as "the predominance obtained by consent, rather than force, of one class over classes."[44] Capitalists mainly rule by disseminating a world view consistent with their interests, which is etched into mass psychology, structured into political and social institutions, and reinforced by popular myths and symbols and evocative language. In time, this world view takes on a life of its own, as those aligned with Critical Theory tell us. "Cultural representations and the psychic makeup of individuals are factors which, instead of merely reflecting material constraints, are integral and defining aspects of a historical situation."[45] The ultimate result of capitalist hegemony is the "friendly fascism" in which elites organize and integrate society for private profit and yet appear to act as if the public good is their central concern, thus winning mass support for their efforts.

If ruling-class hegemony suggests that the United States is moving toward a totally integrated or one-dimensional society, it also generates forces that potentially mean its self-destruction. Early U.S. capitalists, involved in a competitive marketplace, promoted a democratic world view consistent with the marketplace. However, when American capitalism evolved into monopoly capitalism, economic elites were forced to go into partnership with government to engage in systematic planning; but their ability to plan was somewhat constrained by their own democratic world view, now with some life of its own, which introduced mass demands and uncertainty into the planning process. Capitalists now confront their own ideological creation as a hostile force.[46] Similarly, modern capitalists introduced a consumerist ethic consistent with an economy experiencing rapid economic growth and expansion and a need for more market outlets. However, when that growth and expansion gave way to an era of ecological and fiscal limits amidst new international competition, capitalists found themselves in the uncomfortable position of justifying deteriorating standards of living, which contradict their own consumerist ethic. [47] The contradictions that result from capitalists' evolving economic interests and their semiautonomous world views do not produce false consciousness so much as a "contradictory and ambiguous mass consciousness" that is simultaneously integrated into capitalist society and hostile to its current needs. [48]

This reading of capitalist hegemony provides several motivations to politicize American socialism. First, many socialists now fear that capitalist hegemony has the capacity and even the need to absorb not only protest but the idea of protest and critical thought in general. Their view of the new narcissism, for example, is that it represents an extension of capitalist exchange ethics into universities and families, where social frustrations are channeled into forms of self-therapy rather than political thought and action. [49] To combat the capitalist integration of all social life, socialists have increasingly looked to intellectuals and artists, groups on the fringes of American society, and even the inner-directed individual autonomy of an earlier era as forces that carry with them the hope to develop a counterhegemony. [50] The revival of Freudian and Hegelian Marxism (and their variants and syntheses) suggests that the old socialist focus on the working class is being augmented (some say replaced) by a new concern with ideas, voluntary groups, and forms of individualism that have long been the core of liberal politics in the United States.

Second, socialists' growing sensitivity to the contradictions and ambiguities of mass consciousness now makes possible their entrance into the competition for Americans' moral, intellectual, and cultural support. A socialist ethics based on human needs now subversive of of capitalism can be developed as an appeal that cues people to resolve these ambiguities in ways favorable to socialist directions. [51] Relatedly, socialist educational efforts are no longer vain if the contest for intellectual support is no longer epiphenomenal. Moreover, if the ambiguities of moral and intellectual life are deeply embedded in American culture, then socialists have reason to address people on many levels of communication. Ronald Aronson puts it this way: "Since tearing away the veil [of hegemony] is hardly a matter of convincing people's intellects, revolutionary thought must engage the whole person: his feelings, his imagination, his sense of being lost." [52] This is an invitation to set aside "scientific socialism" and to substitute the words and symbols that touch people's everyday lives; this is an invitation to engage Americans in a dialogue in terms that are meaningful to them.

Finally, the combined fear of total societal integration and hope for winning mass support has been the basis for a socialist reanalysis of people's movements as legitimate forms of radical politics. On the one hand, populist movements for consumer rights or ecological sanity may be reformist in an abstract sense, but they are not necessarily reformist in today's historical milieu. These movements preserve and extend public space for thought and action critical of corporate interests at a moment when corporate elites need to manage public space in order to scale down public expectations. Populist movements also provide a public arena in which people can articulate their "shattered expectations" in an era of limits, engage in a dialogue over values and their priorities, and even consider socialist norms that speak to their needs.[53] On the other hand, local movements for community control over schools or utility rates, for tenants' rights, for veto power over the construction of nearby nuclear power plants, or for racial equity can now be considered by socialists as exceptional bases for social transformation. Small-scaled participatory democracies invigorate local politics in opposition to centralized planning or government-corporation partnerships so important to elites. Potentially, they are experiences in egalitarian associations that cause microrevolutions in consciousness, which may organize and spark macrotransformations in society.[54] As American socialists come to appreciate the nonreformist potentials of ongoing people's movements, they become more interested in defending the public space within which these movements struggle and for which they struggle.

One reason socialists are concerned about public space is because it is shrinking. Federal government's expanded powers and integration with multinational corporations has facilitated elite domination. The influence of groups like the Council on Foreign Relations, the Trilateral Commission, and other elite think tanks has waxed; the leverage of labor unions, public interest groups, and other potential representatives of people has waned. The American ruling class is not betraying signs of self-destruction but is becoming more powerful and sophisticated. Neither radical mass consciousness nor socialist class consciousness have appeared in the United States to counter these trends.

Furthermore, ruling-class domination has been augmented by semiautonomous forms of domination. Irving Zeitlin suggests the following:

> Political and military structures may rest at least in some
> degree on an economic class basis and for this reason
> must not be regarded as totally autonomous institutions.
> But this basic Marxian proposition should not obscure the
> fact that they are often sufficiently independent to deter-
> mine the life chances and fate of men.[55]

To economic, political, and military structures of elitism, socialists have added bureaucratic, professional, technocratic, legal and
procedural, racist, and sexist structures of mass subordination.[56]
No believers in iron laws of oligarchy, socialists recognize pervasive
tendencies toward hierarchy throughout American society that systematically reduce the margin of people's choices.

This shrinkage of public space is important to socialists for
several reasons. First, it means that the citizen does "not share in
political power" but, rather, is its object.[57] Political alienation
now augments economic alienation. Second, the objectification of
citizenship suggests that significant change in the United States is
not possible. To the extent that Americans believe this, they will be
unlikely to strive for change. Third, a citizenry that has given up on
change becomes a plastic mass easily molded by elites, who will further reduce public space. Socialist "pessimism of the intellect" fore-
casts greater authoritarianism for the near future. Hopefully, however, this authoritarianism can be contained. Jean Bethke Elshtain
reflects what many socialists believe when she says, "The great challenge facing the women's movement, and American democracy, is
how to prevent further erosion of the 'space' within which democratic
politics can operate."[58]

A slight but significant shift of Marxist emphasis is necessary
to justify the defense of public space as a major priority. One must
downplay historical laws and trends (which is easy if they point us in
authoritarian directions) and instead emphasize human will and choice
as the salient factors in shaping history. Michael Lerner provides an
example: "History is made up of human decisions, which exist in a
certain context. Although that context is not set by us alone, it does
permit us to make choices that can create a new society. The rest
is up to us."[59] It is up to us, for example, to choose against nuclear
proliferation, nuclear power, and the other perils that threaten to
eliminate once and for all any residues of human choice. As socialists give higher priority to defending democratic space and politics,
they become more willing to support political and civil liberties not
as bourgeois democracy or superstructure but as the bases for people to make necessary choices to live together and engage in political
action together.

Increasingly, socialists have adopted the radical liberal strategy of demanding that politicians make good on their promises to defend people's freedoms. To the extent politicians fulfill their promises,
they provide radicals with more elbowroom for dialogue, education,
experimentation, and political action; they provide people some un-
managed space within which to make the hard choices of our times.
To the extent politicians fail to fulfill their promises, which is almost assured if elites have a growing need to manage the public realm

to centralize planning mechanisms, then elites themselves will announce to Americans that capitalism and democracy are at odds with
one another. [60]

Some socialists encourage people to take full advantage of existing rights in ways that undermine elite rule. Suppose that everyone
eligible for government benefits demanded them, or suppose that millions of young Americans appealed their draft status. [61] Elite institutions could not handle the overload. Either elites would have to
make good on established rights and entitlements and, thereby, limit
their own maneuverability; or they would have to retract rights and
entitlements and, therefore, delegitimate their own rule. Finally,
some socialists support mass civil disobedience in defense of endangered freedoms, thereby aligning themselves with American traditions that feed historical rebellions. This puts elites in a somewhat
untenable position. Do they support massive police roundups, which
ignore particular individuals' rights, only to announce that they rule
by force and not consent? Or do elites protect the established rights
of dissidents and, thereby, give free reign to the forces opposing
them? [62] What may be considered a "socialist politics of rights" roots
socialism in American political culture, affirms socialists' support
for democratic rights, and forces elites to make the hard decisions
that may sow conflict among them and weaken their hegemony.

A socialist politics of rights points to a direction for action but
little more. It leaves open questions of strategy and tactics. Some
socialists want to recreate a viable socialist party that internally will
balance leadership and membership and externally will build a socialist constituency. Other socialists are more interested in involving
themselves in single-issue groups, radical union caucuses, feminist
experiments, minority groups, or broader regional movements in
order to accomplish some worthwhile goals and spark greater socialist consciousness in the United States. Some socialists envision
some combination of local and national activism "to preserve a balance between the struggle to force present society to enact reforms
it claims to favor and the struggle to move beyond the limits of society." [63] And, of course, some socialists continue to support revolution. What we may be witnessing is a growing understanding among
socialists that there is no true path to a socialist future and that experimentation, particularly with a mass-based democratic politics,
is in order. This understanding is manifest in the recent merging of
the once-reformist Democratic Socialist Organizing Committee
(DSOC) and the once-revolutionist New American Movement (NAM)
into the Democratic Socialists of America (DSA).

Experimentation in the defense and use of public space forces
socialists to make some hard decisions. When one defends that
space, does one also defend the rights of reactionary groups to abide

there? Staughton Lynd, for example, supports the right to nonviolent civil disobedience, even when applied to "the white Southerner who might wish to disobey a federal civil rights law in a way that would at least immediately harm no one else."[64] More and more socialists argue that their own organizations must be founded on democratic rights, not democratic centralism, in order to foster open discussion and debate, encourage mutual self-education, and elicit the "goodwill" of supporters rather than the halfhearted support of good people bound to a party line.[65] This openness may run against the grain of Weberian efficiency, but socialists consider internal democracy as an important check against elitism among themselves and as a crucial basis for building a bottom-up consensus among themselves.

There is no doubt that American socialism still harbors groups that believe change is possible within the context of the welfare state or that change can come only through a revolution led by Leninist sects with advanced consciousness. Representatives of the latter can be found at almost any gathering of the Left. However, the segment of socialism that I am considering here implicitly recalls Marx's message that political liberation is a prerequisite and a part of human liberation. The shrinkage of public space has alerted many socialists to the fact that political liberation has yet to become a reality; and socialists' "faith" informs them that the struggle for democracy is both a means and an end within the socialist world view.

American socialists have begun to learn faith in several senses. First, a number of socialists have learned to appreciate religious faith as one basis for commitment. William A. Williams applauds efforts "to encourage American radicals to break out of their conception of social change as a wholly secular phenomenon." He adds, "My own sense of being religious has strengthened my commitment to socialist principles and action. . . . I have often found that quietly religious people (as opposed to the 'reborn' or 'churchy' types) are often open to serious talk and action concerning specific social changes."[66] Williams points out that the Mormons of Utah have played an important role in opposing the MX missile. Some Jewish socialists have begun to investigate the relationship between their religious backgrounds and their radicalism. Paul Breines writes, "I wonder more about what a Jew is because I have to wonder more about what a Leftist is."[67] This concern for religious faith partly arises from the fear that the New Right is using religion for reactionary ends without much Left opposition; it partly arises from the realization of the role religious faith has played in the New Left, in Latin America, and in Poland. Maybe more important, socialists' sometime focus on religious faith signifies that they are now interested in a more inclusive politics, one that does not write off religion as false consciousness and, thus, alienates millions of Americans, but one that roots socialism in the wellsprings of everyday life, including everyday religious life. Williams puts it this way: "Religion, after all, is just another word for community. Religion and community have to do with shared values and a daily commitment to those values. . . . If you want to stop nuclear nonsense, then you begin stopping it at home."[68] And, one might add, you draw on people's living faith as one basis for building people's movements at home.

Second, socialists have also begun to nurture a secular faith in the ability of Americans to practice decentralized forms of public control. Increasingly, socialists forsake nationalization of the means of production as a goal that is inherently statist and instead advocate the decentralization of power to local communities.[69] Community control, neighborhood control, worker control, and even consumer control are more and more the preferred mechanisms for the transition to socialism in the United States. But will Americans exercise this control in ways that prefigure socialism? On the one hand, socialists' faith that people will eventually see their interest in opting for socialism is born of necessity. The centralization that characterizes elite power today must be checked, and the redistribution of power to localities seems like the best way to do this. Historically, socialism has fared far better in local than in national arenas. On the other hand, socialists' faith emerges from the ambiguities in mass consciousness today. Certainly people may use newfound power for antidemocratic, antisocialist ends. However, as they participate more in democratic dialogue, as they share the experience of managing their collective lives together, socialists hope they will develop a more intense attachment to values like social equality and policies that enhance public control over resources. Ira Shor's version of socialist pedagogy suggests that mass education must "flow into and through the idiom of mass experiences," because that experience contains an inarticulate egalitarianism that participatory democracy may bring to the surface.[70]

In various ways, socialists' greater faith in Americans is built into their visions of the good society. Paul Sweezy has less faith in leaders than in the masses. "Taking account of the truism that individuals are always fallible, we can carry the reasoning further and say that a government can be relied upon to practice 'from the masses to the masses' consistently and persistently only if in the last analysis it is controlled by the masses."[71] Gar Alperovitz has faith enough to believe that people can voluntarily sustain a socialist economy by allowing individuals the option to exit from it.

Because voluntary individual choice is critical to the development of a new socialist ethic, "a second tier" to the

> economy might be appropriate. . . . Allow that individ-
> uals be free to opt out of the overall economy, if they so
> choose, and that they be guaranteed a minimum subsis-
> tence income much less than the basic economy's
> norm. [72]

The faith here is that people will want and be able to make decisions
for themselves that speak to their egalitarian values and common
needs and, thus, strengthen their ties to a socialist organization of
society.

Third, some socialists have cultivated faith enough in their
own visions and values to be able to admit that many uncertainties
and difficulties will necessarily attend progressive change. There
is no paved road to the socialist future; rather, there will be shifting
degrees of consensus and conflict that must be played out in the process of change. Martin Jay writes, "The belief that political conflict
is epiphenomenal is a fallacy which ought finally to be laid to rest."[73]
Decentralized socialism may fail to solve important social problems;
its solutions may benefit some people at other people's expense; it
may have to coexist with some degree of political centralization and
bureaucracy; it may do more to politicize issues like sexism and
racism than to resolve them; it may have to protect the individual
rights of some groups against the community. It may even have to
face the reality that confrontations between various governments,
groups, and individuals will be the prevailing reality as once-sub-
merged conflicts in capitalist society emerge in socialist society,
as political passivity makes way for mass political energy. Increasingly, a politics without authority is inconceivable to socialists, and
Marx's vision of economic cooperation is being augmented by a new
political vision of egalitarian conflict, subject to democratic discourse
and the object of public decision making. "If one really believes in
democratic ideas and accepts the necessity of chains of command,"
writes Richard Sennett, "these confrontations are necessary."[74] Socialists' faith is that people can engage in confrontations without reproducing hierarchy and elitism, or, as Michael Walzer says, "liberty and equality are the two chief virtues of social institutions, and
they stand best when they stand together."[75]

The socialist transformation discussed here invites dialogue
with radical liberals. Socialists' increasing interest in individual
autonomy, political and civil rights, and voluntaristic politics—that
is, in democracy—provides concepts and language that are accessible
to radical liberals, who then, if they desire, can look more seriously
at the socialist analysis of American society. Thus, Theodore Becker
sees in Marxism "an excellent analysis of the interaction of economics

and politics," which feeds his transformation of radical liberalism.[76] Furthermore, the greater openness of socialist understanding and politics provides space enough for religious radicals and feminists, who fit no categorization, or participatory democrats and populists to enter into a dialogue in which class relations and common human needs play a more significant role than is usually the case. Finally, this politicized socialism is at least partly linked to American democratic traditions and, therefore, provides socialists a means of communication to broader American audiences than they have had in the past; and the messages communicated seem to go beyond welfare-state reformism but stop short of socialist revolutionism in a way that might even be persuasive to many Americans.

In the last decade, American socialists have gone out of their way to open up lines of communication with radical liberals and American audiences. The rather sectarian radical paper, the Guardian, now competes with an independent socialist weekly, In These Times, whose editors reach out to nonsocialists. Revealingly, Socialist Revolution has changed its name to Socialist Review and opens its pages to the discussion of potential similarities and alliances between socialists and populists. Socialists have more often joined into debates in the radical press, where some version of radical democracy forms the foundation for dialogue. This press includes magazines like Radical America, Nation, Mother Jones, Working Papers, Social Policy, Dollars and Sense, and more. January 1981 saw the publication of a new journal, Democracy, which editor Sheldon Wolin has has shaped as a forum in which an array of radicals come together to discuss issues germaine to a politicized Left.[77] To the extent that American socialists have invited and participated in discourse over democracy, they have also firmed up their credentials as democrats, linked themselves to traditions that go back to 1776 and to a politics that is both familiar to Americans and radical.

In 1964, William A. Williams subtitled one of his books An Essay on the Contemporary Relevance of Karl Marx and the Wisdom of Admitting the Heretic into a Dialogue about America's Future. Today, Williams is less concerned with admitting Marxism into American talk and more concerned with Americanizing socialism. He looks to the Articles of Confederation as an indigenous precedent for the confederation of decentralized, regional governments and participatory democracies, which he now advocates; he looks to the conditions under which a constitutional convention would become a serious possibility.[78] In short, he and other American socialists look to radical democracy as one way to lead socialists out of their historical isolation in the United States.

THE LIMITS OF CONVERGENCE

The politicization of the Left and its convergence on the terrain of radical democracy is a limited phenomenon. Radical liberal reformism and socialist revolutionism persist. Many radicals find it unsettling and politically risky to move away from the logicality of the old ideologies; even more radicals hesitate to invest their trust in the demos rather than in Enlightenment rationality or technical historical analysis. Radical liberals who find themselves traversing socialist territory and socialists who find themselves at the border of radical liberalism open themselves up to the Gothic enmity of their old bedfellows. Since political and social ideas have only a very indirect and mediated relationship to political action, it is always tempting to fall back on old loyalties when new ones do not produce obvious results. Let me conclude this chapter and Part II by considering some potential assets of an American Left that coalesces around radical democracy.

A Left convergence on the terrain of radical democracy can conceivably help the Left to stop contributing to its historical failures. It could provide the Left a core identity that opposes elites and also offers a positive alternative that is familiar, persuasive, and radical. Convergence might also mean a narrowing of the gap between Left theory and activism. Demands to politicize social life and to socialize political life may afford activists both a direction for their current political struggles and at least an intuition of what kinds of present-day changes might empower people to make greater changes tomorrow. To the degree that the Left can build mass support for egalitarian ends Left assimilation and isolation become easier to resist. In sum, radical democracy holds the promise of an abiding Left unity that develops ongoing public support and gives weight to demands for more equality in American political and social life.

Of course, a Left convergence on radical democratic terrain is necessarily limited by the historical baggage that radicals carry with them today. Radical liberals remain attached to individualism, consent, and equal opportunity in the economy; they still believe in a universal morality, with liberal freedom at its center; they still want interclass harmony; and they as yet evidence a realism that feeds compromise and distrust of the wider citizenry. Socialists are more concerned with organizing society to meet human needs, establish cooperative community, and generate economic equality; they still conceive of morality as a historical product; their loyalties continue to demand an end to classes; and they remain attached to a teleological vision within which revolution makes the most intellectual sense.

Overall, the politicization of the American Left is located at a point where some experimentation with new ways is justified because of the failures of the old ways. But the old ways persist. This means that any consequent Left unity will be tentative, tense, and, at best, coalitional; and that theoretical issues and political disputes will continue to provide an uncertain direction and future for the Left. I, for one, find this realm of uncertainty pleasing on two counts. First, uncertainty can fuel an openness to democratic debates, to new alternative modes of association and politics, to testing ideas against experiences, and, ultimately, to finding a place for the Left in the contest for democracy. Second, uncertainty invites radicals to open their conversations to the judgment of the American people. Whether the presumptions of radical liberals or those of socialists are most justified should not be determined solely by ideological debate; they should also be submitted to the people, who ultimately determine what ideas will inform their actions and what kinds of relations they want to experience.

As I see it, the significance of radical democracy for the American Left is that it provides a vision, voice, and politics that might help the Left get its ideas on the public agenda. However, the success of radical democracy depends on whether it is useful for locating the cracks in elite hegemony, legitimating egalitarian alternatives to existing power structures, and informing a radical politics that is influential. In Part III, I will focus on radical democracy as a perspective able to enhance the fortunes of the American Left.

NOTES

1. Alan Wolfe, The Limits of Legitimacy: Political Contradictions of Contemporary Capitalism (New York: Free Press, 1977), p. 152.

2. John Rawls, A Theory of Justice (Cambridge, Mass.: Harvard University Press, 1971).

3. Herbert Gans, More Equality (New York: Vintage, 1974).

4. Sanford Lakoff, ed., Private Government (Glenview, Ill.: Scott, Foresman, 1973); and Mark V. Nadel, Corporations and Political Accountability (Lexington, Mass.: D. C. Heath, 1976).

5. Antonio Gramsci, The Prison Notebooks of Antonio Gramsci, ed. and trans. Quintin Hoare and Geoffrey Nowell Smith (New York: International, 1971); and Jurgen Habermas, Legitimation Crisis, trans. Thomas McCarthy (Boston: Beacon, 1975). European thinkers, like Ralph Milliband, Nicos Poulantzas, Louis Althusser, and even Santiago Carrillo, were also important in stimulating debate over Marxism and politics.

6. For examples, see David Gold, Clarence Lo, and Erik Wright, "Recent Developments in Marxist Theories of the Capitalist

State—Parts I and II," Monthly Review 27 (October 1975): 29-42 and 27 (November 1975): 36-51; Alan Wolfe, "New Directions in the Marxist Theory of Politics," Politics and Society 4, no. 2 (1974): 131-59; see also Terry Eagleton, Marxism and Literary Criticism (Berkeley: University of California, 1976) to get a sense of the extent to which American socialists began to take seriously what had once been devalued as superstructural.

    7. See James Weinstein, "Corporate Liberalism and the Monopoly Capitalist State," in The Capitalist System, 2nd ed., ed. Richard Edwards, Michael Reich, and Thomas Weisskopf (Englewood Cliffs, N.J.: Prentice-Hall, 1978), p. 232.

    8. Notice the number of books on political corruption that have appeared in recent years. Increasingly, they focus not on individual cases of corruption but on the institutional forces that continually reproduce it. For example, see Larry Berg, Harlan Hahn, and John Schmidhauser, Corruption in the American Political System (Morristown, N.J.: General Learning, 1976); and John C. Bollens and Henry J. Schmandt, Political Corruption: Power, Money, and Sex (Pacific Palisades, Calif.: Palisades, 1979).

    9. Sheldon Wolin, "The Idea of the State in America," in The Problem of Authority in America, ed. John Diggins and Mark Kann (Philadelphia: Temple University Press, 1981), p. 55.

    10. One of the most popular political science texts of the early 1970s was Thomas R. Dye and Harmon Zeigler, The Irony of Democracy: An Uncommon Introduction to American Politics (Belmont, Calif.: Wadsworth, 1970). The book was important because it compared pluralist and power elite theories and gave equal credibility to the latter.

    11. Compare John Kenneth Galbraith, American Capitalism: The Concept of Countervailing Power (Boston: Houghton Mifflin, 1952) and idem, Economics and the Public Purpose (Boston: Houghton Mifflin, 1973).

    12. Compare Theodore Lowi, The End of Liberalism: Ideology, Policy and the Crisis of Public Authority (New York: Norton, 1969), chap. 10 and idem, The Politics of Disorder (New York: Norton, 1971), p. 180.

    13. Lewis Lipsitz, "Forgotten Roots," in The Frontiers of Democratic Theory, ed. Henry Kariel (New York: Random House, 1970), p. 398.

    14. Ibid., pp. 399-402.

    15. Theodore Becker, American Government: Past, Present, Future (Boston: Allyn & Bacon, 1976), p. 519; see also Harlan Hahn and R. William Holland, American Government: Minority Rights versus Majority Rule (New York: Wiley, 1976), p. 197.

    16. Theodore Becker, Paul Szep, and Dwight Ritter, Un-Vote for a New America (Boston: Allyn & Bacon, 1976), p. 3.

17. Becker, American Government, pp. 513-24.

18. C. B. Macpherson, The Life and Times of Liberal Democracy (Oxford: Oxford University Press, 1977), pp. 17-18. See also chap. 5 for Macpherson's model of participatory democracy.

19. Some of the early collections and essays on participatory democracy include Terrence Cook and Patrick Morgan, eds., Participatory Democracy (San Francisco: Canfield, 1971); J. Roland Pennock and John W. Chapman, eds., Participation in Politics, Nomos 16 (New York: Lieber-Atherton, 1975); Carole Pateman, Participation and Democratic Theory (London: Cambridge University Press, 1970); and Richard Cloward and Frances Fox Piven, The Politics of Turmoil (New York: Pantheon, 1974).

20. Lawrence Goodwyn, "Organizing Democracy: The Limits of Theory and Practice," Democracy 1, no. 1 (January 1981): 42.

21. See Howard Kalodner, "Citizen Participation in Emerging Social Institutions," in Participation in Politics, ed. J. Roland Pennock and John Chapman (New York: Lieber-Atherton, 1975), pp. 161-84. Kalodner concludes, "While we continue to examine what we may do to create direct involvement of all citizens—and particularly the alienated poor—in matters pertaining to neighborhoods, we must more clearly focus on the goals we have often stated but not pursued— a redistribution of wealth and power to achieve greater equality of access to our political, economic, and social institutions."

22. This is especially evident, early on, in C. G. Benello and D. Roussopoulos, eds., The Case for Participatory Democracy (New York: Viking, 1972), where liberal, socialist, and anarchist versions of participatory democracy merge with relative ease.

23. See Todd Gitlin, "New Video Technology: Pluralism or Banality," Democracy 1, no. 4 (October 1981): 60-76; Barry Commoner, The Poverty of Power (New York: Knopf, 1976), chap. 9; or the old "people power" literature represented by Stokely Carmichael and Charles V. Hamilton, Black Power: The Politics of Liberation in America (New York: Vintage, 1967); or Martin Luther King, Jr., "Letter from a Birmingham Jail," in Why We Can't Wait (New York: New American Library, 1964), pp. 76-95.

24. See Jackie St. Joan, "Female Leaders: Who was Rembrandt's Mother?" in Building Feminist Theory, ed. Charlotte Bunch et al. (New York: Longman, 1981), pp. 223-35; and Bertram Gross, "Some Anticrime Proposals for Progressives," Nation, February 6, 1982, pp. 137-40.

25. This distinction is taken from Macpherson, Liberal Democracy, chap. 1.

26. Peter Bachrach, "Interest, Participation, and Democratic Theory," in Participation in Politics, ed. J. Roland Pennock and John Chapman (New York: Lieber-Atherton, 1975), p. 43.

27. Pateman, Participation and Democratic Theory, p. 42.

28. A fine analysis of the dangers of symbolic participation can be found in Murray Edelman, Political Language: Words That Succeed and Policies That Fail (New York: Academic Press, 1977), chap. 7; and Peter Bachrach, "Democracy and Class Struggle," in The Future of American Democracy: Views from the Left, ed. Mark E. Kann (Philadelphia: Temple University Press, 1983), chap. 11.

29. S. M. Shumer, "Machiavelli: Republican Politics and Its Corruption," Political Theory 7 (February 1979): 30.

30. See Fred R. Harris, The New Populism (New York: Saturday Review Press, 1973), p. 11. Other representative works of the new populists include Gans, More Equality; and Jack Newfield and Jeff Greenfield, A Populist Manifesto: The Making of a New Majority (New York: Praeger, 1972). An interesting discussion of the new populism is contained in Harry C. Boyte, "The Populist Challenge: Anatomy of an Emerging Movement," Socialist Revolution 7 (March–April 1977): 39–81; and idem, The Backyard Revolution (Philadelphia: Temple University Press, 1980).

31. Goodwyn, "Organizing Democracy," pp. 48–49.

32. For example, see Fred R. Harris's text, America's Democracy: The Ideal and the Reality (Glenview, Ill.: Scott, Foresman, 1980).

33. See John W. Gardner, "Citizen Action," and Ralph Nader and Donald Ross, "Toward an Initiatory Democracy," in Is America Necessary?, ed. Henry Etzkowitz and Peter Schwab (St. Paul: West, 1976), pp. 576–81 and pp. 581–87, respectively.

34. See Gans, More Equality, pt. 3.

35. Harris argues that the market is the best planning mechanism but, when competition "isn't working, . . . then ownership should be in the people, directly or through consumer-owned enterprises." See his New Populism, pp. 207–8.

36. See Arthur G. Gish, The New Left and Christian Radicalism (Grand Rapids, Mich.: Eerrdmans, 1970), p. 123.

37. Jeff Lustig, "Community and Social Class," Democracy 1, no. 2 (April 1981): 99; and Harry C. Boyte, "Populism and the Left," Democracy 1, no. 2 (April 1981): 65.

38. See Kirkpatrick Sale, SDS (New York: Vintage, 1973), chaps. 1–5; and idem, "A Selective History," Nation, September 26, 1981, pp. 283–84. One might also note that a major lesson of Barrington Moore, Jr., Social Origins of Dictatorship and Democracy (Boston: Beacon, 1967), was that revolutions from above do not produce democracy.

39. Wolfe, Limits of Legitimacy, p. 321.

40. Ibid.

41. For example, see Bruce Brown, Marx, Freud, and the Critique of Everyday Life (New York: Monthly Review, 1973); Ben

Agger, Western Marxism (Santa Monica, Calif.: Goodyear, 1979);
or perhaps Jack Barnes, et al., Prospects for Socialism in America
(New York: Pathfinder, 1976).

42. Agger, Western Marxism, p. 337; see also Stanley Arono-
witz, "Does the United States Have a New Working Class?" in The
Revival of American Socialism, ed. George Fischer (New York: Ox-
ford University Press, 1971), p. 200; Harry Braverman, Labor and
Monopoly Capital (New York: Monthly Review, 1974); Barbara Ehren-
reich and John Ehrenreich, "The Professional-Managerial Class,"
Radical America 11 (March–April 1977): 7–31; and idem, "The New
Left and the Professional-Managerial Class," Radical America 11
(May–June 1977): 7–22. The literature here is vast and still growing.

43. Erich Fromm, "The Application of Humanist Psychoanalysis to Marx's Theory," in Socialist Humanism, ed. Erich Fromm
(Garden City, N.Y.: Anchor, 1966), p. 241; see also Herbert Marcuse, An Essay on Liberation (Boston: Beacon, 1969), p. 30; and
Michael Lerner, The New Socialist Revolution (New York: Dell,
1973), pp. 5, 55.

44. John Cammet, "Socialism and Participatory Democracy,"
in The Revival of American Socialism, ed. George Fischer (New
York: Oxford University Press, 1971), p. 51. More recent discussions of Gramsci's notion of hegemony can be found in Perry Ander-
son, "The Antinomies of Antonio Gramsci," New Left Review, Winter 1976/77, pp. 5–78; and in Martin Clark, Antonio Gramsci and the
Revolution That Failed (New Haven, Conn.: Yale University Press,
1977). Here, too, there has been an explosion of concern and analysis.

45. Brown, Marx, Freud, and the Critique of Everyday Life,
pp. 70, 80–83, 91.

46. See Wolfe, The Limits of Legitimacy, pp. 1–10.

47. See Agger, Western Marxism, pp. 319–20.

48. Carl Boggs, Gramsci's Marxism (London: Pluto Press,
1976), p. 71.

49. For example, see Russell Jacoby, "The Politics of Narcissism," and Jessica Benjamin, "The Oedipal Riddle: Authority, Autonomy, and the New Narcissism," in The Problem of Authority in
America, ed. John Diggins and Mark E. Kann (Philadelphia: Temple
University Press, 1981), pp. 185–94 and pp. 195–224, respectively.

50. This theme is implicit throughout Marcuse's works and especially in his last work, The Aesthetic Dimension (Boston: Beacon,
1978).

51. Marxists are well aware of the difficulties of developing a
socialist ethics of need in a class-based society and, consequently,
have done little to develop that ethics. For the difficulties, see Richard Miller, "Rawls and Marxism," Philosophy and Public Affairs 111

(Winter 1974): 167–91; for the possibilities, see Robert Booth Fowler and Jeffrey R. Orenstein, Contemporary Issues in Political Theory (New York: Wiley, 1977), pp. 111–15.

52. Ronald Aronson, "Dear Herbert," in The Revival of American Socialism, ed. George Fischer (New York: Oxford University Press, 1971), p. 274; see also Marcuse, An Essay on Liberation, p. 6; and Lerner, New Socialist Revolution, p. 233.

53. See Agger, Western Marxism, pp. 336–38; Michael H. Best and William E. Connolly, The Politicized Economy (Lexington, Mass.: Heath, 1976), chap. 6; and Dan Georgakas and Marvin Surkin, Detroit, I Do Mind Dying: A Study in Urban Revolution (New York: St. Martin's Press, 1975).

54. For example, see Kenneth Dolbeare, Political Change in the United States: A Framework in Analysis (New York: McGraw-Hill, 1974), p. 121; or Martin Oppenheimer, "The Limitations of Socialism: Some Sociological Observations on Participatory Democracy," in The Case for Participatory Democracy, ed. C. G. Benello and D. Roussopoulos (New York: Viking, 1972), p. 280.

55. Irving Zeitlin, "The Plain Marxism of C. Wright Mills," in The Revival of American Socialism, ed. George Fischer (New York: Oxford University Press, 1971), p. 237; see also articles by Martin Nicolaus, James Weinstein, and Ronald Radosh in For a New America, ed. James Weinstein and David Eakins (New York: Vintage, 1970); Paul Sweezy and Charles Bettelheim, On the Transition to Socialism (New York: Monthly Review, 1971), p. 25; and Michael Harrington, Socialism (New York: Bantam, 1972), pp. 257–61.

56. For example, see Isaac Balbus, The Dialectic of Legal Repression (New York: Russell Sage Foundation, 1973), p. 13.

57. Michael Walzer, "Politics and the Welfare State," in Essential Works of Socialism, ed. Irving Howe (New York: Bantam, 1971), pp. 817, 823.

58. Jean Bethke Elshtain, "Mr. Right Is Dead," Nation, November 14, 1981, p. 496.

59. Lerner, New Socialist Revolution, p. 229.

60. Compare Irving Howe, "The Welfare State," in The Revival of American Socialism, ed. George Fischer (New York: Oxford University Press, 1971), p. 73; and Samuel P. Huntington, "The United States," in The Crisis of Democracy, ed. Michel Crozier, Samuel P. Huntington, and Joji Watanuki (New York: New York University Press, 1975), pp. 113–41. To an extent, Howe's point is made by Huntington's fears of "an excess of democracy."

61. This thesis is worked out in Cloward and Piven, Politics of Turmoil, pt. 4.

62. See Balbus, Dialectic of Legal Repression, p. 25.

63. Howe, "Welfare State," pp. 79–80.

64. Staughton Lynd quoted in James Finn, Protest: Pacifism and Politics (New York: Vintage, 1968), p. 241.

65. See Cammet, "Socialism and Participatory Democracy," pp. 59-60.

66. William A. Williams, "Backyard Autonomy," Nation, September 5, 1981, p. 161.

67. Paul Breines, "Germans, Journals and Jews/Madison, Men, Marxism and Mosse: A Tale of Jewish-Leftist Identity Confusion in America," New German Critique 20 (Spring-Summer 1980): 103; see also Kenneth Kann, Joe Rapoport: The Life of a Jewish Radical (Philadelphia: Temple University Press, 1981).

68. William A. Williams, "Radicals and Regionalism," Democracy 1, no. 4 (October 1981): 93.

69. Ibid., p. 95; or see Staughton Lynd and Gar Alperovitz, Strategy and Program: Two Essays toward a New American Socialism (Boston: Beacon, 1973), pp. 78, 81.

70. Ira Shor, "No More Teacher's Dirty Looks: Conceptual Teaching from the Bottom Up," in Studies in Socialist Pedagogy, ed. Theodore Mills Norton and Bertell Ollman (New York: Monthly Review, 1978), p. 179.

71. Sweezy and Bettelheim, On the Transition to Socialism, pp. 100, 106.

72. Lynd and Alperovitz, Strategy and Program, p. 87.

73. Martin Jay, "How Utopian Is Marcuse?" in The Revival of American Socialism, ed. George Fischer (New York: Oxford University Press, 1971), pp. 253-54.

74. Richard Sennett, Authority (New York: Knopf, 1980), p. 179.

75. Micheal Walzer, "In Defense of Equality," in Is America Possible?, ed. Henry Etzkowitz, 2d ed. (St. Paul: West, 1980), p. 311.

76. Becker, Un-Vote for a New America, p. 145.

77. Sheldon Wolin, "Why Democracy?" Democracy 1, no. 1 (January 1981): 4.

78. Compare William A. Williams, The Great Evasion: An Essay on the Contemporary Relevance of Karl Marx and the Wisdom of Admitting the Heretic into a Dialogue about America's Future (Chicago: University of Chicago Press, 1964); and idem, "Radicals and Regionalism," pp. 95-98.

PART III

FORTUNES

INTRODUCTION TO PART III

> Even if intellectual dissent flourished, as it began to do
> in the 1960s, and even if it took shape in a coherent criti-
> cal theory, as it has not yet done, this would still be in-
> adequate for the transformation of society. In order to
> bring about radical change there is needed a social move-
> ment which embodies the practical experiences and inter-
> ests of large numbers of men [and women].
>
> T. B. Bottomore

The fortunes of the American Left hinge on its ability to establish some unity, engage Americans in egalitarian talk, and practice
a politics that offers a persuasive means of social change. In Part
II, I extracted from the American Left experience the possibility that
radical democracy could serve as a perspective to unify and identify
the Left as a force relevant to American politics. In Part III, I will
draw out that relevance by suggesting how radical liberals, socialists, and activists can conceivably create an ongoing and visible role
in contemporary political struggles.

Chapter 6 illuminates the cracks in elite hegemony that can be
visualized from a radical democratic vantage point. American elites,
though sharing a world view, are deeply divided on the means for
realizing it. Those divisions are especially important, because the
structures that once made America somewhat exceptional can no
longer accommodate mass discontents. This is a historical opportunity for the Left to promote radical democracy as a familiar vision
that can inspire mass mobilizations in favor of egalitarian alternatives.

Chapter 7 offers a theory of radical democracy, which provides
concepts, words, and lines of thought that may be useful for legitimating egalitarian alternatives among the American people. The theory
is framed in terms of Lockean consent theory but conveys substantive
content and cues that significantly overlap with socialist meanings.
It justifies radical democracy as a set of egalitarian social relations
and government as an instrument for articulating and fostering egalitarian social relations. Furthermore, the theory of radical democracy provides some guidelines for the practice of American Left politics.

Chapter 8 applies these guidelines to American Left politics.
The application includes suggestions about where and how radicals
can participate in the mainstream without being submerged in it. It
also involves an argument concerning when and how radicals can take
part in democratic rebellions, without suffering isolation. The guidelines leave considerable room for dispute. But, I conclude, the American Left can be strengthened by its differences if it recognizes the

possibility of a democratic division of political labor, which ultimate ly, could transform old failures into new fortunes.

I make no predictions as to whether the Left actually will en- hance its fortunes in the immediate future. My historical sense tells me that the Left may very well reproduce its checkered past; but my moral sense tells me that the Left is both free and able to appeal to American's complex attachment to democratic traditions. Like most Americans, I remain ambivalent.

6

CRACKS IN ELITE HEGEMONY

Marx spent a lifetime analyzing capitalism, focusing on its strengths in order to reveal its weaknesses. His theory of capitalist contradictions and class conflict, whatever its merits, announced that liberating changes were possible, even inevitable. This "power of positive thinking" testified to a faith in social change that challenged mass resignation and energized activists. The American Left, to the contrary, has devoted many lifetimes to unveiling the pervasiveness of elite hegemony, giving little notice to elite vulnerabilities. In general, American Left literature testifies to the unity, intelligence, and creativity of U.S. elites in cementing their grip on American life and, except in the abstract and distant future, to the fragmentation, gullibility, and inertia of the American people in consenting to their own subordination. The American Left's "power of negative thinking" implicitly broadcasts the message that progressive changes are unlikely, if not impossible, thereby reinforcing mass quiescence and enervating actual and potential activists.

Radical pessimism can be justified to an extent, but only to an extent. This chapter will suggest that a radical democratic perspective provides some basis for radical optimism. It highlights the fragmentation, uncertainties, and dilemmas that weaken elite hegemony and drive elites to become openly subversive of American democratic traditions; it demonstrates that radical democratic movements, at the very least, are powerful enough to enlarge the cracks in elite hegemony in ways that empower people to take greater control over their lives. To the degree that American exceptionalism once existed, it no longer does; to the degree that elites could once accommodate democratic reforms, they no longer can; and to the degree that the Left identifies itself with radical democratic reforms, it may have discovered for itself its part in the future of the United States.

RADICAL PESSIMISM AND OPTIMISM

American Left scholarship consistently makes the point that
elite hegemony pervades all aspects of American life.[1] It is lodged
in state institutions and private corporations, where the few exercise
it and the many are subordinated by it. It appears in schools and
universities, the media, everyday language, and the broader culture
to outfit most Americans for a quiescent role. It is reproduced in
social relations between the sexes, races, nationalities, and genera-
tions, where many forms of inequality appear as natural facts of life.
Because elite hegemony is manifest everywhere, it is taken for granted
and is, therefore, inconspicuous to most people.

Left analysts are devoted to making elite hegemony conspicuous
and, in the process, often endow U.S. elites with extraordinary so-
phistication.[2] Elites know how to rule and how to insulate their rule
from opposition. They hide the iron fist and use the velvet glove,
minimize coercion and maximize consent. They are brilliant at accommodating minor changes to abort major ones; they can provide
workers and the poor a stake in the political economy that ultimately
impoverishes them; they protect old frontiers that siphon off dissent
and pioneer new frontiers that are safe magnets for idealism. Furthermore, elites encase their hegemony in multiple layers of armor.
Their social networks, recruitment centers, foundations, and think
tanks can be attacked as power elite conspiracies without endangering
the historical structures that reinforce their interests; these structures
can be attacked without denting elites' monopolies in pluralist marketplaces. Radical scholars who peel away the layers of hegemony are
usually impressed by how each one fosters the long-term rather than
parochial interests of the ruling class.

The Left portrait is complete when U.S. elites are presented
as a fundamentally united entity. "It cannot be stressed too highly,"
writes Albert Szymanski, "that when faced with interclass issues (as
opposed to intraclass issues), the upper class is normally united."[3]
Elites do disagree among themselves on some questions but are fundamentally united on end values: Lockean rights that sanctify private
property and accumulation; political institutions that facilitate elite
control but distance people from power; and the ethic of rationality
and efficiency that justifies elite domination, particularly in the economy. When push comes to shove, elites will stand together against
fragmented social protests and, therefore, will usually win out.
Meanwhile, "minor" disagreements among elites on appropriate means
for realizing their common ends give the appearance of pluralism
and competition.

Radicals who ennoble elites with pervasive power, sophisticated
knowledge, and basic unity project so much savvy onto rulers that

little virtue is left for the majority of American people. By comparison, Americans are impotent, ignorant, and fundamentally divided. Elites, who are powerful, create a mass of victims, who are powerless. Elites manipulate their victims to mask alienation and dependence; elites are so successful that American citizens are misinformed and ignorant of their own plight and suffer false consciousness. Unaware of their true interests and common needs, Americans divide against themselves to engage in moral, racial, or perhaps sexual conflicts, which sap their collective strength. Radicals may not blame the victims for their weaknesses, but their portrait nonetheless suggests that most people do not have the qualifications for remaking their own history.

Even when people organize and act in progressive social movements, demonstrate some knowledge of their common plight, and coalesce in opposition to elites, American Left analysts stand ready to accuse them of some degree of gullibility. In the Progressive era, for example, mass movements demanded greater democracy and welfare and won some important reforms. But rather than explore how to build on these reforms, Left scholars are quick to point out that the movements and the reforms played into the hands of elites, who were intent on rationalizing the corporate economy. In the end, Americans are still "prisoners of the system"; their rebellions usually complete rather than contest elite hegemony. [4]

This ennobling of elites gives rise to radicals' exaggerated attachment to American exceptionalism as an excuse for their failures (as discussed in Chapter 1); this impoverished view of Americans gives rise to the politics of devaluation, which distances radicals from the people (as discussed in Chapter 2). While the historical record partly supports this analysis, the Left has little to gain by carrying it so far. By ceding so much savvy to elites and reserving so little virtue for the people, radical scholars undermine the faith in change that is necessary for making change. They transform powerful elites into invulnerable elites. If this is true, then it becomes rational for Americans to choose the lesser evil among elites rather than challenge elite hegemony. Politics is still the art of the possible. Radicals also transform weak people into impotent victims. If this is true, then what do activists have to gain by organizing the victims into a mass movement? Impotence multiplied many times over is still impotence. With some justification, Marx's famous thesis may be rephrased: the American Left has only interpreted the world in various ways; the point is to change it. Radicals have failed to change it, in part, because their traditional pessimism has become a self-fulfilling prophecy.

The Left might learn at least one lesson from the New Right. Phyllis Schlafly's The Power of the Positive Woman and Richard A.

Viguerie's The New Right: We're Ready to Lead are more than evan-
gelical declarations that individuals and nations can be born again. 5
They are also declarations that a specter of change is haunting the
United States, based on the cracks in liberal hegemony and the ability
of conservative populist movements to enlarge them. The New Right
has not taken power; it may never take power. But its optimism regarding change and its search for vulnerabilities in the liberal establishment that make optimism conceivable have helped (along with considerable financial support) to bring it a success the Left can only
imagine; conservative values now occupy a prominent place on the
American political agenda, but radical values do not.

In the last decade, a handful of Left analysts have tried to build
a foundation for radical optimism by highlighting the vulnerabilities
of elites and building strategies that rely on the strengths of mass
movements. It is not surprising that these analysts do not fit traditional ideological labels but, in my opinion, are more properly tagged
as radical democrats. Richard F. Hamilton pointed out the limits of
elites' understanding and the impressive number of failures by them;
he also rooted out some of the progressive elements in public opinion
that might give rise to a left-wing politics. Alan Wolfe mapped elites'
"exhaustion of alternatives in late capitalism," while Frances Fox
Piven and Richard A. Cloward blueprinted the "mass defiance" that
has yielded progressive victories. More recently, Martin Carnoy
and Derek Shearer tried to "redefine what is politically possible" by
tracing the route between today's public policies and tomorrow's radical democracy. 6 On the basis of a radical democratic perspective
that treats elites as fallible human beings and most people as trustworthy, I want to argue that the end of American exceptionalism today is a crisis for U.S. elites and an opportunity for democratic
movements.

LEGITIMATION CRISIS AND OPPORTUNITY

American elites and people's movements renegotiated the American social contract during the first decades of the twentieth century.
The outcome was the welfare state, in which elites won concentrated
political power and the people won government guarantees of social
welfare and rights. The renegotiated contract may now be anachronistic. For elites, this constitutes what Habermas calls a legitimation
crisis;7 for the American Left, it provides an opportunity to articulate growing mass discontents that the political system can no longer
accommodate.

Radical democrats are sensitive to political centralization in
a way that radical liberals and socialists are not. Radical democrats

see political centralization as a direct threat to the ability of people to be self-governing. It distances power from the people in a way that undermines democratic means to change, and it decreases people's ability to participate in decisions that affect their community life. While radical liberals and socialists are also sensitive to political centralization, their sensitivity is blunted by their ideological predispositions. Radical liberals can write off political centralization as a means of concentrating intelligence and expertise, where it might be used to administer people's rights; socialists can ignore political centralization as a reflection of more basic trends in the capitalist economy. My own view, stemming from a radical democratic perspective but consistent with politicized versions of the old ideologies, is that political centralization is key to understanding the prospects for change in the United States.

Dramatic centralization of political power has occurred in the twentieth century in the United States. The Progressive era, the New Deal, two world wars and numerous limited wars, a prolonged Cold War, and the emergence of big capital and big labor are the context in which U.S. presidents have taken over congressional powers, and the federal government has assumed what were once state and local powers. Political elites in Washington, D.C., now make foreign policy choices, economic decisions, and domestic policy judgments that inescapably shape Americans' options. This political centralization, however, was bought at a price. Political elites won centralized power only by granting a series of concessions demanded by mass movements.

The federal government assumed responsibility for the nation's economic health and the people's welfare. It became America's foremost problem solver, "looked to for redress and assistance when the people are threatened by inflation, unemployment, environmental degradation, and crime."[8] The federal government also became the guarantor of people's democratic rights and entitlements. It was responsible for ensuring that women and blacks had voting rights; it was responsible for rooting out corruption in the parties and political machines by authorizing primary elections, standardized ballots, and a meritocratic rather than patronage civil service. More important, the federal government became the legitimate arena in the struggle to extend rights and entitlements, from labor unions' right to collective bargaining to poor people's entitlement to a minimum standard of living.[9]

What may be called a renegotiated social contract gave elites more concentrated power but also more responsibilities that might limit that power, which made it controversial. U.S. elites divided over whether this exchange was in their best interests. At the beginning of this century, the National Civic Federation brought together government, business, and labor elites to work out the terms of the contract and to engineer support for it. However, "the National Civic Federation did not represent all opinions in the business world; the National Association of Manufacturers didn't want to recognize organized labor in any way. Many businessmen did not want even the puny reforms proposed by the Civic Federation."[10] The new contract was no less controversial during the New Deal. The Roosevelt administration represented those elites who favored it, who saw their interests in centralized political power in the Oval Office, in government as an instrument for rationalizing the economy, and in legitimation through welfare measures. But these elites were opposed by those Alan Wolfe calls the precapitalist elites, ensconced in pockets of government and dominant in local governments, who feared their own interests would be undermined by statism, economic rationalization, and new links between federal government and the citizenry.[11] Some social commentators in the 1950s believed that "the genius of American politics" had produced "the end of ideology" and, thus, disagreement among elites. After all, President Eisenhower did not try to dismantle the welfare state. But the candidacies of Barry Goldwater, George Wallace, and George McGovern intimated that intraelite conflict persisted. Certainly, the 1980 election of Ronald Reagan suggests that an important if not considerable segment of U.S. elites may be ready to scuttle the renegotiated contract and write a new one.

Radical analysts sometimes cheapen intraelite conflict by calling it a disagreement over means to common goals. The conflict is over means, but it is important to remember that the means often determine the effective outcomes; the struggle to control the means is often as divisive as the conflict over goals. Recall that Marx, Lenin, Trotsky, and Stalin, in a certain sense, agreed on the end values that made for communism. But disagreement over the means to achieve communism drove a wedge between Bolshevik elites; ultimately, it was the Stalinist means rather than the communist ends that shaped Soviet society. Closer to home, radicals might recall that they have often experienced some unity on end values but nonetheless suffer fragmentation and Gothic enmity over means questions, like reform versus revolution. This should indicate that ongoing intraelite conflict over the means to shared goals is potentially as divisive and important as conflicts over the goals themselves.

The renegotiated social contract was an issue that divided elites because mass movements forced it on them. Discontented masses of American farmers, small businessmen, urbanites, immigrants, minorities, women, and workers—"those near the bottom of the social structure—those who benefitted least from the rapid increase in the productivity of the industrial plant of the United States and from

expansion at home and abroad"[12]—were able to forge enough collective
power, wisdom, and unity in the populist, progressive, and socialist
movements to force the renegotiated contract on hesitant, divided
elites. The millions of Americans who were the rank and file and supporters of militant unions and strikes, share-the-wealth groups, or
Townsend Clubs during the 1930s once again forced hesitant and divided
elites to acknowledge "some federal responsibility for relief of the
poor."[13] Whether or not the resulting reforms were accommodationist, the ability of mass movements to extract them testifies to the potential potency of the American people.

In fact, the reforms were accommodationist and more. In the
short run, political concessions did little to alter the distribution of
power between elites and Americans. Electoral and party reforms
were the means "by which a large and possibly dangerous mass electorate could be brought to heel and subjected to management and control
within a political system appropriate to capitalist democracy."[14]
Woodrow Wilson's statement that "the government of freedom must in
these days be positive" was translated into a regulatory state that
functions to "maintain and increase the efficiency of the existing social order."[15] In the long run, however, the renegotiated social contract increased the costs elites would have to pay for political legitimacy. If the federal government failed to maintain a thriving economy,
ensure expanding economic opportunities, or provide a socially acceptable standard of living for the poor, it would attract blame for the
nation's problems and free individuals from self-blame. If the federal government failed to support people's democratic rights or appeared to retract their entitlements, its concentrated power could
easily be viewed as naked force rather than legitimate authority. To
the extent that people's expectations for economic mobility and democratic rights escalate with each new generation, the federal government must continually upgrade its performance lest the governed
withdraw their consent.

The failure of the federal government to make good on its part
of the social contract combined with Americans' escalating demands
as the price of consent make up today's legitimation crisis.[16] Americans distrust the intentions of governors, question their ability to perform, and increasingly alienate themselves from the taint of mainstream politics.[17] In 1976, Jimmy Carter rode this wave of public
distrust, portraying himself as an outsider untainted by Washington
politics; by 1980 Carter was engulfed by public distrust. Ronald
Reagan, another outsider, capitalized on it by promising to "get government off of our backs"—what John Diggins calls the hunchback
theory of politics.[18]

What is the political monkey on Americans' backs? First, there
is a general feeling that the federal government is not a neutral umpire

of social relations. According to one Trilateral Commission report, an increasing number of Americans feel that "the government is pretty much run by a few big interests."[19] The Reagan administration's overt support for the rich is likely to fuel public suspicions, generated by government bail outs of major corporations, government deals with oil companies, news stories of government corruption and corporate bribery, and perhaps a diffuse cultural combination of old populist fears and more recent power elite perspectives. My own experience as a teacher at a notably conservative university is that my students are often more cynical about who actually runs the federal government than I am.

Second, government performance fails to accommodate public expectations. In 1973 James O'Connor described the performance problem in terms of "the fiscal crisis of the state." Corporate and public demands on the state continue to grow, but no one wants to pay new taxes or higher rates on old taxes to finance these demands. The result is a "tendency for government expenditures to outrace revenues."[20] The difference between expenditures and revenues is made up through deficit spending, which, especially when the economy is doing poorly, deepens problems like inflation, high interest rates, capital shortages, and unemployment. To date, political elites have failed to develop systematic policies that either convince or demonstrate to Americans that the federal government can restore economic opportunities or even cushion the impact of economic ills. In a sense, Americans now expect more from government, only they receive less, especially with cuts in social security and major entitlement programs now considered fair political game.

Third, albeit for differing reasons, very few Americans believe that the federal government is adequately guaranteeing citizens' democratic rights. Conservatives blame the federal government for what George Gilder calls the moral blight of dependency or what M. Stanton Evans describes as the removal of constitutional limits to the exercise of political authority.[21] Many liberals feel that they have overestimated what government can accomplish and, consequently, feel somewhat responsible for having raised public expectations to impossible levels, which guarantee disappointment. They have a new appreciation that ours may be a zero-sum society in which government support for more rights for some people means fewer rights for other people.[22] Civil libertarians and radicals generally fear that the rise of conservatism combined with the paralysis of liberalism is a recipe for greater government coercion and secrecy as well as for fewer democratic rights in the street and in the bedroom.[23] We now lack poets or politicians who staunchly defend the federal government as a Lincolnian government "of the people, by the people, and for the people" that is able to meet up to Thoreau's standard of

allowing us to be "men first, and subjects afterward." We are subjects first.

Political distrust is evidence that political elites are currently
failing to accommodate mass discontents. It also is a problem for
continued elite domination through consent. "Every four years,"
writes Gil Sewell, "we hunt for an authority figure to take command—
and then we spend the next four years denouncing him for his misuse
of power."[24] It is a short step between denouncing political elites
and disobeying them. Conservative government estimates tell us that
nearly one million American males failed to register with the selective
service in the time period provided by law.[25] Everyday experience
tells us that the 55 mile per hour speed limit, income tax laws, and
basic property laws are broken with great regularity and minimal
self-recrimination. Lawlessness is not yet the American way of life;
but it is also not an uncommon American way of life.

Elites may certainly try to restore consent and obedience by
evoking crises, which they then manage. Certainly we have heard
much about the crises in Poland and El Salvador, in the economy, in
America's moral fiber and more; we have also heard that we must
trust government to get us through these crises. The object of this
emotional roller coaster of fear and hope is to justify greater public
unity and patience. However, the "trivialization of crisis" as another
media event increasingly fails on two grounds.[26] First, Americans'
lives are so crisis-ridden that each new crisis is less haunting than
the last; we become innoculated against them. Second, when political
elites portray themselves as crisis managers, they help to undermine
people's belief in "the idea that government can improve the quality
of their lives and extend the realm of social justice."[27] Crisis management is an admission that elites may be bailing water out of a
sinking ship of state.

How can elites restore political legitimacy? Elites split along
the old lines of divisiveness. Conservatives, who have never been
happy with the renegotiated contract, want to devitalize federal government. It should be restricted to its appropriate functions: coercion and adjudication, national defense, and law and order. The welfare state must be contracted so that the federal government plays a
smaller role within American society. This is the basis for the new
federalism, which, like the old states' rights argument, requires a
devolution of political power to the 50 state capitals, where conservative values usually weigh more heavily. It is also the basis for a deregulation of the economy, which frees investors and entrepreneurs
from government intervention to determine the nation's material future according to the unpolluted standards of private profits. In short,
conservatives want to rewrite the social contract to restore political

legitimacy by limiting government and further empowering capitalists.[28]

Conservatives do not agree among themselves on priorities or tactics. Too much emphasis on defense expenditures, for example, may limit opportunities for some capitalists. The new federalism might saddle local politicians with programs they cannot afford to continue but that, if discontinued, will undermine their legitimacy. Deregulation is not necessarily a virtue for conservative businessmen, who regularly rely on government insurance and subsidies to support their profit margins and market shares. And the New Right, neoconservatives, and libertarian conservatives are in fundamental disagreement on many current issues, particularly those pertaining to morality and individual rights. Though conservatives agree that the social contract should be rewritten, they are not close to agreeing on the actual terms.

Liberal elites are experiencing a period of confusion but tend to favor a revitalization of federal government. They want a central power able to balance military threat and diplomacy, state planning and citizen participation, private investment and public interest, or more generally, today's limits and tomorrow's dreams. Federal government's ability to strike such balances depends on it assuming more power and responsibility, on the one hand, and on it inviting more responsible citizen participation, on the other hand. Increasingly, responsible citizen participation refers, for example, to union leaders, who will serve as consultants on the "take aways" now demanded by corporations, or public interest group leaders, who preach that today's limits require fewer material demands and greater spiritual concerns by their members.[29] The theory is that cooperation between government elites and responsible citizens will result in a national consensus on the hard decisions that, perhaps circuitously, will eventually benefit all Americans. The current social contract can be salvaged to strengthen political legitimacy.

If this sounds vague, it is because liberal alites cannot agree on what it would mean in practice. How do national interest and human rights overlap to inform defense strategy? Are state planning and balancing possible if real public participation injects uncertainty into the process? Is national health insurance among the expected benefits? If so, can the federal government afford to underwrite it? Liberal elites want to fortify the federal government but are not quite sure of what they want to do with it. Usually, they find it easier to criticize the conservatives, who now rule, rather than talk about concrete alternatives of their own.

Intraelite conflict—between and within elite clusters—over solutions to the legitimation crisis often deepen the crisis. Recently, former Reagan devotee, Republican Congressman Marc L. Marks, attacked "a President and his cronies whose belief in Hooverism has blinded them to the wretchedness and suffering they are inflicting through their policies . . . on the sick, the poor, the handicapped, . . . the black community, . . . women of all economic and social backgrounds . . . in fact, anyone and everyone."[30] Such immoderate attacks by friends reinforce public beliefs that the federal government, regardless of who is at the helm, is not neutral, effective, or particularly democratic. They are cues to the American public that the U.S. political system, as presently constituted, cannot accommodate their growing discontents. This is an atmosphere in which it is at least conceivable that the American Left can broadcast cues that greater public control is a legitimate alternative and constructive outlet for mass discontents.

Intraelite conflict tends to weaken the checks and balances of government. For example, any modern president must further centralize power if he is to devitalize or revitalize federal government against the wishes of the intraelite opposition. The Reagan administration would make a wonderful case for study of this phenomenon. Its avowed goal has been to exorcise centralized power. But to begin the process, it has had to use the full powers of the executive branch and other kinds of political muscle, both to keep Republicans in line and to ride roughshod over the opposition in Congress, the bureaucracy, and even state capitals. Any foreseeable liberal administration is even more likely to centralize power, in the name of necessary state planning and in opposition to conservative dissent. This tendency toward further political centralization is double-edged. On one side, it provides those elites in power greater maneuverability than historical checks and balances in government might allow; on the other side, it creates new opportunities for the American Left. Elites who centralize power can more easily be portrayed as subverters of democracy, who are taking power away from the people; the Left can be self-portrayed as the primary and perhaps only defender of democracy in politics today. Furthermore, centralized political power, unlike power diffused by checks and balances, provides a distinctive focus for radical democratic movements and, with some imagination, an instrument with which the demos could assert its own authority. Samuel Bowles writes, "While Robin Hood is not about to be installed in the Oval Office, the specter of an interventionist state and a working class majority is hardly comforting, as any British or Italian capitalist will tell you."[31] Centralized power is both necessary and dangerous to elites, as long as they are divided among themselves and potentially threatened by democratic mechanisms for mass power.

Intraelite conflict weakens the two-party system as a mechanism for promoting national consensus and quiescence. William Crotty and Gary Jacobson introduce their American Parties in Decline with the following statement:

The American electorate in the twentieth century is a "turned-off" electorate. It is characterized by low levels of voter participation; a decline in party loyalty, with a concomitant increase in split-ticket voting and wild and unpredictable swings in outcomes and vote margins from one election to the next; an increasing emphasis on issue voting; and claims, at least, of a more ideological nature.[32]

With a turned-off electorate, political elites must take extraordinary measures to win the marginal support necessary for victory against competing elites. They bypass traditional party mechanisms to raise their own funds, produce their own media blitzes, and even take controversial issue positions, as Reagan and others did in the 1980 elections. Furthermore, they politicize electoral competition by advocating ideological positions aimed at luring independents and the apathetic to the polls. This creates a political atmosphere in which people forego their traditional and habitual attachments to middle-of-the-road parties and become accessible to the more issue-oriented and ideological messages of the American Left. Furthermore, this is a political atmosphere that provides several new alternatives for left-wing politics.

First, just as disarray in the Republican party opened up its right wing to ideological conservatives, so too does disarray in the Democratic party open up its left wing to radical activists. Tom Hayden may be among the first of many radicals who root themselves in party politics and yet offer something new to the context. Second, overall disenchantment with party politics by Americans helps to legitimate an alternative politics that Harry C. Boyte calls the Backyard Revolution of community activism. Janice Perlman captures the flavor of this alternative politics in the following:

> The direct-action groups and electoral efforts tend to be more openly anticorporate and antiestablishment, but even the Community Development Corporations and the co-ops feel strongly that neither the public nor the private institutions of this society are concerned with meeting the needs of "the little guy."[33]

In answer to Everett Carll Ladd's question, "Where have all the voters gone?" we might say that they have taken a step away from the consensus politics of the two-party system and a step toward community activism, where radical democratic ideas are more competitive.[34]

To the degree that the U.S. political system was once exceptionally accommodating to Americans' demands and discontents, it
no longer is. The renegotiated social contract that legitimated the
welfare state is now disputed among elites and discredited among
American citizens. This is a legitimation crisis for elites, who now
find it difficult to centralize political power without overtly dismantling
democratic rights and entitlements Americans have learned to take for
granted. This is an opportunity for the American Left to articulate
people's discontents and seek political power through conventional and
unconventional means that promise to enhance American democracy.

CLASS HEGEMONY

The U.S. economy is now in the midst of a crisis that is often
characterized by a "decline in productivity growth."[35] Symptoms include inflation, record interest and bankruptcy rates, massive unemployment, falling real wages, shutdowns, runaway shops, layoffs,
and deteriorating standards of living for millions of Americans. One
effect of the crisis is to broaden the gap between the prosperity that
American capitalists have promised to its workers and the reality of
disappointed material hopes for more and more Americans. Again,
we will see that U.S. elites are deeply divided over the means for
ending the economic crisis to accommodate people's material discontents; we will also see that the failure of elites to end the crisis is an
opportunity for the American Left to build support for a more democratic economy.

The current economic crisis may be more serious and ongoing
than past ones. First, the U.S. economy is experiencing tensions
related to investment and disinvestment patterns. Much U.S. capital
is locked into less productive and nonproductive investments. De-
caying and technologically dated industries eat up much investment
capital; noncompetitive and less competitive businesses consume
more; and massive military expenditures and less massive transfer
payments ingest investment capital in ways that do not increase the
stock of goods and services, which make up people's standards of
living. Abstractly, the economy would be strengthened if such capital was disinvested and then reinvested in more productive enterprises.
But, says Lester Thurow, "disinvestment is what our economy does
worse."[36] Powerful economic and political interests have a stake in
the survival and profitability of these investments, and they protect
them against threats to their survival.
Concomitantly, new innovative and productive investments are
increasingly risky today. Regardless of who foots the bill—the private

or the public sector—new technologies demand huge research and development costs and costs associated with specialized kinds of education; years of planning, experimenting, construction and retooling, and finetuning must be subsidized before any profits are realized; and, as the nuclear power industry has demonstrated, the price tag for errors, unforeseen difficulties, mass marketing and salesmanship, and cost overruns can be immense.[37] Furthermore, the current economic crisis produces a host of uncertainties, ranging from the threat of obsolescence, which comes with new technological breakthroughs, to political unrest and revolution in crucial nations, which make it difficult to acquire bank financing for risky ventures.

Disinvestment resistance and investment risk is a formula for continued productivity growth decline in the United States. Less productive and nonproductive industries must seek government subsidies and protection to safeguard profits, only to lock up more capital in the weaker sectors. Old and new investors may avoid the risks associated with innovation by sinking their capital into profitable, ongoing industries, creating a mania for conglomeration and mergers that do not enhance productivity growth. Furthermore, America's unstable investment atmosphere motivates the owners of profitable, ongoing industries to hedge their bets against the future. Thus, U.S. oil and steel companies are still productive, but Getty Oil is slowly liquidating its oil holdings and getting into the reinsurance business, while U.S. Steel is more rapidly liquidating its steel holdings to buy up chemical companies.[38] Even productive and profitable investments are being cut back. The current economic logic appears to suggest a continuation of America's "sunset" industries, greater monopolization in productive industries, and stillbirths for potential "sunrise" industries.

Second, the U.S. economy is also experiencing tensions associated with the new international economic order. Since World War II, our national economy has increasingly been integrated into the world economy; but its hegemony in the international marketplace has diminished considerably.[39] Business in the United States is clearly dominant in some sectors, but it is only competitive and sometimes noncompetitive in many other sectors. Daily evidence can be seen on American highways, where Chevrolets, Fords, and Chryslers now make room for Toyotas, Datsuns, and Volkswagens. This situation raises some perplexing questions, which lack obvious answers. Should U.S. business enhance its competitive edge through protectionism only to risk an international price war costly to all capitalists? Should it resign itself to a less-than-hegemonic role and work out cooperative agreements with the competition? Can it forge enough unity in its own ranks to follow either tactic? If so, how? If not, should it rely on government intervention to secure class unity? Indeed, is there even such an entity as "U.S. business" in a world of multinational corporations?

Third, the U.S. economy is now experiencing tensions associated with its uncertain relationship to the federal government. Since the beginning of the twentieth century, the federal government has played an increasingly large and crucial role in the economy, facilitating capital accumulation and social control; regulating particular sectors; providing a superstructure of transportation, communication, and education; making the world safe for U.S. investors; cushioning the costs of economic change; and much more. The current economic crisis makes it unclear if the federal government should continue the old ways, seek out a new role, or give up altogether. Should it channel investment capital in growth industries and underwrite the risks of new ventures? Can it afford to assume this responsibility? Should it bail out less productive industries? What position should it take on mergermania? Should it protect domestic industries against international competition? Should it foster the multinationalism that assumes the expendability of some domestic industries? Should U.S. foreign policy carry the big stick that keeps competitors and subversives in line or should it talk softly to create an atmosphere for international economic agreements? Or should it get out of the economy altogether, letting capitalists fend for themselves? Today, political elites are receiving different, even antagonistic messages from different sectors of the economy; this produces a range of political uncertainties, which reinforce capitalists' motivation to hedge their investment bets and look overseas for more stable investment atmospheres.

Elites in the United States have worked overtime to discover a way out of the economic crisis. The American Enterprise Institute, the Brookings Institution, and the Trilateral Commission are just a few of the think tanks and forums that have raised many of the important questions, discussed them, heard expert testimony on them, and worked out strategies for answering them. But no upper-class consensus has emerged. To the contrary, U.S. elites seem to be clustering around polar strategies and, thereby, exacerbate intraelite conflict over the economy.

Conservatives have midwifed the birth of "supply-side" economics, something of a reincarnation of nineteenth-century laissez-faire economics. Their assumption is that the nation's top economic priority is to free up investment capital and to allow capitalists maximal freedom in investing that capital.[40] New capital can be "liberated" by limiting or eliminating costly government intervention in the economy. Deregulation of the savings and loan industry, for example, will make available loan capital once tied by law to home construction and mortgages. The erosion of government transfer payments and entitlements will also free up investment capital. The end of staggering corporate taxation will add more capital to investment pools.

In theory, capitalists will use this capital in ways that catalyze productivity growth, enhance the competitive edge of U.S. business in the world, and expand the economic pie to make Americans less dependent on government and more able to share in the new wealth. Of course, the transition between welfare-state capitalism and the supply-side economy will take some time, causing temporary dislocations that impoverish some Americans. However, Reagan budget director David A. Stockman assures us that high interest rates, record unemployment, and rising bankruptcies are "all part of the cure, not the problem."[41] U.S. investors, who have hit upon hard times, and American citizens, who have lost their welfare cushion and entitlements, must be patient. Eventually, the supply-side strategy will generate the productivity growth that will trickle down to everyone, putting the American Dream back within the grasp of all Americans with enough pluck to reach out for it.

There is a major contradiction built into the supply-side strategy that creates space for significant intraelite conflict. On the one hand, the strategy promises a new freedom for the most powerful economic elites—the multinational corporations—whose interests are transnational. "The multinational corporate system," writes Stephen Hymer, "tends to abolish national capital and create a world system in which output is produced cooperatively to a greater degree than ever before."[42] The logic of the multinational world system is to limit the power of the nation-state, even bypass it through the good offices of international groups, like the Trilateral Commission or financial consortia.[43] On the other hand, supply-siders and their political representatives participate in a nationalist ethic that promises domestic growth and "get-tough" policies in the world. This nationalist ethic is manifest in Reagan administration attempts to use the federal government as a threat against Canadian investors in the U.S. economy or Japanese competitors to U.S. domestic industries. It is also manifest in what Philip Green calls the national-defense state, which necessarily involves continued government regulation of the economy.

> If the nation had only a national-defense sector . . . we would find our politics taken up entirely . . . over the disposition of "defense contracts" (a term that would then be used to cover just about everything but the manufacture of pipe cleaners). The location and closure of "defense" plants, the development and distribution of natural resources, the desire to import versus the drive to self-

sufficiency (at present in the United States tariffs on wrist-
watches, Swiss cheese, and peanuts are justified in the
name of "national defense"), the distribution of income
between "defense" and "nondefense" workers, the question of special preferences and rewards for veterans of
both military fronts and the industrial "home front" and
their dependents, . . . the amount of money to be spent
(and the ways it should be spent) on "vital" services like
education and transportation (like the National Defense
Education Act, the National Defense Highway Act pays for
a much greater proportion of the sector to which it relates
than could possibly be explained by any logistic planner)
—all would naturally fall under the consideration of "national defense."[44]

Should economic deregulation in the interest of multinationals take
place at the expense of national defense? Should conservatives support the multinationalism that harms domestic small businessmen,
who have often been the core of conservative support? Is national
defense such a high priority that government planning and huge budget
deficits are justified despite the ideological and economic costs? The
coalition that helped engineer the Reagan victory and get him through
his first year in office is now fragmenting over questions such as
these.

Liberal elites, in general, continue to advocate the demand-
side economics associated with Keynesian fine tuning of the economy
and welfare-state cushioning for those suffering economic dislocation.
However, armed with the knowledge that the old ways are problematic
and suspect, liberals have increasingly considered the appropriate-
ness of systematic state planning for the reindustrialization of the
U.S. economy. Lester Thurow catches the drift when he says, "We
do need the national equivalent of a corporate investment committee
to redirect investment flows from our sunset industries to our sunrise industries."[45] The drift is toward corporatism. The federal
government must become a gathering place for political, capitalist,
and labor elites to meet, plan the economy for greater productivity
growth, and administer and enforce their plans, despite recalcitrance
among both elites and mass publics. The aim would be to direct
capital investment to high technology and growth industries; conserve
access to depleting, nonrenewable resources and develop renewable
substitutes; make appropriate fiscal adjustments; and maintain aggregate demand. Theoretically, Americans will "consent to a new
set of incentives" because their leaders will represent their interests
in the planning process to assure a smooth transition, a fair distribution of sacrifices, and at least some degree of citizen participation
in the process.[46]

The reindustrialization strategy discussed here also involved a major contradiction that fosters intraclass disputes. On the one hand, though the logic of multinationalism is to transcend national interests, that transcendence is mediated by state mechanisms. Multinational corporations rely on the federal government to provide the foreign aid that stabilizes overseas markets, to facilitate the export of jobs and capital, to support an intelligence network that reveals and sometimes adjusts investment climates abroad, and especially to maintain and use the military to protect foreign investments. "As far as the capitalist state is concerned," suggests Alan Wolfe, "multinational corporate activity has not brought about its end but has given it a new lease on life."[47] But that lease depends on the federal government subordinating national interests to multinational ones. On the other hand, state planning for reindustrialization requires that the federal government have autonomy enough to subordinate multinational interests to domestic ones, if necessary. By locating economic planning of such magnitude in government, reindustrialization strategy opens up the political economy to the "sources of instability" associated with democratic representation and participation in the planning process. To avert this, according to Peter Bachrach, elites must perform a bypass operation, linking state planning to a top-down institutionalized participation, which does not invite public control over the process.[48] The host of uncertainties that would be involved in such an operation motivates some liberal elites to stick by Keynesian incentives, though discredited, rather than risk some form of public participation that might open the door to public control.

The longer that these intraelite conflicts rage, the more pronounced the economic crisis becomes for the Americans who suffer most from it. When intraelite conflict is manifest in the rhetoric of "voodoo" economics, public suspicions that something very basic is wrong with U.S. capitalism are fueled. Calls for patience as old strategies are invigorated or new ones are proposed, without attendent relief of the symptoms in actual life, are only further evidence that the American Dream of material prosperity for everyone is surely slipping away. Meanwhile, what Richard Barnet and Ronald Muller call the Latin Americanization of the United States proceeds apace.[49] Multinationals continue to export jobs and capital to exacerbate the domestic crisis; domestic industries go to bankruptcy courts; and the labor unions, women, and minorities who won some important victories in the 1970s now find themselves with fewer economic opportunities than they had in the 1960s. In addition, the continued multinationalization and conglomeration of the economy has "all but eliminated small business, family farming, and independent professional or artisan work, thus destroying the economic basis of those groups on which the capitalist class has historically counted for . . .

support."[50] Indeed, George Gilder's extraordinarily popular Wealth and Poverty is premised on the notion that even U.S. capitalism's foremost defenders believe that "the capitalist vision" now teeters "so precariously over the . . . ash can of history."[51]

The failure of the U.S. economy to produce up to expectations or to provide hope for improvement in the near future fosters widespread anxieties among Americans, which conceivably open Americans to democratic alternatives. Let me suggest that the American Left, if it looks, can find many entry points for advocating greater public control over the economy.

Conservatives' supply-side strategy constitutes what Robert Alford calls an attack by the capitalist aspect of the state on the democratic aspect of the state.[52] This suggests, to an extent, that political elites are divided among themselves. Those allied with the more democratic aspects of the state, in order to outdo the opposition, may have to look for new constituencies for support. Conceivably, the Left could organize that support, demanding in return a set of democratic reforms, which may include anything from the restoration of entitlement programs to public representation and worker participation in corporations that the federal government subsidizes, protects, or bails out. Liberals' state planning strategy may drive them to seek mass support against conservative opposition. In this instance, the Left might help organize that support, the price being that the participatory mechanism for citizens include some measure of public control over the process.

To the extent that both conservatives and liberals fail to solve the economic problems of the nation, as is likely to be the case in the immediate future, radicals can adopt the ethic of rationality and efficiency as their own, claiming that elites have failed to measure up to their own standards of productivity, and offer as an alternative a set of democratic mechanisms for popular control over investment decisions. Such strategies have already been proposed by economic democrats.[53] Alternatively, radicals can play on the shattered material expectations of Americans to introduce into American dialogue a set of democratic rights intertwined with human needs, decentralized processes of decision making that prefigure public control, and economic reorganization based on community and worker control of the means of production.[54] Such directions have already been articulated as a matter of expedience in places like Youngstown, Ohio, where corporation shutdowns have made local control a matter of community survival.

The internationalization of capital and the fact that multinational interests may require domestic sacrifices creates an environment in which economic elites can be considered treasonous and radical democrats patriotic. If what is good for General Motors is opening up production plants in South Africa and shutting down production plants in Southgate, California, then it can be argued that irresponsible "public" corporations must be subjected to public accountability. Maurice Zeitlin proposes a kind of "reindustrialization of America from below": the development of a Public Investment Reserve System, based initially on government and union pension funds but also requiring corporate contributions as a condition of operating in a particular state or the nation, which will loan scarce capital to responsible firms, penalize irresponsible businesses, and, most important, provide democratic mechanisms for determining what counts as responsible.[55] Of course, corporations could always threaten to disinvest in the United States. But by so doing, they might arouse the mass enmity, translated into political power, which would limit their access to investment capital, eat into their markets, deplete their skilled labor supply, and even generate support for the municipalization of existing plants that are shut down.[56]

Current efforts by corporations to enhance productivity at home are also pregnant with democratic possibilities. The routinization of professional, white-collar, and blue-collar labor is one way in which economic elites have tried to maximize efficiency; however, routinization also destroys many of the stratification distinctions that have divided workers against one another.[57] In a sense, lawyers who work in branch offices in shopping centers, bookkeepers who feed cards into computers, and factory workers on the assembly line, despite income differentials, share a sense of alienation and a sense of job insecurity during today's hard times; conceivably, they could share a sense of wanting greater control over their work lives and, thus, a sense of supporting efforts toward democratic control of their workplaces. Capitalists have sometimes invited their workers to become part-owners through profit sharing, stock distribution, and pension plans in order to stabilize their work force; but they also create a basis for the argument that these part-owners should also have partial control over investment as well as shop floor decisions. Finally, some employers traffic in worker participation plans to increase workers' interest in their job, enhance their productivity, and minimize their absenteeism; by so doing, they introduce the idea of democracy into the workplace and provide workers some incentive to struggle for the reality of worker self-management.[58]

The economic crisis today is evidence that the capitalist class is not as invulnerable, intelligent, or unified as radicals often imagine. There are many cracks in capitalist hegemony, and U.S. elites have divided over the means for sealing them, though the suggested alternatives both involve centralizing economic power—either in the hands of multinationals or corporatist government. Presently, they are unable to accommodate Americans' material demands and frustrations; but they can rightly be accused of subverting democratic norms and, therefore, are vulnerable to the claims of those who defend and hope to extend democracy in the United States.

CLOSED FRONTIERS AND OPENED FRONTIERS

"The end of the frontier," writes Tom Hayden, "is the crucial fact for the next generation of Americans."[59] U.S. elites seemingly have run out of geographical space for expansion, where the discontented can find hope, and of intellectual frontiers that can attract American idealism to safe arenas. The cause, for Henry Steele Commager, is a failure of leadership. "So few of our leaders—and our potential leaders—seem to have any road map. It is hard to lead when you yourself are in a labyrinth."[60] There may be a more basic reason why U.S. leaders have no road map. The old ones have led us to our current legitimation and economic crisis, and U.S. elites do not know of new ones.

Inside the United States, geographical frontiers are less available and less desirable than ever before. In the American West, inexpensive land is scarce, new business opportunities few, and employment diminishing. The soaring costs of family homes and condominiums, high-cost and scarce rentals, staggering interest rates, unpredictable automobile and gasoline costs, and federal and state tax bites conspire to make the American Dream of a place of one's own an increasingly distant prospect for people from Southern California to Alaska, not to mention Hawaii. The residual attraction of the Sunbelt, its beautiful weather and crime-free environment, has been marred by widespread air pollution, repeated droughts, and a spreading of crime that usually comes with high expectations and few opportunities. Paradoxically, the old Lockean option of "exit" for those with a pioneering spirit is now reserved for the survivalists, who are arming themselves for an economic Armageddon.

Outside of the United States, geographical frontiers have become increasingly hostile. What has happened since World War II? The United States did not win a war in Korea; it did lose a war in Vietnam. Although it "won" back Chile from Allende, it "lost" China to Mao, Cuba to Castro, or, more recently, Nicaragua to the Sandanistas. The United States can no longer be the world's policeman, and most Americans do not want the role. They have resisted U.S. intervention in the national liberation struggles of Angola and continue to resist Reagan administration attempts to whip up public fervor for greater U.S. intervention in El Salvador. Furthermore, the United States is not the only hegemonic power in the world system today. The instability of the dollar abroad, the emergence of the Organization of Petroleum Exporting Countries (OPEC), revolutions in supplier nations, and even serious tensions with neighboring Canada and Mexico indicate that the United States does not have the uncontested muscle to impose its will whenever and wherever it wishes. Finally, the United States has lost much of its moral influence as "the first democratic nation" by supporting dictatorial regimes that brutally and consistently violate the most basic human rights or, for example, by being the only nation in the World Health Organization to support Third World sales of infant formula, despite the avowed consequences of malnutrition, disease, and death for children. Certainly, America's outward push into the world will continue to be a source of important wealth, but it may be a diminishing source that causes more conflict than it can buy off.

America's new frontiers have lost much of their capacity to absorb Americans' idealism. "The career," according to Ira Shor, "is the modern form of the [American] Dream."[61] The traditional entrance to the career has been higher education. However, as careers become more routinized and as recession eats into professional and middle-class employment, the career becomes less desirable as a means of satisfying moral values and less attainable as a means of social mobility. One result is the growth of an overeducated, underemployed population without conventional outlets for its dreams.

The frontiers of science are now experiencing something of a drought. Science has become "Big Science," requiring millions of dollars to educate personnel, equip laboratories, and carry on basic research. These dollars are increasingly scarce for basic research and even for applied research, except in the military sector.[62] However, the technological finetuning of the art of global destruction is not likely to excite people's hopes for a better future; it is more likely to generate a nationwide and international movement against ticking off another minute toward the midnight of nuclear holocaust. Moreover, the scientific enterprise has encountered growing public skepticism. Environmental degradation, nuclear power dangers and radiation leaks, toxic waste dumping, carcinogenic drugs and food additives, diseases picked up while in the hospital, and related factors have been well publicized or directly experienced; they contribute to a public fear that scientific advances often outstrip people's ability to control them. Robert Heilbroner says that "the ethos of 'science,' so intimately connected with industrial application" must play a diminished role in the future if we are to survive.[63] Trapped between economic hard times and public skepticism, science has become a poor investment for Americans' hopes for a better future.

To the degree that the traditional frontiers are closed or closing fast, it is increasingly difficult for Americans to ignore or tolerate today's crises, under the assumption that they will disappear during a better tomorrow. Tomorrow, we fear, may be considerably worse. This fear can give rise to two general kinds of survival techniques. One is pessimism. It is pessimism that informs much of what is called the New Narcissism; and it is pessimism that gives rise to radicals' predictions that social fascism, friendly fascism, or plain old authoritarianism lie just ahead. Let me close this chapter by suggesting that the closing of traditional frontiers is an opportunity for the Left to open up new frontiers, radical democratic frontiers.

A second survival technique is based on stubborn optimism fueled by anger. We can witness it in the lives of some of the survivors of the Nazi concentration camps or of the atomic bombings of Hiroshima and Nagasaki or of the meaningless war in Vietnam. Rather than try to escape the pain of an experience that destroys the traditional pillars of meaning in their lives, the survivors are angered by their experience and seek to give it meaning in a lifelong search for social justice. They use the past in the service of a better future. One might refer to Robert Jay Lifton's studies or to Barbara Meyerhoff's brilliant study of an aging community of Jewish "survivors" in Venice, California.

> Here was a community, then sewn together by internal conflict, whose members were building and conserving their connections using grievance and dissension. Anger welded them together, fulfilling many purposes at the same time: asserting autonomy over themselves and their circumstances; demonstrating responsiveness to each other; clarifying the community's membership boundaries; displacing resentment from absent, vague targets toward nearer safer ones; and denying that they shared a common, hideous fate. [64]

Meyerhoff's gerontological survivors drew strength from the shtetl or community life of their childhood to give meaning to old age in a society that casts aside its elderly. They denied having been cast aside in order to create for themselves a profoundly democratic existence, where autonomy and community fed on each other.

It seems to me that the American Left has a choice. It can look to history as an excuse for failure and look to the future with pessimism, or it can draw strength from America's democratic past, deny its own impotence, and commit itself to offering radical democracy as an alternative for Americans' future. In this chapter, I tried to show that there are cracks in elite hegemony that make radical democracy a viable political perspective for the Left. In the next chapter, I will try to show that a theory of radical democracy can be useful for articulating and focusing people's frustrations in egalitarian directions.

NOTES

1. For example, see Richard Ohmann, English in America: A Radical View of the Profession (New York: Oxford, 1976), p. 189, where the author suggests language styles in the United States are best suited to those with power and privilege, because "this is a rhetoric that masks power and privilege."

2. In part, C. Wright Mills set the tone in The Power Elite (New York: Oxford, 1956), p. 3, where he applies Burckhardt's saying about great men to the power elite: "They are all that we are not." Mills immediately adds that the power elite "is composed of men whose positions enable them to transcend the ordinary environments of ordinary men and women" [emphasis added].

3. Albert Szymanski, The Capitalist State and the Politics of Class (Cambridge, Mass.: Winthrop, 1978), p. 40.

4. For example, see Howard Zinn, A People's History of the United States (New York: Harper & Row, 1980), pp. 341, 582.

5. Phyllis Schlafly, The Power of the Positive Woman (New York: Harcourt Brace Jovanovich, 1977); and Richard A. Vigeurie, The New Right: We're Ready to Lead (Falls Church, Va.: Viguerie, 1981).

6. Richard F. Hamilton, Class and Politics in the United States (New York: Wiley, 1973), p. 517; Alan Wolfe, The Limits of Legitimacy: Political Contradictions of Contemporary Capitalism (New York: Free Press, 1977), p. 253; Frances Fox Piven and Richard A. Cloward, Poor People's Movements: Why They Succeed and How They Fail (New York: Vintage, 1977), p. xv; and Martin Carnoy and Derek Shearer, Economic Democracy: The Challenge of the 1980s (White Plains, N.Y.: M. E. Sharpe, 1980), p. 394.

7. See Jurgen Habermas, Legitimation Crisis, trans. Thomas McCarthy (Boston: Beacon, 1975); see also Wolfe, Limits of Legitimacy, chap. 10.

8. Michael Best and William Connolly, The Politicized Economy (Lexington, Mass.: Heath, 1976), pp. 172-73.

9. See Alan Wolfe, "Closures and Openings: Political Responses to the Current Crisis," in U.S. Capitalism in Crisis, ed. The Union for Radical Political Economics (New York: URPE, 1978), pp. 323-30; Edward Greenberg, Serving the Few: Corporate Capitalism and the Bias of Government Policy (New York: Wiley, 1974), pp. 89-94; and idem, The American Political System: A Radical Approach

(Cambridge, Mass.: Winthrop, 1977), pp. 268-69; and T. B. Bottomore, Critics of Society: Radical Thought in North America (New York: Pantheon, 1968), p. 33.

10. Zinn, A People's History, pp. 344-45.

11. See Alan Wolfe, "Presidential Power and the Crisis of Modernization," Democracy 1, no. 2 (April 1981): 23.

12. James Weinstein, "Corporate Liberalism and the Monopoly Capitalist State," in The Capitalism System, ed. Richard Edwards, Michael Reich, and Thomas Weisskopf, 2d ed. (Englewood Cliffs, N.J.: Prentice-Hall, 1978), p. 232; see also Fred Block, "The Ruling Class Does Not Rule," Socialist Revolution 7 (May-June 1977): 6-28.

13. Joe R. Feagin, Subordinating the Poor: Welfare and American Beliefs (Englewood Cliffs, N.J.: Prentice-Hall, 1975), p. 44; see also Greenberg, Serving the Few, pp. 103-25.

14. Walter Dean Burnham quoted in Greenberg, American Political System, pp. 268-69; see also Wolfe, Limits of Legitimacy, p. 293.

15. Compare Greenberg, Serving the Few, p. 102, and Weinstein, "Corporate Liberalism," p. 233.

16. I have dealt with this at greater length in "Consent and Authority in America," in The Problem of Authority in America, ed. John P. Diggins and Mark E. Kann (Philadelphia: Temple University Press, 1981), pp. 59-83.

17. The data that substantiate growing political distrust and alienation are vast. Perhaps a more interesting indicator is that U.S. presidents usually affirm it and them blame the press for it. Johnson's and Nixon's attacks on the press have now been augmented by Reagan's criticisms that the press too often dwells on the negative and portrays his administration's policies in a poor light.

18. See John P. Diggins, Los Angeles Times Book Review, February 28, 1982.

19. Cited in Samuel Bowles, "The Trilateral Commission: Have Capitalism and Democracy Come to a Parting of the Ways?" in U.S. Capitalism in Crisis, ed. Union for Radical Political Economics (New York: URPE, 1978), p. 263.

20. James O'Connor, The Fiscal Crisis of the State (New York: St. Martin's Press, 1973), pp. 1-10.

21. George Gilder, Wealth and Poverty (New York: Bantam, 1981), p. 14; and M. Stanton Evans, Clear and Present Dangers: A Conservative View of America's Government (New York: Harcourt Brace Jovanovich, 1975), p. 33.

22. Compare Samuel P. Huntington, "The United States," in The Crisis of Democracy: Report on the Governability of Democracies to the Trilateral Commission, ed. Michel Crozier, Samuel P.

Huntington, and Joji Watanuke (New York: New York University Press, 1975), pp. 59-115; and Lester C. Thurow, The Zero-sum Society (New York: Penguin, 1981).

23. For example, see articles by Mark Green, Martin Carnoy, and Derek Shearer, Frances Fox Piven and Richard A. Cloward, Patricia Derian, Ralph Nader, and James Ridgeway in a special November 7, 1981, issue of Nation entitled "Reagan Rated."

24. Gil Sewell, "To Obey or Disobey?" Newsweek, May 5, 1980, p. 83; see also Wolfe, "Presidential Power," p. 20.

25. Reported in the Los Angeles Times, February 27, 1982.

26. Sheldon Wolin, "Theme Note," Democracy 1, no. 1 (January 1981): 7; see also Murray Edelman, Political Language: Words That Succeed and Policies That Fail (New York: Academic Press, 1977), chap. 13; and Mark E. Kann, "Consent and Authority in America," pp. 69-70.

27. Philip Green, "Redeeming Government," Nation, December 12, 1981, p. 625.

28. This is meant to be a composite portrait, general enough to represent strains of thought promoted by Milton Friedman and Ayn Rand, William Buckley and Barry Goldwater, Richard Viguerie and Phyllis Schlafly, Irving Kristol and Edward Banfield, and Ronald Reagan and David Stockman, not to mention Alexander Haig and Casper Weinberger.

29. This, too, is a composite portrait, one that draws heavily on the early thrust of the Trilateral Commission and its emphasis on international and domestic cooperation. Perhaps most interesting is how liberal elites define responsible public participation in a way that undermines its democratic elements. See Carl J. Friedrich, "Participation without Responsibility: Codetermination in Industry and University," in Participation in Politics, ed. J. Roland Pennock and John W. Chapman, Nomos 16 (New York: Lieber-Atherton, 1975), pp. 195-212, for a relevant example.

30. Quoted in William Schneider, "For Many Americans, Reagan's Ends No Longer Justify His Means," Los Angeles Times, March 14, 1982.

31. Bowles, "Trilateral Commission," p. 264.

32. William J. Crotty and Gary C. Jacobson, American Parties in Decline (Boston: Little, Brown, 1980), p. 3; see also Richard Edwards and Michael Reich, "Party Politics and Class Conflict," in The Capitalist System, ed. Richard Edwards, Michael Reich, and Thomas Weisskopf, 2d ed. (Englewood Cliffs, N.J.: Prentice-Hall, 1978), pp. 252-62.

33. Janice Perlman, "Grassrooting the System," in U.S. Capitalism in Crisis, ed. Union for Radical Political Economics (New York: URPE, 1978), p. 321; see also Harry C. Boyte, The Backyard Revolution (Philadelphia: Temple University Press, 1980), chap. 1.

34. Everett Carll Ladd, Jr., Where Have All the Voters Gone? The Fracturing of America's Political Parties (New York: Norton, 1978), pp. ix-xxiv.

35. This may be the only point of agreement among U.S. economists today. Compare Gilder, Wealth and Poverty, chap. 12, entitled "The Economy of Frustration"; Thurow, The Zero-sum Society, chap. 1, entitled "An Economy That No Longer Performs"; and "What Makes It a Crisis?" in U.S. Capitalism in Crisis, ed. Union for Radical Political Economics (New York: URPE, 1978), pp. 1-2.

36. Thurow, The Zero-sum Society, p. 77.

37. See Barry Commoner, The Poverty of Power: Energy and the Economic Crisis (New York: Bantam, 1976), chap. 5.

38. For example, see Staughton Lynd, "Reindustrialization: Brownfield or Greenfield?" Democracy 1, no. 3 (July 1981): 22-36.

39. For a summary perspective, see Marty Landsberg, "Multinational Corporations and the Crisis of Capitalism," Insurgent Sociologist 6 (Spring 1976): 19-33.

40. See Gilder, Wealth and Poverty, chap. 4, for a statement and defense of supply-side economics.

41. Stockman quoted in the Los Angeles Times, March 5, 1982.

42. Stephen Hymer, "The Internationalization of Capital," Journal of Economic Issues 6, no. 1 (1972): 101.

43. See Landsberg, "Multinational Corporations," p. 29; and Carol Thompson, "The Politicization of Monopoly Capital: The Trilateral Commission and Bank Consortia," Transition 2, no. 1 (1979): 21-39.

44. Philip Green, "In Defense of the State(I)," Democracy 1, no. 2 (April 1981): 8.

45. Thurow, The Zero-sum Society, p. 95; see also Felix Rohatyn's numerous articles and speeches in the 1980 and 1981 New York Review of Books, Economist, and the Harvard Business Review.

46. See William E. Connolly, "The Politics of Reindustrialization," Democracy 1, no. 3 (July 1981): 15.

47. Wolf, Limits of Legitimacy, p. 241.

48. See Peter Bachrach, "Democracy and Class Struggle" and Maurice Zeitlin, "The American Crisis: An Analysis and Modest Proposal," in The Future of American Democracy: Views from the Left, ed. Mark E. Kann (Philadelphia: Temple University Press, 1983), chaps. 5, 11.

49. See Richard Barnet and Ronald Muller, Global Reach: The Power of Multinational Corporations (New York: Simon & Schuster, 1974), chap. 9.

50. Bowles, "Trilateral Commission," p. 264.

51. Gilder, Wealth and Poverty, p. 3.

52. Robert Alford, "Whither Capitalism, the State, and Democracy," in The Future of American Democracy: Views from the Left, ed. Mark E. Kann (Philadelphia: Temple University Press, 1983), chap. 2.

53. For example, see Carnoy and Shearer, Economic Democracy, part II.

54. See Ben Agger, Western Marxism (Santa Monica, Calif.: Goodyear, 1979), pp. 316-39.

55. See Zeitlin's "American Crisis" and note that the state of California is considering a facsimile of his proposal.

56. Jack Newfield has used his Village Voice articles to arouse public opinion in favor of municipalizing Consolidated Edison. For example, see his July 17, 1978, article entitled "Con Ed Cons the 'Times.'"

57. See Harry Braverman, Labor and Monopoly Capitalism (New York: Monthly Review, 1974); and Stanley Aronowitz, False Promises: The Shaping of American Working Class Consciousness (New York: McGraw-Hill, 1973), chap. 6.

58. See Carnoy and Shearer, Economic Democracy, chap. 3; and Bachrach, "Democracy and Class Struggle," in The Future of American Democracy: Views from the Left, ed. Mark E. Kann (Philadelphia: Temple University Press, 1983), chap. 11.

59. Tom Hayden, The American Future: New Visions Beyond Old Frontiers (Boston: South End Press, 1980), p. 12.

60. Henry Steele Commager, "Our Leadership Crisis: America's Real Malaise," Los Angeles Times, November 11, 1979.

61. Ira Shor, "The Working Class Goes to College," in Studies in Socialist Pedagogy, ed. Theodore Mills Norton and Bertell Ollman (New York: Monthly Review Press, 1978), p. 110.

62. See Robert H. Kargon, "The Future of American Science: An Historical Perspective," in The Future of American Democracy: Views from the Left, ed. Mark E. Kann (Philadelphia: Temple University Press, 1983), chap. 6.

63. Robert L. Heilbroner, An Inquiry into the Human Prospect (New York: Norton, 1974), p. 139.

64. Barbara Myerhoff, Number Our Days (New York: Simon & Schuster, 1978), p. 187.

7

A THEORY OF
RADICAL DEMOCRACY

What is radical democracy? I have indicated that it involves egalitarian discourse, widespread citizen participation, and the extension of public control over social life. To this point, I have purposefully not given radical democracy a more precise definition to avoid premature closure on what I take to be an essentially open-ended perspective. To an extent, radical democracy will be whatever the demos itself decides. Nonetheless, there are two compelling reasons why an explicit theory of radical democracy should be developed.

First, more precision is needed if radical democracy is to identify the Left as an autonomous political force, with its own alternative viewpoint that is appealing to public audiences. Vague renderings of radical democracy lend themselves to strictly proceduralist interpretations, like majority rule or public control. These procedural norms are adequate for condemning elite hegemony and pointing out its vulnerabilities, but they are not adequate as a foundation for relative Left unity or for legitimating Left alternatives among American citizens. On the one hand, radical democratic procedures in themselves can be and usually are assimilated to mainstream politics, without affecting substantive inequalities in the distribution of power and wealth in the United States. Socialists, who are particularly sensitive to the problem, and some radical activists, who have had souring experiences with procedural reforms lacking substantive results, are unlikely to cast their lot with radical democracy unless

An earlier and considerably different version of this chapter was published as Mark E. Kann, "The Dialectic of Consent Theory," Journal of Politics 40 (May 1978): 386-408. Sections of that article are reprinted here with permission of the Journal of Politics.

it is explicitly linked to new directions for social life. On the other hand, new procedures, even ones that provide mechanisms for direct mass participation, are not likely to spark much commitment among Americans unless it is clear to them that the results will be beneficial for them. After all, mass participation has been known to generate informal modes of elitism that are resilient as well as policies that are repressive. "I think," says William A. Williams, "procedure determines substance."[1] If so, the American Left must state outright the relationship between radical democratic procedures and radical democratic society.

Second, greater precision is needed if radical democracy is to be a useful perspective for guiding Left political practices. At most, a vague definition indicates that American Left politics must use democratic means to achieve democratic ends; it must eliminate elitism and vanguardism in its own ranks and replace them with mass organizations and participation. But what should be the focus of mass movements? What is their relationship to government or to direct action in society? Unless there is some closure on these questions, radical democracy could become another label that justifies Left fragmentation and Gothic enmities that are self-defeating. The challenge of radical democratic theory is to provide guidelines specific enough to provide a common direction for radical activism but general enough to allow for the experimental politics that is part of radical democracy.

In this chapter, I will develop a theory of radical democracy that provides concepts, terms, and lines of thought that might be useful in establishing an American Left identity and in cuing Americans to support egalitarian alternatives to present political and social relations. My intention is mainly to develop a theory that will be a useful legitimation device. In the next chapter, I will apply the theory as a set of guidelines for directing Left politics along what I consider the most useful avenues of change in our time.

CONSENT THEORY AND RADICAL DEMOCRACY

Let me begin by affirming a common Lockean assumption, which will serve as a familiar foundation for a theory of radical democracy. Locke and his heirs argue that individuals are in a position to give their consent when they are "free, equal, and independent." They must be situated to make the informed, voluntary choice that constitutes consent. On this familiar foundation, I will argue that power and wealth in the United States must be redistributed in egalitarian ways as a prerequisite to consent of the governed as the legitimate basis for government.

Are Americans socially situated to be able to consent today? Conservatives argue that the welfare state has sapped individuals' freedoms, while liberals feel that people's political rights, entitlements, and civil liberties are under attack. Groups that speak for women, minorities, the aged, and other significant groups of Americans testify to fears that they are less free to pursue their interests than they were a few years back. The continuing centralization of political and economic power, under both Republican and Democratic administrations, has shattered most people's illusions about equality in the United States. A few people decide what kinds of options are available to the majority, and the majority sees its options narrowing amid social crises. Furthermore, the independence long associated with individual ownership of a farm, a small business, a profession or career, and a home of one's own (let alone a room of one's own) is increasingly hard for young Americans to achieve. Instead, big government, big bureaucracy, and big business nourish widespread dependence among Americans. In a very real sense, few Americans can lay claim to the self-mastery Locke assumed for consent.

Does this diminished sense of self-mastery mean that most Americans are not situated to make the willful, conscientious, rational choice to consent or not? Certainly, Americans' disinterest in conventional politics indicates that their quiescence to it may be more a matter of habit or fear or resignation than of choice. However, before pursuing this possibility, let me cut a path through the conventional arguments that obscure the social prerequisites to consent. This is necessary both to appreciate their merits and to make explicit their limits.

The first argument, often made by conservatives, is that freedom, equality, and independence are above all else states of mind. Individuals have free will.[2] Regardless of adverse social circumstances, individuals can stand on their own feet and master their environment. They can be like the Founding Fathers, who fought for their freedom; the immigrants, who earned their equality; and the pioneers, who forged their own independence. Through self-reliance, Americans can rediscover the Yankee ingenuity or the "true grit" that enables them to become autonomous masters of their own fate, to become reborn Americans.

It may be true, the argument sometimes continues, that powerful elites manipulate people's consciousness and reinforce among them habits of quiescence and dependence. While such ideological hegemony "is an evil," suggests John Plamenatz, "it does not affect the question of consent."[3] Just as each of us must take responsibility for earthly acts on the day of judgment, so must we take full responsibility for our political beliefs and behavior today.

This argument has several merits. It evokes Locke's familiar state of nature, outside of history, and ennobles individuals as free moral agents. The claim to free will, individual responsibility, self-help and self-reliance strikes responsive chords in U.S. social history and is one important basis for political commitment. It suggests that people can always make and remake their own history. However, the argument meets its limits at people's daily experiences. For example, individuals with grit may discover ways to cut through bureaucratic red tape to solve personal problems, but they are born into a society in which there is virtually nothing they can do as individuals to avoid being on the receiving end of computer errors and bureaucratic snafus, and the indignities that attend them. As the crises that wrack American society expand in scope and impact, the arenas in which individuals can exercise free will, feel personal responsibility, or benefit by ingenuity diminish.

The second argument is one that liberals have made in many variations. It suggests that the best cure for people's sense of impotence is a proper civic education. Joseph Tussman says that an "act can only be properly taken as 'consent' if it is done 'knowing,'" as opposed to involuntarily, unconsciously, without foresight, or accidently.[4] Unfortunately, social circumstances sometimes conspire to make individuals act out of habit and ignorance. Tussman recommends that we consider these individuals to be political minors. They are like children who have the potential to be insightful citizens but have not as yet developed that potential into political maturity. Civic education can help the maturation process.

Education can set people free. It can alert them to the received habits that limit their options and, thus, empower them to make new choices and develop a more independent sense of self. It can inform people on the meaning of consent as a legitimate basis for incurring the obligations of political membership. It can teach people the skills necessary for taking full advantage of their membership. Most important, civic education can alert individuals to the benefits of consent—compared with other bases for political obligation and in relation to their own enlightened self-interests. All of this new knowledge will generate in people's lives a sense of efficacy and skillfulness, which they can translate into active and conscientious citizenship.

The liberal argument finds some support in empirical data, which indicate that education plays an important role in motivating people to participate knowingly and skillfully in the political arena. The very notion of education implies that people do have human capacities that can be developed and that particular kinds of skills can be important for mastering one's personal and political environment. Nonetheless, the utility of civic education stops at the border of public distrust. Who are the civic educators? Elites are so busy arguing

among themselves that they destroy their own credibility as teachers
of citizenship. Politicians who portray themselves as crisis managers lack the vision and values that might inspire an educated sense
of citizenship. Someone like Ronald Reagan, who would gladly play
the role of the Great Educator, is more readily cast as the Great
Communicator of public relations images, which are no more believ-
able than the images broadcast in television commercials. How much
can civic education accomplish? Public schools have taught it for
years, but Americans still resist playing conventional citizenship
roles. One of the lessons of the narcissism literature is that highly
educated Americans, with advanced citizenship skills, often experience
overwhelming feelings of dependence.[5] How much trust should people
invest in education, civic or not, when people with college degrees
are often jobless? The connection between liberal education and informed citizenship is, at best, an obscure one.

The third argument may simultaneously be the most interesting
and the most inconsequential. John Rawls recognizes that adverse
social conditions deprive people of the ability to practice the self-
mastery necessary for consent. Rather than question those social
conditions, he abstracts individuals from society; relocates them in
an Original Position, where hypothetical freedom, equality, and independence exist; and then considers what these fictive creatures might
find worthy of their consent. His argument is that they will find it
rational to agree on his principles of justice as fairness. The argument involves a philosophical sleight of hand.

> Yet a society satisfying the principles of justice as fair-
> ness comes as close as a society can to being a voluntary
> scheme, for it meets the principles which free and equal
> persons would assent to under circumstances that are
> fair. In this sense, its members are autonomous and the
> obligations they recognize self-imposed.[6]

In other words, a society based on Rawls's principles would be legitimate because it would be as if individuals, once they cast off their
social baggage, had consented to it. Rawls substitutes what is rational or hypothetical consent for actual consent.

Rawls's argument has the merit of fidelity to familiar values
like fairness and reason, liberty and equality. It is especially attractive to philosophers, intellectuals, and even bureaucrats, who "know"
better what rational people would choose than the irrational masses.
But what works in the higher circles of culture may not work in the
streets. Rawls's dismissal of actual consent runs against the grain
of U.S. history. For Locke, consent was an affirmation of the social
contract; for Jefferson, it was an agreement on a particular form of

government; soon, consent was linked to popular suffrage and the right to choose one's governors; and in the twentieth century, consent was vested with more direct forms of popular participation, even in actual policy-making processes.[7] It is difficult to imagine why Americans would return to an anachronistic version of hypothetical consent when they have spent the last two centuries struggling to increase the price of their actual consent.

The arguments for free will, civic education, and hypothetical consent are not wholly persuasive in our present social circumstances. They are half steps on the road to overcoming social impotence. For the American Left they are important half steps, because they are familiar, continue to have some evocative power among American audiences, and as we will see, are sometimes mistaken as whole steps by radicals themselves. Furthermore, they are important because they can be used in particular ways to justify changes far more radical than their authors intend. Radicals might ask what kinds of social changes would be necessary to extend the space for exercising free will, responsibility, and self-reliance; radicals could argue for substantive reforms that enable people to become self-educators in American civics; and radicals can suggest that the principles of justice can be found in the social conditions that nourish the freedom, equality, and independence necessary for consent.[8] Radicals who focus their attention on the social prerequisites to consent develop a more distinctive view of their radical democratic commitments and make explicit the links between consent procedures and radical substance.

It is beyond the scope of this book to present a fully developed sociology of consent, but I can indicate a range of social relations that now inhibit the self-mastery necessary for consent and require a redistribution of power and wealth, if they are to be an adequate foundation for consent. I will consider three interrelated aspects of our social worlds to suggest the kinds of changes that would be necessary: family life, daily social intercourse, and power relations.

Family life is the social incubator within which children develop their internalized, preconscious worlds, which predispose them to particular kinds of relations in later life. While these predispositions are not necessarily permanent, they are highly resistant to change by external forces. Historically, family life in the United States has been patriarchal. Males have been dominant, females subordinate, and children expected to learn their appropriate gender role. Given this form of family life, childhood learning has generally consisted of the internalization of asymmetries in power relations, which are then reinforced once children enter into broader social and political worlds. Boys are predisposed to play autonomous roles out in the world and dominant roles in their own families; girls are predisposed to assume a dependent position in both spheres. Most important, neither boys nor girls are predisposed to recognize equality or practice reciprocity across gender lines. [9]

The psychodynamics of patriarchy in American society produce individuals who are not predisposed to exercising the self-mastery necessary for consent. First, males can be expected to assert their freedom and independence but, lacking a predisposition to equality and reciprocity, in a way that denies equal personhood to male competitors and to all women. This is freedom and independence purchased at others' expense. In addition, males in American society increasingly find themselves in an external world, where very few men have the opportunity to practice freedom and independence. Most men are slaves to their bosses, their routinized work, and their monthly or weekly paychecks. Frustrated outside of the family, men may increase their aggressiveness and domination inside the family as a compensation for failure. But compensation is often an illusion. Men who practice physical or emotional cruelty in their families destroy whatever residual harmony exists between the genders and, today, often come home to discover their wives and children have up and left. Second, females can be expected to fit the role of social dependents who receive male support in return for nurturance and motherhood; they are ill-prepared for freedom, equality, and independence, particularly outside the family. Within a social context where males have difficulty providing that support, owing to male frustrations or perhaps the need for a second income, women will be forced to exercise a degree of autonomy and self-support. This is a direct challenge to conventional male roles and is likely to exacerbate tensions between the sexes; it is a role that women are likely to fill with great ambivalence, which may condemn them to do poorly in it. Finally, children who are raised in this cauldron of domination and subordination, frustration and tension, are likely to arm themselves against making emotional commitments that can be painful, to fixate at what psychiatrists call the preoedipal stage of development, and to serve as potential recruits in the army of social and political apathetics in the United States.

Patriarchal family life based on sexual inequality provides virtually no one with the rudimentary sense of self-mastery necessary for consent. It must be changed if it is to predispose people to cooperate with one another on equal terms to determine the nature of their political association. One might use an abstract logic to justify revolutionizing family life by eliminating it. However, this alternative is likely to win little support among Americans, who may divorce at record rates, but who also remarry at record rates. It is also an attack on family life, which continues to be one of the few strongholds in our society against depersonalized authority.[10] In my view, the Left should defend family life and argue against the inequalities structured into its patriarchal form. It should stress role sharing and egalitarian interdependence both as a means for improving parents' lives and as the foundation of an institution that frees male and female children to test their will, respect one another regardless of gender, and stake out their own sense of authority and independence. Furthermore, the Left might argue that family life is so important to future citizenship that facilitating mechanisms, like job sharing, accessible day-care centers, and related services, are social necessities.

Childhood predispositions are elaborated and sometimes changed in daily social intercourse outside of family life. Daily social intercourse is mediated by language, symbols, and expectations, which at least partly shape people's perceptions and cognitions. How Americans speak, think, and act toward one another is important in terms of their ability to be receptive to civic education or to educate themselves about civic duties and rights. Let me suggest that class inequalities in American society limit the ability of a majority of Americans to become active and knowledgeable citizens.

Roughly speaking, middle-class Americans—including workers who have risen to the middle class or identify with it—learn the language games (or what is sometimes called Standard Dialect) that emphasize empirical, positivistic, and pragmatic meanings. They tend to occupy symbolic and mythic worlds that valorize feelings of efficacy and engagement in social action. They are apt to work and play within a framework of social expectations that reinforces instrumental attitudes, including conventional attitudes toward health, sanity, happiness, and success, that are goal oriented. In sum, middle-class Americans perceive the world in terms of getting things done; they are problem solvers and expect that hard work will result in solutions.[11]

However, life on Main Street is sustained by an identifiable closure of perceptions and cognitions. Middle-class Americans have a difficult time expressing noninstrumental feelings of affection or community, either because the words are not there or because they are ritualized as popular psychology. Middle-class people often screen out perceptions that might conflict with their view that individual hard work will pay off; rather, they are likely to see individual laziness or ignorance at the root of failure. Finally, middle-class Americans are quite intolerant, myths to the contrary notwithstanding. They often condemn unconventional behavior as idiosyncratic, sinful, or sick, calling for therapeutic treatment. Let us not forget that the intolerance that fed McCarthyism yesterday and the New Right today stems mainly from the middle class.[12] This composite portrays the middle class as efficacious and active but also as one-dimensional in its view of society.

Lower-class Americans—including unskilled workers, the under-employed, and the permanently unemployed—inhabit very different worlds of social intercourse. They are more likely to learn language games and nonstandard dialects that facilitate the expression of affection and community, which are for them necessities for everyday survival. They are more adept at creating symbols and myths that make conspicuous their poverty in order to make poverty bearable by humorizing it or by fateful resignation to it. In a certain sense, lower-class Americans tolerate an extraordinarily broad range of behaviors; these are part of people's attempt to cope with marginality and impoverished lives. [13] Put another way, poor people do not have much sense of efficacy, but they do have a fairly accurate understanding of their subordination in American society and a fairly sophisticated set of skills for surviving it.

If these class portraits are roughly accurate, then it follows that a majority of Americans are ill-prepared to learn the most fundamental lessons of citizenship. Middle-class Americans are best outfitted to participate actively in what Murray Edelman calls symbolic politics. They are politically active in an uninformed way. They rally behind politicians whose promises mean the most to them but whose actions produce the least for them; they direct their activism toward government agencies that sound powerful but are not, while government agencies and private institutions that are powerful are usually insulated from middle-class activism. [14] Lower-class Americans rarely take an active role in shaping social life, if only because they are overwhelmed by the demands of everyday survival. At times, they may avoid political engagement even when it offers opportunities for change; at times, they may tolerate and even applaud the guile of the ghetto hustler who uses political influence to line his own wallet. [15] Working-class Americans occupy an ambiguous position in the social structure between middle-class aspirations and ever-present lower-class realities. This generates an ambivalence that makes working-class people vulnerable to elite-dominated cuing processes, which intensify feelings of efficacy or apathy in ways that suit elites' interests. In sum, class society in the United States prepares a majority of people to participate in the illusions of symbolic politics, to participate little if at all, or to suffer the ambivalence that deprives them of autonomy; class society in the United States does not make people receptive to combining activism and accurate knowledge or political power and community support and tolerance as the bases for conscientious consent and citizenship.

Class society must be changed if it is to serve as a foundation for conscientious consent and citizenship. Since class revolution is not in the offing, change must involve reforms that redistribute power and wealth in ways that blunt the negative effects of class variations and build on the positive aspects of class differences. The middle class needs more power in order to combine its activism with an experiential education in self-management, which might alert it to the benefits of mutual aid and tolerance in a community of decision makers; the lower class needs more power in order to put its concerns on the national agenda and more wealth to free its members to participate in the making of that agenda; and the working class needs more power and wealth with which to found the autonomy necessary for resisting elite hegemony and for developing its own perspective on citizenship. Where is this power and wealth to come from? The Left should argue that the U.S. upper class is the only class to benefit from current class divisions and Americans' inability to be conscientious citizens, and that the upper class must be forced to cede its concentrated power and wealth if consent of the governed is to be a reality.

Ultimately, the concentrated power and wealth of elites is an assault on all prerequisites to consent. It allows elites to withhold information necessary for informed consent; it denies the political equality assumed by consent; and it undermines the economic independence that makes voluntary consent possible. However, concentrated power and wealth is an assault that is less threatening to white Americans than to American minorities.

Elites in the United States are white elites who have grown up in white families and generally in white communities; they take for granted many of the rights and opportunities that American minorities have barely known and have never been secure in; they have virtually no experience in and little awareness of the special problems plaguing minorities. In this sense, U.S. elites make decisions that are informed by a distinctly "white perspective" and that are, therefore, more representative of the interests of white people than of minorities.[16] Furthermore, the fact that these elites wield power of a nationwide scope ties them even more closely to white interests. They are open mainly to the demands of white Americans, who constitute the majority of voters, petitioners, and consumers in the country as a whole. Because white Americans are comparatively well-off, they are likely to make the most moderate demands on elites and are, therefore, the most likely to win concessions from elites. These concessions may bear little relationship to the needs of minorities, who for example, might find demands for environmentalism or the Equal Rights Amendment extravagances, when better public housing or municipal transportation are immediate, pressing concerns.[17]

Concentrated power and wealth are far removed from the local arenas, where minorities have some leverage. White elites secluded in their Washington offices or Wall Street boardrooms have little com-

merce with minorities, whereas white elites situated in communities
and neighborhoods sometimes come into daily contact with the minorities whose lives they affect. National elites are not particularly vulnerable to minorities, who have little national voting power or buying
power, whereas local elites are more likely to be sensitive to minority votes and dollars, which are aggregated in small geographical
areas. Centralized elites can usually meet minority demands with
symbolic gestures, whereas local elites are forced to confront the
frustrations or tangible dissatisfactions of minorities. In April 1982
the official unemployment rate for the nation was a catastrophic 9 percent; for American blacks, it was 18 percent. [18] These very conservative figures indicate, quite simply, that white Americans are less
unfree, unequal, and dependent than black Americans.

Minorities must be situated to be more free, equal, and independent if they are to play their appropriate role in the United States
as consenting citizens. The Left might argue that a decentralization
of political and economic power to minority communities is a necessary first step. It would provide minorities with the resources necessary to defend their own rights, to shape the content of their own
political associations, and to begin to solve many of the social problems elites either ignore or have an interest in continuing. The American Left might emulate the black power militants of the 1960s by advocating community control of political, economic, and social relations as a justifiable and necessary condition for enhancing the autonomy of millions of Americans.

This brief journey into American social life is admittedly sim-
plistic. It does not encompass the complex interrelations between
sexual, class, and racial inequalities; it does not consider other important inequalities that impoverish American political life, citizenship, and the conditions for consent. However, this analysis should
indicate that most Americans are born into a set of social relations
that combine to deny them the freedom, equality, and independence
at the very heart of Lockean consent theory. These social relations
must be changed, democratized in radical ways, if men and women;
middle-class, working-class, and lower-class Americans; and American minorities are to play their rightful role as conscientious citizens. Greater sexual, class, and racial equality, mediated by values
like reciprocity, community, and decentralization, give substance
to radical democracy as an American Left identity and to the legitimate prerequisites to the actual consent Americans continue to demand as their procedural right.

RADICAL DEMOCRACY AND GOVERNMENT

The legitimation of radical democratic society has two implications for how the American Left should understand political processes of change. First, the American Left must advocate notions of free will, individual responsibility, and self-reliance; of self-education and civic education; and of reason and fairness as necessary conditions for democratic change. Second, however, the Left must avoid the trap of considering these necessary half steps as sufficient conditions for democratic change. Rather, it must come to terms with government as a potential instrument for democratic change and as a potential arena for democratic practices.

There is no question that the impetus for democratic change must come from the bottom up. Democratic means for change are most consistent with achieving democratic ends, and equally important, the demos itself is the only force in society with an interest in democratic changes. Certainly, political and economic elites do not want them.

Bottom-up changes involve democratic dialogue as a means and as an end in itself. Kenneth Dolbeare writes, "As one becomes more aware of the nature and limiting effects of one's present consciousness, and begins to take part with others in the process of self-reconstruction, one also begins to have a consciousness-changing impact on those others."[19] In a sense, individuals must free their wills from illusions, take responsibility for their lives, and engage in the self-help necessary for overcoming adverse social conditions. They can work together in small groups in ways that illuminate their preconscious, symbolic, and social worlds; sensitize their perceptions and cognitions to the politics of social life; and elucidate the power relations that constrict social interaction. By so doing, these individuals free themselves to explore the fuller range of their human selves and to appreciate the human needs they share with others. In the process, they may serve as examples for their neighbors to emulate.

Democratic dialogue can then inform democratic participation in individuals' everyday lives. As individuals work together to unveil the biases of patriarchal family life, they may participate in experiments to create nonpatriarchal families that enrich relations between genders and better prepare children for active, informed citizenship. They may investigate their own language games and cognitive screens and even create new language patterns (for example, the counterculture), new symbolic mediations (for example, the closed fist of black militants), and new modes of acceptance (for example, gay liberation). In their interpersonal relations, they can develop alternative power structures, which foster open discourse rather than silence or equal respect in place of domination and subordination. Through their own participation, individuals can educate themselves to the rights and responsibilities as well as the skills of citizenship.

Furthermore, democratic participation can be the basis for democratic political organizations involving Alinsky-style mobilizations of neighborhoods and communities. These organizations can provide people a fair sense of the different ways religious groups, racial groups, and others view community life and of the common concerns that cut across social barriers. They can provide people with a reasonable understanding of politics, political skills, and political leverage, which might empower them to exercise greater influence in their own localities. Moreover, they may serve as mechanisms for winning small but important victories that, according to Harry C. Boyte, are "the lifeblood of successful grassroots organizing, the only way that those accustomed to defeat and disunity can be welded together into a powerful collective acting in their own behalf."[20]

Boyte may be right in estimating that more than 20 million Americans have become involved in such neighborhood groups, composed of relatively powerless people hoping to empower themselves. This is a positive sign that American democratic traditions persist and can be invigorated, but its meaning and potential should not be overestimated. Consciousness raising in small groups can easily backfire. For example, feminists today sometimes feel that their forays into women's consciousness raising in the 1970s often provided people with tools and arguments for personalizing change rather than cooperating to alter adverse social conditions.[21] Even skilled participation in local politics is unlikely to provide the kind of education that would enable people to assert power over the political and economic elites who determine the parameters of local decisions; it may even help people accommodate themselves to those parameters. Alinsky-style mobilizations, even when combined in local or regional coalitions, do not offer to accomplish much more than to make people's movements more competitive in the pluralist arena. Bottom-up changes are important for initiating mass support for radical democracy; but they are likely to be temporary phenomena, assimilated to mainstream politics, unless explicitly connected with a theory of radical democracy that focuses on citizen activism.

The immediate focus may be on the social institutions where people spend most of their time: schools, workplaces, and communities. These institutions certainly reproduce the inequalities that impoverish democracy, but they also contain democratic potentials that can be drawn out and politicized. Schools may prepare individuals to fill corporate slots, but they also provide spaces for critical thinking and questioning; workplaces may be the location where economic sub-

ordination is practiced, but they also afford worker grievance and
participation procedures, which give the economy democratic content;
communities are usually on the receiving end of externally determined
elite decisions that constrict community power, but communities also
have leverage over local land usage and resources, which can be used
to publicize and contest elite decisions. Perhaps equal in importance
to the minor democratic victories to be won is the politicization of the
social institutions and issues that most concern Americans.

Politicization takes once-silent concerns and converts them into
disputable issues that are potentially subject to change. Politicization
relocates issues from the private realm to the public realm, where
government must act on them. Politicization of issues is a test of
government's democratic credentials. Does government as a whole
articulate, act on, and administer the will of the people? Or does
government as a whole deny consent of the governed by ignoring or
silencing the public? In large part, citizen activism must be focused
on government, because it is the one ongoing institution in American
society powerful enough to make significant changes in American social relations.

If existing social conditions in the United States do not provide
people with the rudiments of consent, then most people have not consented to be governed. When they take oaths of allegience, vote and
petition, or accept government benefits, their actions should be construed as measures of expedience rather than as declarations of consent. However, I do not want to carry this argument to unreasonable
extremes. Social conditions in the United States do not entirely conspire against the freedom, equality, and independence required for
consent. In important ways, Americans are better positioned to consent than most people in the world. This is why, in fact, a bottom-up
mobilization for radical democracy is conceivable in the United States.
Consequently, it is fair to say that Americans are partially situated
to consent; are partial participants who give their partial consent;
and therefore, have partially legitimated the U.S. government. What
is the function of a partially legitimate government? Is it to administer natural law and rights, as Locke suggested, for a fully legitimate
government? If so, what natural law and rights are at stake?

In modern America, the most fundamental truths or natural
rights are disputed. Creationists find one set of truths in the Bible,
while evolutionists discover a different set of truths in modern scientific theory. Neither religious people nor advocates of modern science
agree among themselves on which stories or interpretations best capture truths. Similarly, the most "self-evident" rights are disputed.
Prolife groups believe in self-evident rights for fetuses, while pro-
abortion groups articulate self-evident rights for women; landlords

claim rights to dispose of their property without constraints, but tenants claim rights to security from unjust evictions. The contest for law and nature and rights is carried on in almost every pocket of American life.

These disputes take an acute political form when they spill over into considerations of government's appropriate function in society. If its proper role is to administer natural law and rights, it is not obvious which natural law and rights are the authoritative ones. Should government avoid the dilemma by simply maintaining peace and order? What kind of peace inside of what kind of order? Perhaps government's main job is to manage crises. Which crisis, how, and with whose resources? Today, Americans do not agree on what their government is about, proving Tocqueville correct to worry that a society without traditional authority lacks the spiritual cement to bind its members together.

Scholars provide us two main routes for bypassing this dilemma. First, Michael Walzer argues that "consent theory suggests a procedural rather than a substantive ethics."[22] From this perspective, those who consent to be governed also determine how they are to be governed. Their various modes of participation, ranging from intense commitments to voluntary groups to more routinized involvement in elections, are the procedures by which people define for themselves the substantive direction of government. Since there is likely to be substantial disagreement, people must have maximal freedom to practice civil disobedience in order to keep the dialogue going. In large part, the function of government is to protect people's right to civil disobedience, so that political conflicts can be worked out in society.

The main problem with this route is that the same social conditions that impoverish consent also militate against public agreement either on the norms that define political society or on the processes that allow people to define government's function for themselves. As we have seen, men and women, people from different classes, and whites and minorities are predisposed to view the political world through different lenses, each of which inhibits their autonomy. While they may be able to coalesce in small, limited groups to work out a consensus on political norms, that consensus is likely to be opposed by other groups, and group competition itself may take place in a vacuum created by powerful elites. Furthermore, there is little reason to believe that Americans can agree on a set of adversarial procedures, including ones for civil disobedience, for articulating or tolerating their different viewpoints. "It is a very 'low' order of consent," writes P. H. Partridge, "which constitutes the foundation of support for the most general forms of procedure and processes of government."[23] No matter how fair, any procedure can be disputed because it can be contaminated by the superior ability of elites to use it to their advantage; it will be disputed if it generates policies at odds with Americans' diverse notions of how government should be functioning.

Second, Alan Gewirth tries to avoid this dilemma by augmenting the processes of consent with a lowest-common-denominator standard of common good. He writes, "It is not contradictory to say that the decision reached by the democratic process turned out not to be for the common good. And it is not tautological to say that what the democratic process was trying to achieve, or at least the standard by which it is to be evaluated, is the common good."[24] Gewirth believes that the common good should inform people engaged in consent processes and serve as a standard to judge their outcomes. This is possible because the essentials of the common good are obvious. "Many interests are obviously common to a whole society," Gewirth suggests, including "clothing, food stuffs, reading matter."[25] Thus, government should be understood as an arena serving public choice and adjusting it to the common good.

However, the common good is not obvious to Americans. At an academic level, the debates between Rawls and his critics demonstrate fundamental disagreement over the nature of the common good. In Washington, the current battles over which welfare programs should be gutted without alienating too many constituents reveal a serious lack of agreement in this country regarding what aspects of the common good are worth saving. In the end, the common good is another name for natural law and rights, which by any other name, are still disputed.

The problem with both ways of defining the role of government is as old as Rousseau. "Doubtless, there is a universal justice emanating from reason alone; but this justice, to be admitted among us, must be mutual."[26] Any standard of good that informs government can be undermined if people consent on other terms; and any process of consent is endangered if it is challenged as resulting in something other than what is good. Philosophically, Rousseau solved the problem by posing the General Will, but in the United States the social preconditions for creating a General Will do not exist. What, then, is the mandate of a partially legitimate government? Let me suggest that it has an obligation to foster greater freedom, equality, and independence in society so that people can become consenters and present government with a legitimate mandate. In other words, the U.S. government today must be a force for democratizing society.

When individuals consent to government, a reciprocal process occurs. Individuals take on the obligations of political membership, which includes a duty to obey government; and government, as the official representative of other members, has the right to expect that individuals will honor their duty to obey. Just as corporations can be considered legal persons, governments can be considered moral agents. "There is a sense in which an institution is an agent. For it operates by imposing obligations on persons who participate in it, so that the latter are in a position of recipients of the institution's operations."[27] Furthermore, the U. S. government should be considered a moral agent. To turn Tussman on his head, the U. S. government should be considered a politically immature moral agent. Because consent of the governed is at least partial in the United States, government is not purely an instrument of a ruling class; because consent of the governed is only partial, government is not purely an instrument of people's will. Located at the intersection of mass demands and elite interests, U. S. government has an uncertain range of autonomy in mediating social relations. This autonomy is the foundation of its moral agency. Can government be "educated" to become a mature moral agent?

As a moral agent, government can be held responsible for the persistence of social conditions that undermine full consent. Either through its active participation or tacit tolerance, the U. S. government has reinforced patriarchal family life; it has propagated terms, myths, and symbols that foster symbolic participation and mass quiescence; and it has been complicit in the centralization of power, which impoverishes political life in general and minority influence in particular. Certainly, government cannot be held responsible for all social relations that undermine self-mastery, but it is powerful enough and autonomous enough to have left its mark on American social life.

Government has played a major role in diminishing public authority and empowering private corporations. Originally, the Anglo-American idea of the corporation was "an exclusive grant by the state to a private company for the purpose of providing something that was in the common interest of the whole society."[28] Corporations were viewed as special creations of the state, agents responsible to the state, and instruments for achieving state-mediated goals of public welfare; they were to pursue public purposes first, private profits second. In the course of U. S. history, government took an active part in converting corporations from public-oriented agencies into limited liability ventures for private profit. "By the end of the Civil War," writes Alan Wolfe, "the notion of the corporation as an agency of public good was as dead as chivalry."[29] Government created the monster and then set it loose to achieve unlimited accumulations of wealth, which now allow it to assault people's freedom, equality, and independence. To the extent that government continues to subsidize and support corporations, it must bear part of the responsibility for mass impotence.

In our courtrooms, it is common to expect that moral agents who err have an obligation to undo their mistakes, if possible; thus, the convicted thief must restore stolen goods to their owner. Similarly, it is reasonable to expect that a government that errs has an obligation to undo its mistakes, in this case, by actively defending and extending the radical democratic relations necessary for consent. [30] It can enact and administer a number of reforms that have precedence and do not directly challenge existing social structures. Its tax laws, marriage and family laws, zoning laws, and inheritance laws could be rewritten to facilitate experimentation with nonpatriarchal family life. Government could support and subsidize middle-class groups, which enrich social life with new language games, symbols, and roles; lower-class groups, which foster political involvement and self-management skills; and working-class groups, which stop shutdowns by taking over ownership. Furthermore, government could take the lead in enacting reforms that decentralize significant powers to communities and thus provide minorities or Alinsky-style organizations greater political and economic leverage. None of these suggestions are new or even particularly radical; most of them have been tested in the welfare state. Taken together, however, they do imply a new understanding of the function of government; its main job is not to engage in social control by engineering consent but to be an agency that uses its power to enhance democratic dialogue, participation, and control.

At a second level, government could serve as a vehicle for people to articulate their economic will and to regain control over their material lives. Government could be a force for reestablishing the principle that corporations are state creations, state agents, and instruments for achieving public goals. On the basis of this principle, government could initially enact and enforce open disclosure laws, which would reveal the true nature, extent, and impact of corporate activities today. If Left analyses of corporate capitalism are only half correct, then disclosure should make clear that most corporations are publicly irresponsible and thus generate a wave of anticorporate sentiment far greater than at present. Emboldened, government might pursue any number of policy avenues that converge in attempts to subordinate corporate elites and diminish corporate autonomy. Regulations could be fortified, antitrust laws enforced, worker and consumer representation on investment boards institutionalized, shutdowns forbidden or perhaps turned over to workers and communities, and more. Simultaneously, government could become a champion of people's economic rights, which might include rights to national health insurance, healthy work environments, worker participation in shop floor decisions, or community control over local business practices. Again, none of these suggestions are new or untried;

they do imply that government efforts ought to be directed toward sapping corporate power by supporting democratic planning and participation mechanisms.

At a third and progressively more radical level, government could be considered obligated to lead the way in restructuring American social institutions, which now deprive people of the ability to consent. This is a reciprocal process whereby people free themselves from old constraints and are freed by a government of their own making. John Wild puts it this way: "Individuals are not innately free and responsible. If they are to become free, they must decide this on their own. They may be helped, however, by the processes of formal and informal education."[31] Americans must demand democratic freedoms in order to get government to fulfill its obligations, and government must take the lead in educating society by changing undemocratic institutions or facilitating group efforts to do so. This may entail a redistribution of wealth from the top down to provide wealth enough for workers and lower-class people to assert their independence, demand the equality they have been promised, and take full advantage of the freedoms they could never quite afford. This may also entail a redistribution of political power from the top down to guarantee that the privileged will be in no position to defend the reproduction of mass dependence. One might go so far as to argue that the U.S. government is obligated to help free people to consent by leading the way to democratic socialism in the United States, the final wedding between Locke and Marx.

In the hypothetical event that the U.S. government actually recognized such obligations and acted to fulfill them, then it would certainly foster the social conditions that better situate people to consent. But would people so situated actually give their consent? Would they be in a better position to agree on procedures for defining government's function or on substantive standards of justice? Conceivably, most Americans would recognize that they have benefited, both personally and socially, from the radical democratization of society and would therefore consent to the government processes and policies that enhance continued democratization. In this sense, radical democracy could be the means and ends of government. However, it is also true that people who are well situated to consent are well situated to dissent, too. They may contest particular government actions with some regularity. Would regular dissent make society ungovernable, as Samuel P. Huntington recently argued?[32]

Dissent is not an antisocial act. To the contrary, it is a conscientious, voluntary act that calls on other members of society to reevaluate the norms that inform government and the actions that issue from government. Dissent is a plea to expand democratic dialogue, to extend modes of democratic participation, and to recognize that the people, not government, are sovereign. Regular dissent may even be taken as evidence that consent is alive and well. According to Hannah Arendt, "Dissent implies consent, and is the hallmark of free government; one who knows that he may dissent knows also that he somehow consents when he does not dissent."[33] Dissent does create disorder, which does not fit neatly into abstract logic; but it can create the disorder of a people struggling to define its life together. Democracy and dissent require one another.

My goal in this chapter is to develop a theory that legitimates democratic mobilizations in society and government as an agent for democratizing society. I am not predicting that ambivalent Americans are prepared to enroll in such mobilizations or that a U.S. government held captive by elites is likely to recognize its function as a democratic agent. I am not suggesting that Americans cannot take democratic initiatives or that the U.S. government is hopelessly bound to elite hegemony. These are simply possibilities that can be explored in the future. The object of a theory of radical democracy is to see that they are explored. It is to articulate a Left vision that identifies radicals with American traditions, which can be communicated to attract popular support and encourage Americans to test whether this society and government can be educated to practice radical democracy and, thus, to reunite popular consent and popular control.

THEORY AND POLITICS

Lockean consent theory provides grounds for political obligation and government legitimacy. People are obligated to obey government when they have consented to it; people are not obligated to obey when they have not consented. Government is legitimate when founded on popular consent; government is illegitimate when popular consent is lacking. The radical democratic version of consent theory developed in this chapter also contains notions of political obligation and government legitimacy, which can be used as practical guidelines for Left politics in the United States.

In political arenas where Americans have maximal freedom, equality, and independence, and have consented to government, radicals have an obligation to respect conventional political processes. This is a moral obligation that should be fulfilled, at the very least, because most Americans believe in it. Fulfillment testifies to radicals' respect for people and for their preferred ways to articulate and administer their needs and desires; it announces that radicals are democrats. This is also good politics. People who are socially situated to practice informed, democratic dialogue are likely to be receptive to radical messages, which are broadcast through electioneering, petitioning, door-to-door canvassing, and voluntary organizations. People who are socially situated so that their consent gives them a measure of control over government can conceivably use government as an arena and means for converting radical messages into everyday realities. In the next chapter, I will argue that such political arenas do exist in the United States, though mainly at the level of community politics.

Conversely, in political arenas where Americans have minimal freedom, equality, and independence, and therefore, have minimally consented to government, neither they nor radicals have an obligation to obey government or recognize its legitimacy. In these arenas, Left politics can be guided by expedience alone. Because a politics of expedience involves a high degree of uncertainty, radicals should expect it to be characterized by considerable disagreement and disorder. That may be good. Disagreement and disorder can be the basis for a commitment to recognize that THE WAY still does not exist and that democratic experimentation is required if the Left is to avoid reproducing its history of failures. Furthermore, disagreement and disorder, though following no neat logic, may be the means by which to politicize social issues, like worker control, and to socialize political issues, like foreign policy. I will argue that these political arenas exist mainly at the level of national politics.

Finally, in political arenas where Americans' self-mastery is subject to dispute, the degree of their consent questionable, and government's legitimacy open to question, one can expect radicals to disagree on how to apply these guidelines. Predictably, radical liberals will prefer to work within mainstream politics, socialists in opposition to it, and activists caught somewhere in the middle. This is a situation when Left unity around some notion of radical democracy is crucial. If radicals can agree to keep the conversation going among themselves, they may discover a Left division of political labor that enhances mainstream participation without assimilation and opposition without isolation, which combine to make the Left a visible force in the contest for democracy.

NOTES

1. William A. Williams, "Procedure Becomes Substance," Democracy 2, no. 2 (April 1982): 102.
2. See Robert Booth Fowler, "Political Obligation and the Draft," in Obligation and Dissent, ed. Donald Hanson and Robert Booth

Fowler (Boston: Little, Brown, 1971), p. 47; see also Robert Nozick, Anarchy, State, and Utopia (New York: Basic Books, 1974); and George Gilder, Wealth and Poverty (New York: Bantam, 1981).

3. John P. Plamenatz, Consent, Freedom, and Political Obligation (London: Oxford University Press, 1968), p. 11.

4. Joseph Tussman, Obligation and the Body Politic (London: Oxford University Press, 1960), p. 36.

5. See Russell Jacoby, "The Politics of Narcissism," in The Problem of Authority in America, ed. John P. Diggins and Mark E. Kann (Philadelphia: Temple University Press, 1981), pp. 185-94.

6. John Rawls, A Theory of Justice (Cambridge, Mass.: Harvard University Press, 1971), p. 13; for an earlier but related argument, see Hanna Pitkin, "Obligation and Consent—I," American Political Science Review 59 (December 1965): 990-99.

7. For further discussion, see Mark E. Kann, "Consent and Authority in America," in The Problem of Authority in America, ed. John P. Diggins and Mark E. Kann (Philadelphia: Temple University Press, 1981), pp. 70-76.

8. In part, these reformulated questions are consistent with Jurgen Habermas's interest in ideal speech situations as prerequisites to social justice.

9. See Jane Flax, "Tragedy or Emancipation?: On the 'Decline' of Contemporary American Families," in The Future of American Democracy: Views from the Left, ed. Mark E. Kann (Philadelphia: Temple University Press, 1983), chap. 4.

10. For an interesting and innovative analysis, see Zelda Bronstein, "Psychoanalysis without Father," Humanities in Society 3, no. 2 (Spring 1980): 199-212.

11. This portrait is drawn from a rather large and, unfortunately, amorphous literature. Some of the references are the May 1978 issue of Radical Teacher on the politics of literacy; Kenneth Dolbeare, Political Change in the United States: A Framework in Analysis (New York: McGraw-Hill, 1974), pp. 92, 106 ff.; Melvin Kohn, Class and Conformity: A Study of Values (Homewood, Ill.: Dorsey Press, 1969); Thomas Szasz, Ideology and Insanity (Garden City, N.Y.: Doubleday, 1970); Sidney Verba and Norman Nie, Participation in America (New York: Harper & Row, 1972); and Edgar Litt's classic study, "Civic Education, Community Norms, and Political Indoctrination," American Sociological Review 28 (March 1963): 69-75.

12. See Richard F. Hamilton, Class and Politics in the United States (New York: Wiley, 1972), pp. 115 ff.; Bonnie Cook Freeman, "Antifeminists and Women's Liberation: A Case Study of Paradox," unpublished paper; and the classic article by S. M. Miller and Frank Riessman, "'Working-class Authoritarianism': A Critique of Lipset," British Journal of Sociology, September 1961, p. 272.

13. In addition to the literature cited in note 11, I have found these works useful: J. L. Dillard, Black English: Its History and Usage in America (New York: Vintage, 1972); Elliot Liebow, Tally's Corner (Boston: Little, Brown, 1967); Joe R. Feagin, Subordinating the Poor: Welfare and American Beliefs (Englewood Cliffs, N.J.: Prentice-Hall, 1975); and Richard A. Cloward and Francis Fox Piven, The Politics of Turmoil: Essays on Poverty, Race, and the Urban Crisis (New York: Pantheon, 1974).

14. See Murray Edelman, "The Future of American Politics," in The Future of American Democracy: Views from the Left, ed. Mark E. Kann (Philadelphia: Temple University Press, 1983), chap. 10; see also idem, The Symbolic Uses of Politics (Urbana: University of Illinois, 1964); idem, Politics as Symbolic Action (Chicago: Markham, 1971); and idem, Political Language: Words That Succeed and Policies That Fail (New York: Academic, 1977).

15. See Edelman, Politics as Symbolic Action, pp. 116–17.

16. "Our basic need," wrote Stokely Carmichael and Charles V. Hamilton in 1967, "is to reclaim our history and our identity from what must be called cultural terrorism, from the depredation of self-justifying white guilt." Their point was that even ostensible white friends to black people's movements do not easily, if at all, understand minorities' situations, interests, and needs. See their Black Power: The Politics of Liberation in America (New York: Vintage, 1967), pp. 34–35.

17. See Lester Thurow, The Zero-sum Society (New York: Penguin, 1981), p. 105; and Karen Kollias, "Class Realities: Create a New Power Base," in Building Feminist Theory: Essays from Quest, a Feminist Quarterly, ed. Charlotte Bunch et al. (New York: Longman, 1981), pp. 125–38.

18. Reported in Los Angeles Times, April 3, 1982.

19. Dolbeare, Political Change in the United States, p. 21; see also Christian Bay, The Structure of Freedom (Stanford, Calif.: Stanford University Press, 1958), p. 267.

20. Harry C. Boyte, The Backyard Revolution: Understanding the New Citizen Movement (Philadelphia: Temple University Press, 1980), p. 51.

21. See Nancy Hartsock, "Political Change: Two Perspectives on Power," in Building Feminist Theory: Essays from Quest, a Feminist Quarterly, ed. Charlotte Bunch et al. (New York: Longman, 1981), p. 7.

22. Michael Walzer, Obligations: Essays on Disobedience, War, and Citizenship (New York: Clarion, 1970), p. viii.

23. P. H. Partridge, Consent and Consensus (New York: Praeger, 1971), pp. 57–58; see also Samuel P. Huntington, "The United States," in The Crisis of Democracy: Report on the Govern-

ability of Democracies to the Trilateral Commission, ed. Michel Crozier, Samuel P. Huntington, and Joji Watanuki (New York: New York University Press, 1975), pp. 75-76.

24. Alan Gewirth, "Political Justice," in Social Justice, ed. R. B. Brandt (Englewood Cliffs, N.J.: Prentice-Hall, 1962), p. 160.

25. Ibid., pp. 161-62.

26. Jean-Jacques Rousseau, Social Contract and Discourses, trans. G. D. H. Cole (New York: Dutton, 1950), p. 34.

27. Alan Gewirth, "Obligations: Political, Legal, Moral," in Political and Legal Obligation, ed. J. Roland Pennock and John W. Chapman, Nomos 12 (New York: Atherton, 1970), pp. 72, 80.

28. Alan Wolfe, The Limits of Legitimacy: Political Contradictions of Contemporary Capitalism (New York: Free Press, 1977), p. 21.

29. Ibid., p. 22.

30. I make this argument in greater detail in Mark E. Kann, "A Standard for Democratic Leadership," Polity 12, no. 2 (Winter 1979): 202-24.

31. Compare John Wild, "The Need for a Philosophy of Democracy," in Existential Phenomenology and Political Theory: A Reader, ed. Hwa Yol Jung (Chicago: Regnery, 1972), p. 384; and Robert Paul Wolff, In Defense of Anarchism (New York: Harper & Row, 1970), pp. 18-19.

32. Huntington, "United States," pp. 113-15.

33. Hannah Arendt, Crises of the Republic (New York: Harcourt Brace Jovanovich, 1972), p. 88.

8

POLITICAL
FORTUNES

U. S. elites are vulnerable to schisms in their own ranks and
to the public distrust, which makes their rule by consent increasingly
difficult. Radical democracy is a perspective that is potentially useful for taking advantage of elites' vulnerability and for providing an
alternative, egalitarian construction of American reality. This is
not the first time in U. S. history that elites have faced a crisis of
consent and that the American Left has had a new array of opportunities. But this may be the first time that the American Left is prepared to practice a politics that may give it permanent visibility,
significant public support, and ongoing influence. To the extent that
the American Left recognizes its historical failures and converges
on radical democratic terrain, it has a good chance to renew its political fortunes.

MAINSTREAMING WITHOUT ASSIMILATION

Should the American Left participate in mainstream politics?
Absolutely! Its choice is ceding the mainstream to conservatives and
liberals, who will surely use institutionalized power to shore up elitist structures and to occupy people's political thinking, or to enter
into mainstream contests, condemn elitism, and offer alternatives to
it. Conventional politics, after all, remains the most visible and
potent arena for shaping people's conceptions of what is possible and,
therefore, for molding America's future. The more interesting questions involve where the Left should enter into the mainstream and
how it can do so without reproducing its history of assimilation.

My theory of radical democracy suggests that the Left should
enter into the mainstream in arenas where people have enough self-

mastery to exert some control over decision making and actually do so. These arenas provide public space for the growth of democratic grass-roots movements in which people begin to restructure social relations from the bottom up and for the transformation of government into a democratic forum, which might be useful for restructuring social relations from the top down. One can often locate these arenas at the level of community politics.

Consider the recent experience of Santa Monica, California, a city of 90,000 people who are mostly in moderate income brackets and are mainly renters.[1] In the 1970s radicals began to organize around the issue of rent control. They formed the Santa Monicans for Renters' Rights (SMRR) in 1979, which brought together left-wing Democrats, activists from Tom Hayden's Campaign for Economic Democracy, and the youthful and aged members of the Santa Monica Fair Housing Alliance. In time, the coalition expanded its focus beyond rent control to community control issues and grew to include progressive labor locals as well. Using Alinsky-style tactics, the SMRR helped to build community support for democratic control over local social life and for electing progressives to city government. By April 1981 this grass-roots movement succeeded in winning a strong rent control charter amendment, a city council majority, a progressive mayor, and majority representation on the elected rent control board. What some people call the People's Republic of Santa Monica was established.

Local government changed in two ways. Once a forum for discussion among developers and real estate interests, it now became a sphere for expressing, discussing, and compromising the perspectives of diverse community groups. In addition, local government became a force for democratizing community life. It redirected Community Development Block Grant funds to neighborhood organizations in the poorer and minority sections of the city. It helped to involve people in neighborhood crime control programs. It named citizen task forces to consider innovative housing policies, which include city-financed and tenant-managed apartments and new zoning laws, or to work out plans for upgrading the status of women in the community. It organized an open-air farmers' market. It began to institute worker participation and self-management among city employees. It declared in word and deed its support for union rights, and it served as one base for opposition against irresponsible corporate decisions that affect city residents. The important point to note is that Santa Monica is not unique. Cities like Berkeley, California, and Hartford, Connecticut, have recently had similar experiences with progressive government.[2]

Grass-roots movements have been the foundation for many progressive electoral victories in the last decade. Electoral victories have gone to Mayors Paul Soglin of Madison, Wisconsin, and Dennis Kucinich of Cleveland, Ohio; to Judges Justin Ravitz of Detroit, Michigan, and Jose Angel Gutierez of Zavala County, Texas; and to scores of city council members throughout the nation. In addition, more than a few feminist candidates and progressive minority candidates now occupy local offices once reserved for white males only. Many of these electoral victories have allowed radicals to fill appointive offices with other radicals or people sensitive to radical concerns. The message that I read from this experience is that community politics is one arena in which Americans can exercise some free will, educate themselves in participation and citizenship skills, and use conventional procedures to capture local governments and use them as the bases for winning more democracy.

Grass-roots politics provides people some influence within and even beyond their own communities. Massachusetts Fair Share helped get utility-rate reforms on the ballot; Chicago's Citizen Action Program thwarted the political machine's attempt to build a crosstown expressway, which would have destroyed multiracial neighborhoods; tenants' groups throughout the country have won legislation to limit owners' power to raise rents indiscriminately, to discriminate against various social groups (including children), and to ignore building maintenance.[3] Since 1971 Seattle's Public Health Care Coalition has worked with great success to prevent the Public Health Service from turning over its local hospital to private entrepreneurs.[4] Dennis Kucinich was able to use his political position to organize pressure against tax abatements in Cleveland.[5] Harry C. Boyte's The Backyard Revolution chronicles many grass-roots successes, the evolution of citizen activism from community to regional associations, and their influence on statewide and even national issues.[6] Elites may dominate the interest-group marketplace, but the experiences of the 1970s demonstrate that elite hegemony is far from complete. Community activism and regional coalitions have competed in the interest-group marketplace with remarkable success.

Several lessons can be learned from these experiences. One lesson, according to Derek Shearer, is that "a democratic movement, which argues that a city exists first for the needs of its citizens rather than for the needs of capital, has the potential of winning majority support in municipal elections."[7] Radical democracy can be a useful perspective for articulating people's concerns and involving them in an egalitarian movement to replace elitism with greater sharing of power and wealth. Another lesson is that this perspective can be communicated to people in familiar ways that do not compromise radical meanings. The SMRR coalition connected patriotic symbols, like the Statue of Liberty and the American flag, to radical causes; Dennis Kucinich used social justice quotes from the Bible;

and Nicholas Carbone of Hartford spoke directly to the American
Dream that crumbles before people's eyes. [8] A third and essential
lesson is that radicals cannot afford to invest all of their hopes and
energies into electoral victories. Progressives in Berkeley and
Hartford no longer dominate local government, and many of the reforms they enacted have been reversed by their successors. The significant question that is as yet unanswered is, Have they left a radical
democratic legacy—continuing support among people for taking control
of their communities and some experience with government that empowers people to shape their own future? Without this legacy, the
activist Left will have failed to identify itself, to build a growing base
of public support, or to have exerted real influence. It will have, instead, assimilated.

There are obvious limits to what the American Left can hope
to gain by participating in mainstream politics in communities. Local
governments have very little power compared with state and national
governments or to national and international corporations. What,
for example, can communities do about the nuclear arms race?
They can take votes detesting it, build momentum for some sort of
nuclear freeze, and make life a little difficult for local defense con-
tractors. While this is not unimportant, its value should not be overestimated. The federal government generally has power enough to
ignore local protests, and large corporations usually control enough
jobs to take the sting out of community resistance. Robert Ross argues that "the global scope of capital mobility is able to take advantage of every shade of local difference, pitting states, localities, and
countries against one another for the favors of the goose of investment so that it might lay the golden egg of employment." [9] On the
one hand, community activism is important because it has historically
been the foundation for politicizing issues, like racial equality or nuclear peril. On the other hand, community activism can do little to
challenge the concentrated powers of national elites, where decisions
regarding race or armaments are located. Consequently, the American Left must consider eking out a role for itself in the national
political arena.

Radical politics at the national level is far more problematic,
if only because the stakes are higher. Despite some weakening in
the two-party system, U.S. elections are still biased in favor of the
established parties. Statewide primaries are expensive propositions,
which party stalwarts and corporate contributors usually control
through their purse strings. Even when a progressive candidate wins
a major party nomination, party leaders and corporate backers may
throw their support to the opposition, regardless of their party identification. National elections are still based on winner-take-all con-

tests and single-member districts, which all but cripple third-party efforts. Thus, the most influential third-party candidates still get absorbed into the major parties. Campaign spending reforms have not necessarily improved the situation, for example, because the lion's share of public funding still goes to the two major parties. [10]

Similarly, radical interest-group activity at the national level is not very promising. It is extremely difficult to fund, organize, and sustain a mass movement around single issues that only peripherally affect the lives of people around the nation. However, it is relatively easy for elites with special interests to muster the efforts and resources necessary to exert influence or to defeat initiatives that challenge their interests. For example, national survey research has shown that a vast majority of Americans have favored strong gun control laws for many years; but this diffuse support is no match for the National Rifle Association, the major arms manufacturers, and their congressional allies, who have much to lose by these laws. [11] National environmental groups, anticorporatist groups, pro-Equal Rights Amendment groups, or anti-imperialist groups face the same dilemma.

One might argue that Americans, at best, are minimally free, equal, and independent in national politics. Thus, they have not consented and, therefore, have no obligation to follow the conventional rules of the political game. In general, I think this argument is correct, but some precision is needed here. Despite obstacles, Americans have been able to exercise some influence over national politics and to use government to enhance that influence. There are progressive people in Congress, like Ron Dellums, and there have been electoral races where radicals, like Tom Hayden and Zolton Ferency, have made strong showings. There are national networks of radical politicians, like the Conference on Alternative State and Local Public Policies, which may serve as a breeding ground for skillful national candidates in the near future. Left-oriented pressure groups have won some national victories, like defeating the supersonic transport, supporting the Environmental Protection Agency (EPA) and the Occupational Safety and Health Administration (OSHA), or pressuring government agencies to administer affirmative action guidelines. The fact that Americans are not wholly impotent in national politics means that the American Left has at least a minimal obligation to test the democratic potentials of the mainstream. Otherwise, its own democratic credentials are deservedly suspect.

Where should the Left enter into the national mainstream? According to the theory of radical democracy, the Left should enter in those places where people seem to have the greatest choice. Let me suggest two possibilities, more as a basis for further dialogue than as a set of definitive recommendations. First, radical messages are sometimes heard and discussed in primary elections and in the left wing of the Democratic party. Primary elections can serve as a platform for encouraging democratic dialogue about public control and even about socialist redistributive policies. Henry Etzkowitz and Peter Schwab write the following:

> Electoral platforms give socialists the opportunity to present their ideas and political alternatives to the public. These opportunities to make socialism a public issue are not ignored by committed socialists. . . . Socialists must recognize that they are forced to risk open and direct political activities if they are to advance their cause. Otherwise, socialist groups remain simply educational societies, social and cultural groups, or minor parties. [12]

G. William Domhoff adds that socialists need to present the American public with some blueprints for egalitarian society in order to dissociate themselves from Stalinism and cold war images of statist socialism and to demonstrate that their vision is constructive and desirable. While these blueprints should be developed through community participation, they should be disseminated in the national electoral arena. Domhoff suggests that socialists should run as candidates in Democratic party primaries. Because they have virtually no chance of winning at present, they have no need to moderate their viewpoints to accommodate more voters; because they would drop out after having lost the primaries, they would not alienate working-class voters, who fear that third-party efforts on the Left produce Republican victories. Hopefully, these electoral efforts will expand the scope of democratic dialogue and cue Americans to "see the world through anti-capitalist perspectives."[13]

Many radicals, including socialists, believe that the left wing of the Democratic party may be a useful place for radical participation. Paralyzed by today's legitimation crisis, Democratic party leaders have yet to unite around a set of reforms that promise to strengthen their waning legitimacy and solve pressing social problems. This tends to alienate the labor groups, feminists, and ethnic coalitions on the party's left wing. Conceivably, these left-wing Democrats are more amenable than ever to radical democratic and socialist analyses. Were the left wing to become radicalized, some party leaders might fear an internal split, which would ensure electoral defeat for Democratic candidates, grant concessions to keep the left wing in the fold, and thereby enable radicals to run for office and convey public control messages under the party's own imprimatur. In this way, radicals might avoid the barriers associated with third-party politics. Michael Reich and Richard Edwards, thinking along these lines, conclude that "electoral activity is very significant for a viable socialist movement in the present-day United States."[14] Furthermore, the left wing of the Democratic party could provide space for building progressive coalitions, for example, between environmental groups and progressive labor unions based on some notion of how conservation efforts could enhance rather than threaten jobs. These coalitions, in turn, might "contain the seeds for a new radical party or a movement to transform the Democratic Party."[15] At the very least, these coalitions might inject increasingly radical brands of participation into conventional national politics.

Second, some segments or pockets of the federal government are more open to public influence than others. The Left, in my view, has some obligation to pinpoint which segments are most susceptible to public pressure and then strive to apply it. Because susceptibility is a matter of degrees and because this book is not focused on the intricacies of the U.S. government, let me throw out some possibilities to indicate the kind of discussion that might be germaine: The presidency is less susceptible to public pressure than Congress; the Senate is less susceptible to public pressure than the House; both Senate and House members are less susceptible to public pressure on foreign policy issues than on domestic policy issues. The Defense Department is less susceptible to public pressure than the Department of Education; the Federal Reserve Board is less susceptible than the OSHA or the Social Security Administration. These discussions might be considerably more precise, focusing on particular congressional committees, domestic policies, or subagencies. Furthermore, this "descent" into the nitty-gritty of national politics may reveal pockets of democratic space that can be mined with profit and bring victories that convince Americans that elites are not invulnerable and that mass action can work. While such victories are likely to be minor and reversible, they can be used to drive a wedge between elites, while fostering majority unity in favor of radical democratic change.

Perhaps more important than where the Left should enter into the mainstream is how the Left can do so without assimilating. There are no surefire guarantees against assimilation. Reformers can always become reformists, just as successful revolutionaries once in power can become positively reactionary. With this in mind, let me suggest that radical democratic perspectives provide a few counterweights.

One counterweight is the radical democratic understanding that distinguishes reformism from reforms. Reformism benefits people but does not empower them; reform benefits and empowers people. Charlotte Bunch has constructed a list of questions feminists ought to ask themselves about any particular reform, which is equally applicable for all radicals who engage themselves in conventional politics.

1. Does it materially improve the lives of women and if so, which women, and how many?
2. Does the reform build on an individual woman's self-respect, strength, and confidence?
3. Does working for reform give women a sense of power, strength, and imagination as a group and help build structures for further change?
4. Does the struggle for reform educate women politically, enhancing their ability to criticize and challenge the system in the future?
5. Does the reform weaken patriarchal control of society's institutions and help women gain power over them? [16]

One might condense these questions into one: Does the reform and the struggle for reform empower people to take greater control over their own lives and over their government? If so, the action is nonreformist and extremely difficult for elites to assimilate to their own interest in domination. Furthermore, if the Left were to build a mass movement based on radical democracy, it would be forced by its own constituency to answer this question; if the Left fails to build such a constituency, it will have no need to ask it.

Another counterweight to assimilation is contingent on the Left's willingness to practice democratic dialogue rather than Gothic enmity in its own community. If it does so, then virtually every foray into the mainstream will be disputed by radicals with a less optimistic view of conventional party or interest-group politics. Such disputation can be a counterweight to assimilation. On the one hand, those entering the mainstream, aware of the Left's history of assimilation, should welcome such argument, if only to keep themselves honest and alert to their goals. Naturally, some radicals prefer unqualified support to honesty. On the other hand, those entering the mainstream have a concrete interest in keeping the dialogue with the Left opposition going. Quite often, radicals are able to win elections or reforms because they appear to be a safe alternative, when compared with radicals who are more militant in their demands. In the late 1960s, for example, a number of black reformers were able to attain public office and make changes because the black power movement seemed to be the pending alternative. [17] In a sense, it is in the interest of reformers to help to sustain oppositional groups by engaging them in dialogue and thereby legitimating them; the major cost to reformers is that they must be willing to defend their policies as nonreformist.

An additional counterweight should be mentioned. Radical participants in the mainstream need allies. In the past, they usually looked to conventional liberals; compromised their proposals; and thereby allowed their allies to absorb, moderate, and institutionalize changes in ways that left power relations intact. The predictable result was assimilation. However, when today's radical participants look for allies among conventional liberals, they have a difficult time finding suitable ones. Conventional liberals are preoccupied with outdoing conservatives at their own game or are paralyzed by their inability to imagine alternatives to the welfare state. Consequently, radicals must look elsewhere for support. If they are converging on radical democratic terrain, they are likely to look to the American people for that support; but the American people distrust conventional politics enough to be grudging in their support. To overcome this distrust, radicals must go out of their way to demonstrate that their policies are different from conventional ones, perhaps that they mean less centralized power and more public control. One might argue that this is precisely the path followed by Saul Alinsky and Ralph Nader in the 1970s, and that growing public distrust today makes this route one of the few available for garnering public support. Furthermore, one might argue that the pull from the demos will grow stronger if the American Left also builds support for an oppositional politics, predicated on the inability of the U.S. government to accommodate public frustrations and needs.

OPPOSITION WITHOUT ISOLATION

Should the American Left engage in unconventional politics outside of the mainstream and in opposition to it? Should the Left cast its lot with protests and demonstrations, dissent and disobedience, confrontational politics, and even self-defensive violence? Should the Left identify itself with the rebellions and rebelliousness that Americans have long practiced? The theory of radical democracy justifies challenges to the mainstream, where people lack the self-mastery to control government and government does not act in ways that facilitate greater public power. In these circumstances, expedience becomes a prime criterion and isolation the major peril for Left politics.

John Gardner may speak for liberals far more radical than himself when he writes the following:

No citizens' movement should assume that it has some
divinely inspired grasp on what is "in the public interest."

> It must have the courage of its convictions, but it must
> present those convictions in the public forum where all
> other groups can debate their validity. Everything it
> does it must do openly. And though it is a petitioner (and
> therefore often an adversary) in relation to government,
> it must ultimately respect the public process. [18]

Gardner presumes that the public process is relatively fair and flexible, open to a broad spectrum of ideas and demands. He clearly pre-
fers due process and, in this, he is not alone. Nonetheless, there
are many instances in American politics when open dialogue is difficult and consistently ignored by those who govern, when due process
protects elites' interests and prolongs antidemocratic injustices.
During such times, we can expect that many radical liberals as well
as socialists will find it expedient to opt for greater militancy.

Long-standing injustices in the United States are generally not
amenable to reform efforts alone. Racism is a good example. A
violent war was required to end slavery, but overt manifestations of
racial inequalities persisted for more than a century afterward. In
the 1960s civil rights activists pointed out that legal avenues of redress had been tried for years and had failed to provide black people
with equal civil rights or equal control over their community and personal lives; they also suggested that government efforts in behalf of
racial equality were mainly symbolic, too little and too late, and
largely ineffective. Boycotts, sit-ins, teach-ins, freedom rides,
mass marches and protests, civil disobedience, and other creative
tactics were employed, with great success, to politicize racial inequality and to drum up mass support for eliminating it. These "undue" processes forced the issue. Furthermore, the repressive tactics of political officials, like Bull Connors, and the self-defense
tactics of groups, like the Black Panthers, as well as the emergence
of black power militancy and an oppositional minority culture, symbolized by the Black Muslims, combined to dramatize the failure of
the U.S. political and social systems to accommodate black interests
or to ease black alienation. Similarly, the early labor movement,
the antiwar movement of the 1960s, and to a degree, today's antinuke
movement have been predicated on the failure of conventional reform
efforts and have won significant public support by forcing the issue
through confrontational politics.

Furthermore, political movements in the United States have
had some success legitimating unconventional protests in policy areas
that prove to be insulated from public accountability and that are used
by elites to reinforce striking forms of inequality. Foreign policy is
the most poignant example. During the Carter administration, it became apparent to many Americans that multinational corporations

and banks based in the United States were "investing in apartheid" in South Africa, despite the federal government's human rights rhetoric. Either economic elites were able to overpower the federal government, which indicated that political equality in the United States does not exist in foreign policy, or the federal government was a partner in promoting injustice regardless of its rhetoric, which meant that it was an opponent of democracy in foreign policy. Both interpretations justified protests that bypassed normal political channels. Students used sit-in tactics to pressure university trustees to withdraw their investments from companies that truck with apartheid; church groups and anti-imperialist coalitions used proxy power to get into corporate board meetings, raise the apartheid issue, and sometimes disrupt the proceedings; regional federations, which include progressive labor unions, have sometimes stopped or at least made difficult the unloading of South African goods and athletes on U.S. shores. The fact that the Reagan administration has dropped the human rights rhetoric and cemented ties with the racist South African regime is a further indication that U.S. foreign policy is extremely insulated from the American public and is antidemocratic in content and consequence.[19] Radical democratic criteria justify protests against such a policy and provide a line of reasoning that may legitimate protests among more general American audiences.

Oppositional politics can also be justified when elites themselves preach democracy and then proceed to erode democratic space. This has happened throughout U.S. history.

> With all the controls of power and punishment, enticements and concessions, diversions and decoys, operating throughout the history of the country, the Establishment has been unable to keep itself secure from revolt. Every time it looked as if it had succeeded, the very people it thought seduced or subdued, stirred and rose.[20]

However accommodating that government has been in the past, its complicity in the erosion of democratic space is a signal that it will be less accommodating in the future. Assaults on established and expected democratic rights generally come at a time when elites must centralize their control because they have failed to ease frustrations, solve important problems, or fulfill widespread democratic hopes. Elite coercion waxes when popular consent wanes. In an important sense, elite coercion functions as a public announcement that elites have failed to legitimate their rule by consent. If their rule is not legitimate, then people are free to confront them. Howard Zinn observes that Americans have taken advantage of such freedom.

> Blacks, cajoled by Supreme Court decisions and congres-
> sional statutes, rebelled. Women, wooed and ignored,
> romanticized and mistreated, rebelled. Indians, thought
> dead, reappeared, defiant. Young people, despite lures
> of career and comfort, defected. Working people, thought
> soothed by reforms, regulated by law, kept within bounds
> by their unions, went on strike. Government intellectuals,
> pledged to secrecy, began giving away secrets. Priests
> turned from piety to protest. Prisoners, isolated in cages,
> organized. [21]

Whenever elites have tried to turn back the democratic clock by with-
drawing past concessions, especially by using coercion to enforce
their will, a great many Americans have been prepared to rebel in
defense of democracy.

The American Left should recognize, however, that abstract
justifications for dissent and disobedience do not make them expedient.
There are many areas of everyday social and political life in which
people have little control and are the object of domination but, nonetheless, are not interested in rebellion. The American Left must be
more discriminating and less self-righteous, pinpointing degrees of
mass impotence and frustration as well as respecting Americans'
perceptions regarding which injustices are important enough to legitimate unusual political tactics. Otherwise, the Left will again find
itself isolated.

The American Left should also recognize that the rebellions
justified by radical democratic theory are inherently limited by that
theory. "What is a rebel?" asks Albert Camus. "A man who says
no, but whose refusal does not imply renunciation. He is also a man
who says yes, from the moment he makes his first gesture of rebellion."[22] I do not quote Camus to evoke his debate with Sartre over
Algeria or to take sides in it; the debate over rebellion versus revolution may be germaine to Europe but, at the moment anyway, has no
bearing on American politics. In this country, militancy means rebellion. It means saying no to antidemocratic structures and practices while saying yes to radical democracy as the boundary of rebellion. I propose this as a gauge that radicals can use in measuring
the expedience of their opposition to the mainstream.

Rebellions usually have a specific focus. The Anti-Renter
Movement considered earlier, for example, focused on land monopolies and tenant evictions. This specific focus does not necessarily
imply the parochialism of single-issue politics. The Anti-Renter
Movement produced a sense of solidarity among its participants,
which extended to related issues; the movement generated remedial

legislation, which provided general guidelines for state regulation of owner-tenant relations and land access. One can extract several lessons from the limited nature of rebellions.

First, it is not particularly expedient for radicals to try to mobilize rebellions against the system, the Establishment, monopoly capitalism, or institutional racism and sexism. For most people, these are simply theoretical abstractions, with no clear and immediate relation to the problems they directly face. Americans do not rebel against abstractions but against concrete realities.[23] It may be more fruitful to mobilize against U.S. foreign policy in El Salvador as an extension of Vietnam War policies, with which many Americans are familiar; against particular budget cuts that Americans experience directly; against corporate shutdowns and take-aways, which have immediate consequences for whole communities and unions. While these directions are narrow and miss the structural sources of elite domination, it is likely that the people who enroll in such mobilizations will be in a better position to educate themselves about the broader lines of elitism. This has been the experience of organizers, like George Wiley of the National Welfare Rights Organization, who begin with localized minority strategies but then branch out to broader majoritarian efforts.[24] One of the promises of rebellions is that the people involved in them connect their personal dilemmas to collective struggles; one of the limits of rebellions is that people's experiences, not ideological truths shared by the knowing few, are the basis for social understanding and legitimation.

Second, the specificity of rebellions is an opportunity for radicals to oppose antidemocratic injustices and to affirm democratic practices simultaneously. Radicals who mobilize against government support for building breeder reactors and against the corporations that build, install, and profit by them have the potential to win regional support among Americans who will live in their shadow but have not been consulted about them. At the same time, radicals can use conventional political tactics to win the support of local governments and community businesses, which are threatened by nuclear power interests. This two-pronged approach taps into Americans' ambivalence, protesting against threats to democracy and demonstrating attachment to democratic participation, which Americans still treasure. Similarly, radicals might rebel against particular banking practices and also underwrite the voluntaristic establishment of "people's banks" as a democratic alternative. In this way, the Left can strengthen its own democratic credentials, which I have argued, need strengthening.

Third, the limited nature of rebellions is expedient in terms of buffering against Left fragmentation. What can any rebellion hope to accomplish? The process of rebellion can generate understanding of elitism and support for egalitarian alternatives; it can politicize once silenced issues, open them to democratic dialogue, constrict elites' options, and force a response. But rebellions are not revolutions that overturn the political and economic systems or that suddenly reverse centuries of racism and sexism. They are, instead, political levers that make it possible to wrench concessions from elites. If those engaged in rebellion hope to have any influence over the nature of those concessions or how they are to be administered, they must keep open lines of communication with the radical reformers who actually mediate the process. They must exert pressure on the reformers to negotiate for concessions that simultaneously provide people with benefits and further empower people to extract greater concessions. Charlotte Bunch's list of questions with which to distinguish reformism from reform is as important to rebels as it is to reformers.

In addition to their specific focus, rebellions are generally based on building and sustaining widespread public support. Particular events, individual actions, and even vanguardist incitements may spark rebellions; but mass commitment and support are the factors that determine if rebellions will be influential. This suggests that radicals involved in rebellions must be willing to say yes, at least to a degree, to the subjective perceptions and demands of those Americans who are the rank and file of rebellions.

Saying yes involves a willingness to justify rebellions in the democratic concepts, language, and political analysis that are familiar to Americans. This is no less true in revolutionary situations, as Thomas H. Greene suggests in the following:

> Revolutionary ideology enhances its own legitimacy and
> threatens the legitimacy of the existing regime insofar
> as it can claim continuity with the fundamental values
> and goals of society. Even leftist revolutionary ideolo-
> gies frequently cite traditions of the past and argue that
> revolution is only the necessary means of realizing so-
> ciety's basic cultural identity and historical purpose. [25]

There is, however, a crucial difference between revolutions and rebellions. Some revolutions, like the Bolshevik Revolution, can be carried out by small groups of people in the name of the larger populace. Rebellions must be carried out by the larger populace itself. Consequently, radicals who participate in rebellions must say yes to democracy both in theory and everyday practice. Radicals certainly should bring their own ideologies and logics to mass mobilizations, but they must also be willing to engage in democratic dialogue and to alter their own viewpoints on the basis of others' perceptions and experiences. The best chance for radicals' success might be to work out an experimental meeting point of ideas and actions; the surest route to radical isolation is to try to impose THE WAY on unwilling participants.

From a Weberian perspective, rebellions and mass mobilizations that suffer the disorders of democratic discourse are not likely to be very efficient in achieving their goals. I am not convinced. Whenever the American Left has tried to impose THE WAY on mass movements, it has failed to have much impact. The rise and fall of Students for a Democratic Society (SDS) is a good example.[26] Oftentimes, the American Left has supported highly centralized and undemocratic organizations to lead mass movements only to alienate the masses who might breathe life into those movements. From a radical democratic perspective, the disorders of democratic discourse are virtues that test old theories against current practices, that prefigure greater democracy within present-day society and provide people invaluable experience in self-government, and that testify to Left involvement in the American democratic tradition, which is necessary for winning sustained public support. Furthermore, the unpredictability that stems from these disorders may motivate elites to grant concessions, lest mass mobilizations take a significantly more dangerous course.

CONFLICT AND CONSENSUS IN LEFT POLITICS

Even if the American Left were to identify itself with radical democracy and apply the political guidelines discussed above, there exists considerable room for conflict. Those with radical liberal propensities are likely to apply the guidelines in ways that favor mainstream participation; they have a larger reservoir of faith in the potentials of conventional politics. Socialists are more apt to apply the guidelines to justify opposition movements; they are especially sensitive to the pervasiveness of elite power and the inability of the state to exercise enough autonomy to make a major difference. Even when radicals agree that conventional politics or confrontational politics is justified and expedient, they will certainly disagree on which issues have the highest priority, which elite vulnerabilities should be tested, which segments of the population are most likely to give their support, and which tactics are most promising. Once we get beyond the conservative Lockean myth that the U.S. political marketplace is neutral and the orthodox Marxist myth that it is epiphenomenal, we are left with a broad sphere for legitimate conflicts among radicals. Must this sphere be cultivated to fragment the Left or can it nurture the growth of a general Left consensus?

The theory of radical democracy offers a guideline for intra-Left conflict: dissent implies consent. Within any community, dissent can be considered a conscientious act of loyalty. It is aimed at persuading other members to reconsider their values and actions and to experiment with new modes of understanding and social relations. This guideline is more than a moral shibboleth that demands conflict be accommodated by tolerance. It is also a practical political lesson U.S. elites have understood for years. Within limits, dissent is a means of recognizing and adjusting to social change, reconciling short-term interests with long-term interests, and communicating a democratic openness.[27] What elites have reaped by inviting dissent within their own ranks, radicals should begin to sow.

U.S. elites regularly sit down together in social clubs, policy centers, and think tanks to consider the pressing social issues of the day and to work out positions that reflect their overall interests. The success of these elite groups has depended on their willingness to question received truths and to stir up some new perspectives. At the turn of the century, the American Bankers' Association and the National Civic Federation dissented from conventional laissez-faire beliefs, worked out support for government regulation in their own interests, and laid the groundwork for the renegotiation of the social contract.[28] More recently, the Trilateral Commission has served as an elite forum to discuss and debate whether the received notion that capitalism and democracy are reinforcing is still appropriate to elites' interests.[29] Within these higher circles, toleration of dissent has been key to adjusting elite hegemony in ways that make conservative use of social change.

What can the American Left hope to gain by extending the limits of its own tolerance to encompass dissent? Consider the current issue of the relative autonomy of the state. Radical liberals usually assume that the state is a useful instrument for challenging elite power; socialists presume that the state is primarily an instrument of elite power; neither view is consistently tested against experience because radical liberals and socialists rarely engage one another and debate and defend their viewpoints. Mutual tolerance and discourse, however, might provide interesting payoffs for Left theory and politics. Conceivably, it would produce a historical understanding of shifting state autonomy. Perhaps the state was less autonomous in the 1880s, when it was hamstrung by decentralization and checks and balances, than in the 1980s, when political power is more centralized and irreverent of checks and balances. Perhaps the current threat of nuclear holocaust or ecological catastrophe empowers the state in ways never before known. Intellectual conflict between radicals, mediated by democratic discourse, may add new and needed dimensions to Left analyses and thereby provide a better understanding of the ways in which the state is or is not a useful focus for radical activism.

Elites also tolerate conflict as a basis for working out their long-term interests. For example, export-oriented industries generally prefer low tariffs as a means of persuading other countries to keep their tariffs low; industries that produce for the domestic market, however, want high tariffs to protect their markets from foreign competition. In the short term, these two segments of the capitalist class have antagonistic interests and compete against one another. According to Albert Szymanski, "The state operates to 'aggregate' the diverse interests and wills of the different segments of the capitalist class—that is, form the capitalist class will—so that the state can implement unified compromise policies tempered by the demands of other classes."[30] The effect of elite competition mediated by the state is to produce compromises that give partial satisfaction to both segments of the capitalist class to reinforce class unity and that are palatable to the American people to reinforce popular consent. In a sense, short-term competition is in elites' long-term interests.

The same reasoning can be applied to the American Left. Despite some convergence, radical liberals and socialists have antagonistic political interests. Radical liberals have some chance of winning victories and public support if they do not contest elite power or elite repression and isolation of socialists. Socialists continue to have a stake in opposing radical liberals as reformists who convince American audiences that the nation's political and economic systems can accommodate their demands without making substantive changes. Conceivably, friendly competition between radical liberals and socialists need not be self-destructive if a third force, equivalent to the elites' state, can be located to effect the compromises that are in the long-term interests of the Left as a whole. Let me consider two candidates for the position.

The first candidate is progressive government in communities like Santa Monica and Hartford. Radical liberals and socialists could compete for community support and political influence; progressive government would use its power and resources to pressure radical liberals to make good on the more substantive aspects of their ideology and to demand that socialists take seriously the more procedural aspects incorporated into their ideology. By working out compromises on particular issues and policies, progressive government could articulate a general will for the Left that provides partial satisfaction to both segments and is intelligible and acceptable to members of the community. Conflict can thus be the basis for temporary unity; continuous conflict can be the basis for a more continuous unity.

The second candidate is presently a latent one. Throughout the United States are groups, like the Alliance for Survival, as well as community activists that consider themselves "radical, independent left, or even socialists, but they are so committed to consciousness through experience that they are often unwilling even to discuss their own ideology in the abstract."[31] We can also find larger and smaller scatterings of New Left dropouts, whose dissatisfactions with radical liberal reformism and socialist revolutionism and their failures have become radical apathy and cynicism, resignation, personalized politics, or Left sympathy without distinct outlets. If my analysis of radical democracy and Americans' ambivalence is partly warranted, it should be possible to locate a considerable number of Americans willing to lend their support to democratic dialogue, participation, and control. Were radical liberals and socialists to compete for support among activists, apathetics, and alienated Americans rather than adhere to their logics regardless of people, the competition might produce "invisible hand" compromises among radicals, which benefit the Left by aligning its theory and practice in ways that can win mass constituencies.

Perhaps most important of all, elites tolerate dissent in their own ranks to present a public face of pluralist competition. They then unite in the argument that this competition represents the tug and pull of the diverse interests of the American people. "The image that emerges," writes Michael Parenti, "is of an array of groups competing on an array of issues."[32] This image allows elites to legitimate their own rule as democratic because it is based on adversary procedures that raise the crucial issues, bring out the most intelligent and systematic arguments for resolving them, and ultimately depend on intense and widespread public support for decision making. The reason that elites can effectively promote the pluralist myth is because pluralism among elites is a partial reality.

The American Left would benefit considerably by turning the pluralist myth into its own reality. An American Left that openly engages in democratic dialogue may achieve more than a new understanding of social change; it might also strengthen its democratic image among skeptical Americans. Moreover, an American Left that openly competes for influence in progressive government or for mass support does more than work out its long-term interest; it also demonstrates that it has no monopoly on radical truths and is open to learning from its participants and supporters. Ultimately, conflict among radicals can be the basis for a consensus that the American Left is itself subject to public control. After all, the demos is sovereign.

THE DIVISION OF POLITICAL LABOR

The political fortunes of the American Left depend on its members recognizing that a division of political labor is necessary. Radicals can participate in the mainstream and against the mainstream without necessarily reproducing old Gothic enmity; radical liberals, radical democrats, and socialists can compete with one another for political influence and mass support and simultaneously benefit the American Left as a whole. What makes any division of labor workable is that each segment is oriented toward a common goal. Let me conclude by stating what I consider an essential but easily forgotten "truth" that defines that common goal: U.S. elites need democracy far less than the American Left.

Elites in the United States have profited greatly by wearing a democratic mantle. It has veiled their more ruthless side and has helped them to rule by consent; but U.S. elites do not need to rule by consent. Their dominance over the means of gathering and disseminating information empowers them to define what options are realistic and, thereby, to eliminate alternative conceptions of reality; their control over major political institutions empowers them to use the carrot of public revenues and the stick of police coercion to enforce mass subordination; and their location at the commanding heights of the economy affords them the opportunity to use employment as a loaded pistol held at people's heads. Strip away elite authority founded on consent and considerable naked power remains. There are limits as to how elites can employ naked power without fomenting rebellion, but the limits are indistinct and distant as long as Americans perceive no viable alternatives. Jessica Mitford's The American Way of Death brilliantly highlights this dynamic on a smaller scale. The U.S. funeral industry uses its power over relevant information, related law, and considerable wealth in ways that make U.S. funerals the most expensive in the world. Most of us do not consent to such funeral practices; many of us think them hideous; but virtually all of us go along with them because, in the midst of crisis, we see no alternative.[33]

The American Left does not control information gathering and dissemination, major political institutions, or the economy. Unlike the conservatives who now assault democracy and the liberals who fail to defend it, the American Left cannot rely on corporate contributions to finance its struggle for influence. It cannot "buy" the national media, political offices, or economic leverage. Furthermore, starting from a position of weakness, it cannot hope to make deals with "friendly" elites without coming out on the short end of the bargain.

The only significant resource the Left can claim as its own, in the end, is a moral vision, which I have called radical democracy. This vision is certainly no competition for elites with naked power. But it can be a key to winning access to Americans' aggregate intelli-

gence, combined political force, and collective economic power.
The American Left needs to lay claim to radical democracy because
it is a meaningful moral vision in the American context; and the American Left needs to practice radical democracy because it is the only
means available for placing radical perspectives on the American
agenda.

Such a moral vision and political practice can become the seed
of power when the old ways of satisfying people's desires no longer
work and when new ways promise to build on the past, inform the
present, and point toward a better future. I have argued that the exceptional ways in which U.S. elites have accommodated people's desires no longer work. Elites are now divided. Millions of unemployed people, workers, and minorities are suffering under the lash
of the Reagan administration. Even groups who are better off are experiencing rising anger. Environmentalists, religious and student
groups, civil rights organizations, union and nonunion laborers, white-
collar workers, bureaucrats and their clients, and even state and
local governors are living with dashed hopes and shared disasters.[34]
These are historical circumstances in which radical democratic politics and values might help to focus people's suffering against elitism
and channel their rising anger toward the democratic reconstruction
of American society.

In my view, the major virtue of Lockean liberalism is that it
takes seriously the individual rights and fair procedures that socialist societies too often dismiss; the major virtue of Marxism is its
concern for communal cooperation and the fulfillment of human needs,
which are given little support in capitalist societies. The major
virtue of radical democracy is that it combines liberal and socialist
virtues in a flexible package, which invites Americans to determine
for themselves the precise nature of their association. From the
perspective of the Left, radical democracy should be seen as a morally
desirable and politically expedient goal, one that can capture Americans' imaginations and make public control a serious option for the
immediate future.

NOTES

1. See Derek Shearer, "How the Progressives Won in Santa
Monica," Social Policy 12, no. 3 (Winter 1982): 7-14.
2. See Eve Bach, Nicholas R. Carbone, and Pierre Clavel,
"Running the City for the People," Social Policy 12, no. 3 (Winter
1982): 15-23.
3. See Janice Perlman, "Grassrooting the System," in U.S.
Capitalism in Crisis, ed. Union for Radical Political Economics Col-

lective (New York: Union for Radical Political Economics, 1978), pp. 306-8.

4. See David Loud, "Saving Public Health in Seattle," Dollars and Sense 74 (February 1982): 12-14.

5. See Todd Swanstrom, "Tax Abatement in Cleveland," Social Policy 12, no. 3 (Winter 1982): 24-30.

6. See Harry C. Boyte, The Backyard Revolution: Understanding the New Citizen Movement (Philadelphia: Temple University Press, 1980), chap. 2.

7. Shearer, "How the Progressives Won," p. 14.

8. See Harry C. Boyte, "Neighborhood Politics: The Building Blocks," Social Policy 12, no. 3 (Winter 1982): 4.

9. Robert Ross, "Regional Illusion, Capitalist Reality," Democracy 2, no. 2 (April 1982): 96.

10. See Michael Reich and Richard Edwards, "Party Politics and Class Conflict in the United States," Socialist Review 8 (May-June 1978): 50-53.

11. See Michael J. Harrington, "The Politics of Gun Control," in Is America Necessary?, ed. Henry Etzkowitz and Peter Schwab (St. Paul: West, 1976), pp. 296-303.

12. Henry Etzkowitz and Peter Schwab, "Congress," in Is America Necessary?, ed. Henry Etzkowitz and Peter Schwab (St. Paul: West, 1976), p. 287.

13. G. William Domhoff, "Blueprints for a New Society," in Is America Necessary?, ed. Henry Etzkowitz and Peter Schwab (St. Paul: West, 1976), pp. 596-602.

14. Reich and Edwards, "Party Politics and Class Conflict," pp. 54-57.

15. Perlman, "Grassrooting the System," p. 322.

16. Charlotte Bunch, "The Reform Tool Kit," in Building Feminist Theory: Essays from Quest, a Feminist Quarterly, ed. Charlotte Bunch et al. (New York: Longmans, 1981), pp. 196-98.

17. See Manning Marable, "Black Power—Its Past and Its Promise," Moving On 2 (July-August 1978): 18-20; relatedly, see Richard J. Barnet and Ronald E. Muller, Global Reach: The Power of the Multinational Corporations (New York: Simon & Schuster, 1974), p. 250; and James Weinstein, Ambiguous Legacy: The Left in American Politics (New York: New Viewpoints, 1975), chap. 3.

18. John W. Gardner, "Citizen Action," in Is America Necessary?, ed. Henry Etzkowitz and Peter Schwab (St. Paul: West, 1976), p. 580.

19. See Bernard Magubane, "The United States and Southern Africa in the International Division of Labor," in The Future of American Democracy: Views from the Left, ed. Mark E. Kann (Philadelphia: Temple University Press, 1983), chap. 12.

20. Howard Zinn, A People's History of the United States (New York: Harper & Row, 1980), p. 573.

21. Ibid.

22. Albert Camus, The Rebel, trans. Anthony Bower (New York: Vintage, 1956), p. 13.

23. See Frances Fox Piven and Richard A. Cloward, Poor People's Movements: Why They Succeed and How They Fail (New York: Vintage, 1979), chap. 1.

24. See Boyte, Backyard Revolution, p. 53.

25. Thomas H. Greene, Comparative Revolutionary Movements (Englewood Cliffs, N.J.: Prentice-Hall, 1974), p. 57.

26. See Kirkpatrick Sale, SDS (New York: Vintage, 1973).

27. For a general analysis, see Fred Block, "The Ruling Class Does Not Rule: Notes on the Marxist Theory of the State," Socialist Revolution 7 (May-June 1977): 6-28.

28. See Edward S. Greenberg, Serving the Few: Corporate Capitalism and the Bias of Government Policy (New York: Wiley, 1974), pp. 94-100.

29. See Samuel Bowles, "The Trilateral Commission: Have Capitalism and Democracy Come to a Parting of the Ways?" in U.S. Capitalism in Crisis, ed. Union for Radical Political Economics Collective (New York: Union for Radical Political Economics, 1978), pp. 261-65.

30. Albert Szymanski, The Capitalist State and the Politics of Class (Cambridge, Mass.: Winthrop, 1978), p. 25; see also p. 44.

31. Perlman, "Grassrooting the System," p. 308.

32. Michael Parenti, Power and the Powerless (New York: St. Martin's Press, 1978), p. 27.

33. See Jessica Mitford, The American Way of Death (New York: Fawcett Crest, 1978).

34. See Frances Fox Piven and Richard A. Cloward, "The New Age of Protest," Nation, April 17, 1982, pp. 447, 463-65.

INDEX

Bill of Rights, 19, 22
Black Economic Development Conference, 83
Black Liberation Army, 62
Black Muslims, 218
Black Panthers, 218
Bluhm, William T., 30
Bolshevik party, 111
Bolshevik Revolution, 109
Boorstin, Daniel, 1, 23
Bottomore, T. B., 155
Bowles, Samuel, 167
Boyte, Harry, 27, 168, 197, 211
Braverman, Harry, 47
Breines, Paul, 140
Brookings Institution, 171
Brown, John, 108
Bryan, William Jennings, 35
Bunch, Charlotte, 92, 215-16, 222

Callenbach, Ernest, 127
Cammet, John, 135
Campaign for Economic Democracy (CED), 113, 114-15, 210
Camus, Albert, 220
capitalism: and corporations, 201-3; and crisis, 169-71, 176; and democracy, 23, 43, 224; and growth, 26-27; and Lockean liberalism, 76-78; according to Marxism, 47-49, 86-87, 105-6; and social control, 26, 47-48; and the state, 23, 48, 225 (see also elitism)
Carbone, Nicholas, 211-12
Carnegie, Andrew, 15
Carnoy, Martin, and Derek Shearer, 113, 114-15, 160
Carter, Jimmy, 2, 115, 163
Castro, Fidel, 35
Channing, William Ellery, 73
Chavez, Cesar, 131
Cincottà, Gale, 131
Citizen Action Program, 211
Civil War, 15, 17, 201

Clarke, Lorenne M. G., 73
Clecak, Peter, 4, 23
Cole, G. D. H., 35
Commager, Henry Steele, 177
Commoner, Barry, 84
Communist party, 18
Conference on Alternative State and Local Policies, 59, 213
Connors, Bull, 218
consent: and economic democracy, 113; and education, 188-89; engineering of, 100-1; and families, 73, 190-92; and the founding of America, 71-72; and government, 198-201; and hegemony, 158, 165, 187, 219, 225, 227; hypothetical, 189-90; and popular control, 71-72, 78-79, 202, 204; and radical democracy, 155, 186-95, 202; and radical liberalism, 41-44, 126, 144; and reindustrialization, 173; and socialism, 106-7, 111, 135, 139, 203, 224; and Vietnam War, 56-57, 58; and welfare state, 163 (see also radical democracy; social contract)
conservativism: and democracy, 2, 3, 164; and dissent, 203-4; and economic strategies, 171-73; and free will, 187-88; and language, 99-100, 102; and optimism, 159-60; and political strategies, 165-66, 209; and values, 15
Council on Foreign Relations, 137
counterculture, 21, 58, 127
crisis, 16-17, 101-2, 179, 188, 199; economic, 169-72; political, 160, 163-65, 166, 169, 214
Crotty, William, and Gary Jacobson, 167-68

Daniels, Norman, 82
Debs, Eugene V., 15, 29, 69, 98;

ABOUT THE AUTHOR

MARK E. KANN is Associate Professor of Political Science at the University of Southern California in Los Angeles. He is also Editor of Humanities in Society, an interdisciplinary journal concerned with the legitimacy of ideas and social action.

Dr. Kann is author of Thinking about Politics: Two Political Sciences and editor of The Problem of Authority in America (with John Diggins) and The Future of American Democracy: Views from the Left. He has also published numerous articles on political theory in academic journals. Currently, he is engaged in a study of radicals in power in Santa Monica, California.

Kann was at the University of Wisconsin—Madison in the 1960s, participating in and studying the antiwar movement. He then spent three years as a sixth-grade teacher in Chicago's ghetto schools. He returned to the University of Wisconsin in the more sedate 1970s and received his Ph.D. in political science in 1975.